Hitler
The Führer and the People

J. P. Stern, who has been Professor of
German at the University of London since
1972, was born in Prague and educated
there and at St John's College,
Cambridge. During the war he served in
the Czech Army and the Royal Air Force.
He was for many years Fellow and Tutor
of St John's College and Lecturer in the
Department of German at Cambridge,
and he has been Visiting Professor at the
City College of New York, the University
of California at Berkeley, the State
University of New York at Buffalo, the
University of Virginia at Charlottesville,
Göttingen University and at Cornell
University.

Among Professor Stern's other books
are *Ernst Jünger: a writer of our time* (1952),
*G. C. Lichtenberg: a doctrine of scattered
occasions* (1963), *Re-Interpretations: seven
studies in nineteenth-century German
literature* (1964), *Thomas Mann* (1967),
*Idylls and Realities: studies in nineteenth-
century German literature* (1971), *On
Realism* (1973), *Nietzsche* (Fontana
Modern Masters, 1978), and *A Study of
Nietzsche* (1979).

Hitler: the Führer and the People has
been published in German, Japanese and
French. J. P. Stern's interest in the topic of
this book is of long standing. As a boy he
listened to one of Hitler's election speeches
in a tent on the Oktoberwiese in Munich;
five years later he watched the Viennese
offer an enthusiastic welcome to the
German Army as it entered their city; and
a year after that, in March 1939, he was in
Prague when the German Army occupied it.

J. P. Stern

HITLER

The Führer and the People

UNIVERSITY OF CALIFORNIA PRESS
Berkeley and Los Angeles

UNIVERSITY OF CALIFORNIA PRESS
Berkeley and Los Angeles, California

Updated Paperback Edition, 1988

ISBN 0-520-02952-6
Library of Congress Catalog Card Number: 74-30535
Copyright © J. P. Stern 1975

5 6 7 8 9

Printed in the United States of America

Contents

Preface to the First Edition

This is an essay in historical reconstruction. But since its arguments are frequently illustrated or guided by literary parallels, and some look to German literature for their confirmation, a word in explanation of my undertaking may be in order. In the course of my ordinary avocation, which is the study of literature, there arose the need to provide, for myself and others, including a circle of friends at the State University of New York at Buffalo, something in the nature of an historical background against which German literature in the first third of the twentieth century might be interpreted and understood. When I began, I shared the conventional view that the great writers of the age were either not concerned with political issues at all or in complete and implacable opposition to Hitler's National Socialism, its doctrine and practice. There was a difficulty about this view, since it did nothing to explain the apparently genuine enthusiasm, short-lived though it was, of a very small number of writers whom it was clearly impossible to lump with the very large number of third-rate hacks from Dr Goebbels's stable. In order to resolve this difficulty it became necessary to look more closely, not so much at Hitler the man as rather at the appeal he exercised through his speeches, writings, and conversations, through his promises and achievements. This in turn led me to enquire what connection there was between his professed beliefs and affirmations on the one hand, and on the other the traditional beliefs and affirmations of the society into which he, the ideal-type outsider, made his way and which he came to dominate. 'My business is to record what people say', writes Herodotus, 'but I am by no means bound to believe it';

or necessarily to disbelieve it, I should add in the present context.

However, my preoccupation with what people said is open to a misunderstanding. It might appear to some that while criticizing the old-fashioned historical determinism of the German 'twenties and 'thirties, I myself have succumbed to the fashionable linguistic determinism of the French 'seventies. At no point has it been my intention to suggest that the language of National Socialism (or indeed any other language) is a closed 'semiotic' system the speakers of which are damned. On the contrary, it is my belief that one may use a language and remain a free man. I agree that in using a given language a man will find himself constrained to adopt the moral and ideological outlook of those who have shaped that language, but I wish also to insist that he retains the choice of saying Yes or No to the options they put before him, for the grounds of his choice are not linguistic. It is, as I have shown by the example of Johann Georg Elser, a desperate choice, but that is not a good reason for thinking it chimeric.

I wish to thank my friend John Sugden for reading the book at the type-script stage, for suggesting a number of alterations in order to make its arguments clearer, and for helping to unravel the notes which are placed at the end.

The topic of this book is peculiarly apt to excite the mind and paralyse it at the same time. The truth of this will not have escaped several members of my family. To them, accordingly, I am grateful for their forbearance, without which this state of mind would have lasted even longer.

Unless otherwise acknowledged, all translations are my own. Those from *Mein Kampf* and other National Socialist sources, which I have kept as close to the originals as possible, don't make for easy reading. There is no reason why they should.

J.P.S.   *Easter Sunday 1974*

Preface to the Fifth Printing

While preparing this new edition of a book written almost ten years ago, I had to ask myself whether any of the views I had put forward were undermined by writings published since that time. As was to be expected, some new details of Hitler's biography have been unearthed, but since my intention was only incidentally biographical, these details do not materially affect my argument. There have of course been attempts at 'revising' the history of the Third Reich, of Hitler's own rule and especially of his conduct of the war. Thus David Irving's *Hitler's War* (1977) attempts to show Hitler as a weak leader, as one who not only failed to impose his 'will' on the generals and on his subordinates in the Party, but who knew little or nothing about some of the most momentous measures taken in his name. In particular, the fact that no document exists in which he himself is seen to have ordered the extermination of the Jews is used by Mr Irving as proof of Hitler's ignorance – and thus of his innocence – of that crime and of the bureaucratic machinery devised for its execution. A challenge to Mr Irving's astonishing thesis (a thesis which, as far as I know, no German historian, however 'revisionist', has dared to advance) was undertaken at length by Gerald Fleming in his *Hitler und die Endlösung* (Hitler and the Final Solution) (1982). All that need here be said of that outstandingly sober and accurate book is that its author refutes Mr Irving's thesis by basing himself on analyses of extant documents as well as on the personal testimonies of numerous survivors, victims and perpetrators alike. Mr Fleming has not unearthed the document containing 'the Führer's order'. But he has shown in great and convincing detail how 'the Führer's directives' and 'the Führer's wish' were transmitted through the various Party hierarchies; and he has given good reasons for the belief that such a document is unlikely ever to have existed.

The aim of the present book is to show why Hitler came to power and what kept him there. Certainly, no single cause provides an adequate explanation. Hitler's promise and achievement of full employment and a stable currency, revenge for Versailles and the appeal to German nationalism in its most extreme form are among the causes which have been mentioned by other writers, and I have not ignored them. If I have concentrated on the motive of destruction – of sacrifice and self-sacrifice, what Nicholas Mosley calls 'the black hole of willed self-destruction' – it is because this motive appears to me as the most powerful element in that 'hellish brew' which constituted the ideology of National Socialism; because there is abundant evidence to show that this motive had a special attraction for Hitler's contemporaries; and because justification through sacrifice has its roots in the German past.

I see no 'direct line from Luther to Hitler'. The sacrificial motive with its roots in Judaism and Christianity is a phenomenon of European culture. But only in Germany after the end of the Great War did this motive coincide with a situation of anarchy in which everything seemed possible because, as Nietzsche had said, 'everything is permitted'.

The myth of the weak leader (see below, page 14) and the belief that 'the Führer does not know' (pages 113, 214) are not discoveries of Mr Irving's. These are old myths, to be found in German medieval literature as well as in some major writings from Weimar classicism onwards. Again it should be emphasized that such myths are not mentioned in order to suggest that 'the whole of German history' points to and culminates in National Socialism. No historical necessity need be brought in to explain the Third Reich; nor, however, should it be seen as a mere fortuitous episode. My thesis is that Hitler and his henchmen owe their place in German history to his intuitive understanding and exploitation of an important aspect of that history – to his understanding of what was possible in Germany and Europe in his time.

J.P.S.   *December 1983*

1 The Representative Individual

The elements of the popular image are readily assembled. They include the famous laundry-blue eyes, whose supposedly hypnotic spell is mentioned by a variety of witnesses; the unruly forelock and moustache, intended as emblems of Southern artistic genius and the Prussian military spirit respectively, dating back to the period of early films ('*der schöne Adolf*' of the Munich circle mingles with the figure of Adolphe Menjou); the Leader's stance, right hand raised in salute, left hand clasped over the belt-buckle in a gesture intended for resoluteness, in reality disguising the hand's tremor; the strained smile of the lover of blond children, his arms full of alpine flowers arranged in the manner of a Wilhelminian still-life. His private secretaries invariably speak of Hitler's elaborate, Old Vienna courtesy, his considerateness and charm. A Munich historian who attended Hitler's speech in the Bürgerbräukeller on 8 November 1923 was struck by his 'childlike, frank expression of happiness that I shall never forget'. A colleague, professor of racial hygiene at Munich University, giving evidence at Hitler's trial in February 1924, describes him in the language characteristic of the age, the language which Hitler and National Socialism made peculiarly their own: 'For the first time I saw Hitler at close quarters. Face and head: bad race, mongrel. Low, receding forehead, ugly nose, broad cheekbones, small eyes, dark hair. Facial expression: not of a man commanding with full self-control, but betraying insane excitement. Finally, an expression of blissful egotism.'

Above all there is, during all but the last stages of Hitler's career, the public orator. The staccato invective begins slowly,

rises to abuse and vituperation. A hoarse, grating voice with a
narrow range of pitch and strained beyond its natural volume
explodes and breaks, is quickly cleared, breaks again. The long,
conscious pauses which free the waves of thunder from the
public in front of him and below are used with great deliberation to scan the next part of the script, his hand raised to calm
the roar when he is ready to proceed, the crescendos of abuse
alternating with harsh, hectic avowals and public declarations
of an intimate, personal commitment and manly sincerity.
Inalienably part of the European experience of the 'thirties
and 'forties, the true nature of the man is trivialized and ob-
scured rather than illuminated by the antics of Charles Chaplin
and the deeply unfunny comedy of Bertolt Brecht.

To most German audiences the voice was enigmatic, its
manner of speech strangely vertiginous and synthetic. Characteristic not of a local dialect or class but of some Southern
German social no-man's land, it is the voice of no one and all.
Liberal intellectuals were not impressed:

> Then Adolf Hitler steps forward and has to wait five minutes
> for the tumult to die down. He is pale, nervous; and words are
> not immediately at his command. The first few sentences he
> speaks with notes in his hand . . . and then he launches into
> the tone of his popular harangues. What do they consist of,
> where does their effectiveness lie? Those hearing him for the
> first time are a little disappointed. His voice hasn't a full, clear
> sound, it seems hasty and hoarse; Hitler's German – unmis-
> takably Austrian in origin but not Viennese, reminiscent rather
> of the High German of Vienna civil servants who come from
> German-speaking Bohemia. . . .
> A 'stodgy' [*knödlig*] language, as they call it in Austria. Com-
> prehensible all the same, and indeed audible over a range of
> 60 metres. To a Munich audience this German-Bohemian
> officialese sounds like cultured speech. . . . In view of this
> easy susceptibility to words among the lower middle-class
> masses, one finds it doubly regrettable that the Germans
> completely lack orators with the gift of saying something
> intelligent in popular, graphic terms. Set beside the stutterers

of today, Hitler is an orator. And yet his command of rhetoric, his art of arranging and constructing his speech and leading up to his main points in a logical sequence, is very limited. It also lacks the best seasoning – humour. Hitler is wholly humourless, just bombastic. His climaxes consist in a redoubling of the bombast . . .

Rhetorically weak, thought-content nil; there only remains, as the most effective factor in Hitler's speech, his capacity to convey transports of feeling. The Greeks are known to have valued euphony above all else in speech, which they thought of as 'beautiful song'. The Italians and French have a similar attitude; their great orators are singers. The German is won over by feeling, because, with his aversion for histrionics, he looks for the man of faith, of character. Perhaps Hitler believes what he says; at any rate, it's the tone of impassioned conviction which brings him success. What it comes to is the art of rhetoric at its most primitive level, and politics surely fit for the kindergarten. . . .

But then, 'liberal intellectuals and pen-pushers' are the last people he would *wish* to impress.

These are the outward signs, consciously organized into a configuration, a *Gestalt* of unparalleled efficacy. Never before in history has *the idea of an image* been introduced into politics and exploited with comparable purposefulness.

All these features are deeply familiar to several generations of Hitler's contemporaries; for the post-war generations they are fast turning into the simplified outline of a horror comic. What does the figure amount to? Is it no more than the *grand guignol* of a bygone age? Historical research is doing its best to stem the tide of simplification. As we go down the list of the more important biographers, from Rudolf Olden (1936), Hermann Rauschning (1940), Konrad Heiden (1936, 1944) to H. R. Trevor-Roper (1947), Alan Bullock (1952, 1962), W. A. Jenks (1960), B. F. Smith (1967), and Werner Maser (1971), we find each more meticulous than his predecessor in the sifting of fact

from fiction, of documented evidence from inference and interpretation. Seeing what falsehoods were perpetrated by the
hagiographers of Hitler's regime, such accuracy is only to be
welcomed. Yet there is a point at which it is apt to defeat its
own purpose, which I take to be an understanding of the
past. A montage of biographical minutiae – including for instance a list of all the subjects set at the entrance examinations
into the painting class of the Viennese Academy of Fine Arts
which Hitler failed in 1907 and 1908; or again, a list of all the
medicaments (virility pills, anti-flatulence tablets, cardiac
stimulants and all) which the insalubrious Dr Morell prescribed
for him during the last six years of his life; not to mention the
story of the missing testicle – all this does not necessarily lead
to better insight. More details often entail less sense. Both
Bullock and Heiden (Bullock's main single source, deserving
fuller acknowledgement than he receives) may occasionally
get a fact wrong, but unlike Maser they are attempting a
coherent historical portrait, not just a series of biographical
fragments. The facts of the case – chief among them the
metamorphosis of the Nobody of Vienna into the Leader
of Greater Germany – are so extraordinary that where they
are left to 'tell their own story' they make hardly any
sense at all.

A host of German, English and American scholars are at
work on accounts of specific aspects of Hitler's rise to power
and of his rule. Diaries, memoranda, police dossiers, Hitler's
speeches, notes, and table-talk have been and are being edited
in great numbers, though it is doubtful whether new facts of
great significance are likely to come from these labours. Social
historians and sociologists, on the other hand, have been
revising the evidence offered by Hitler's own contemporaries
and stressing the importance of socio-economic trends at the
expense of the man and his career as 'Leader of the Nation,
Supreme Commander of the Armed Forces, Head of Government and supreme executive chief, Supreme Judiciar and
Leader of the Party'. The apparent banality and low intellectual

content of Hitler's own views as well as the derivativeness and self-contradictions of his regime have led some scholars to conclude that Germany under the National Socialists was a vast network of interlocking organizations with a ghostly Nothing at its core. The passing of time, as well as modes of enquiry rooted in a wholly different social situation, have brought about a sort of Tolstoyan foreshortening: a perspective in which the individual recedes behind 'the accidents of history' or 'the forces of society', his role restricted to the episodic.

This view appears to be corroborated by the failure of creative literature to add very much to our understanding of Hitler's personality. The literary imagination has on the whole found itself outstripped by the facts of the case. In July 1933 (the date may surprise those who are given to post-dating the horrors) the famous Viennese satirist Karl Kraus wrote, '*Mir fällt zu Hitler nichts ein*' ('As to Hitler, I have no comment to make'). And although this is followed by an essay of more than 300 pages which constitutes one of the greatest political and cultural polemics ever written, there is poetic truth in Kraus's famous dictum. The satirist whose incomparable wit and articulate indignation had commented on the follies and outrages of thirty years of Central European history now acknowledges that what is happening in 'the New Germany' is beyond the reach of satire, beyond the meaning that literature can encompass. And, apart from a few pages by Richard Hughes and Günter Grass, creative literature has failed to illuminate the central figure of German and European history in the first third of the twentieth century. Here again, then, we seem to be left with a phantom, a centre of Nothing. Yet this relative failure is characteristic of the travail of literature in many other areas of the modern world – the world which is what it is partly as the result of Hitler's acts of destruction. Tolstoy's historico-philosophical epilogue, in which he argues for the notion of impersonal historical forces, contradicts but does not invalidate the bulk of *War and Peace*, a panorama of living persons. If there were no other differences between Hitler and Napoleon, the existence of *War and Peace* and Beethoven's Third Symphony alone would make any significant comparison problematic. But even though it may be impossible to represent it through a panorama of living persons, the Hitler phenomenon – its reality and myth – remains the most important single phenomenon of its age.

The military and paramilitary organizations that combined in the structure of the Third Reich did not make Hitler's leadership redundant, nor did they make him into a mere figurehead. On the contrary: the more we come to know about these groups and organizations, the more clearly we perceive the astonishing fact that this huge array of jealous and mutually hostile factions, beset with internecine conflicts, plots and counterplots, was held together, until April 1945, by the promises and cajolings, the threats and tantrums, the appeals to loyalty and invitations to expedient betrayal, the contempt and praise, the self-assurance, the realism and fantasies, the cynicism and professed commitment, of one man. The hostility between the Army and the SS, or between the SS and the Security Police (SD) in the Russian campaign was hardly less violent than had been the open war between the SA and the SS which in 1934 led to the 'Night of the Long Knives'. Precisely because any one ideological element was likely to be contradicted by another, precisely because all institutional patterns were fragmentary and only fortuitously related to the political practice of the Party (except for anti-Semitism, and even there differences of emphasis can be found), the figure at the centre alone guaranteed the survival of the state.

When Mussolini suffered the traditional manner of death of the deposed dictator, the Fascist Grand Council survived; and the ministers of the short-lived Republic of Salò could claim with some justice that they were trying to resuscitate certain social ideas of early fascism which Mussolini had once believed in and later betrayed. Nothing of this kind happened in Germany. Visitors in the late 1940s were often told that the Third Reich had been an era of faith: 'What we believed in was misguided, perhaps wicked', one often heard it said, 'but our good faith, the sincerity of our belief – how *that* was abused and exploited . . .!' Yet the actual content of that belief remained mysterious. And the reason why it proved next to impossible to find out *what* people had believed in was not so much their disingenuousness and wilful forgetting as rather their real difficulty in recalling the message now that the voice was gone. Just as Hitler's suicide – the mode of death of one who yielded to outside pressures and an inner voice but was never deposed – was followed by a collapse of the state he created, so nothing remained of the structure of ideas and opinions, of the views and resentments with which he had created and governed that state.

If sociological interpretations lose sight of the man behind the trends, it is the common failing of biographies that they abstract a man from his world – a procedure that is particularly misleading in the case of one whose every public word and every political act expressed for almost the whole of his career the fears and aspirations of his contemporaries. And the distorting effects of biography are magnified in the disclosures of psycho-pathology where these are offered as substitutes for historical studies. What they purport to explain are individual reactions and deeds, while wholly ignoring the historical and social matrix on which the deeds are imprinted, and the resistance of the social fabric at which the deeds were directed and which therefore co-determines the outcome. A view of Hitler as a psychopath or paranoiac fails to account for the fact that for a quarter of a century – from the early years of his political career in Munich to the end of 1944 – he was capable of entirely rational and realistic views based on objective appraisals of a variety of political situations. His manner in discussion was determined by tactical considerations as well as by long-term objectives. The notorious hysterical outbursts in personal encounters were for the most part as perfectly controlled as was the public oratory, the appearance of spontaneity giving way, at a moment's notice, to a sober acknowledgement of an opposing opinion if the situation demanded it. Not only could these outbursts be switched on and off at will, but in more continent moods, too, the men around him were favoured with confidences which varied according to a perceptive and accurate understanding of their personalities and positions: perceptive and accurate, that is, in relation to his own ends in view.

Since my main purpose is to describe the creation, substance and a reception of a myth, and the man behind it only in so far as he helps to explain the myth, I don't propose to add to the speculations about Hitler's psychic regressions, childhood deprivations, and deviant sexual habits. It may be (as the 'psycho-historians' assure us) that the pursuit of political power is 'really' a way of satisfying anal-erotic desires, or that Hitler's outlook was 'basically infantile'. It is far from clear how such explanations are to account for his political success, which is unprecedented in German history, or his military success, which is unparalleled in the history of modern Europe. We may not be sure whether he really was 'a haunted man obsessed by fantasies about the Jewish world conspiracy', but we can determine with some certainty why he chose to make anti-Semitism his main political platform and what need it fulfilled in contemporary German society. Our concern is not with the psycho-pathology of the man but with the public presentation of his intimate thinking in the form of a system of values with a claim to objective validity. Given the circumstances for which it was designed, it is in no sense the system of a madman.

The society whose leader Hitler became was one which, for all the chaos and violence it indulged in, aspired to no radical social or economic reforms, and looked askance on political changes. 'Reared in an age of security', Hitler's generation experienced the collapse of the Wilhelminian Empire as an unprecedented disruption of its social bonds. Even in that disrupted world, however, it seems doubtful whether a mere hysterical fanatic, let alone one clinically insane, could have gauged and exploited the situation so accurately and consistently over a period of more than twenty-five years. A very few of the people with whom Hitler associated after his return to Munich in 1918, and among whom he found his later collaborators, were initially criminal and may have been insane. But this must not blind us to the fact that the views he held and shared with his associates had been without exception the staple of extremist German right-wing politics for some fifty years before 1918; that in his rise to power Hitler appealed not only to the destructive instincts of a vanquished nation but also to certain personal values, values of a traditional kind, acknowledged and accepted by German – and to a lesser extent European – society at large. Firmness of purpose, seriousness, devotion to a cause – to mention but the most obvious – have their place on a European table of values.

The time for accusations and the apportioning of blame is past. The common view of the moral dimension in which Hitler moved – summed up in Bullock's phrase 'moral . . . cretinism' – does not need revising. Yet if it is too late in the day to emphasize moral judgements, likewise there is no point in avoiding them. Thus (to guard against one kind of misunderstanding) it is worth pointing out that to designate Hitler as the central agent of a policy of destruction on a European scale is very far from absolving the German society of his time from its responsibility for that policy. Among the most interesting passages of his writings, public speeches and private conversations are those in which he explicitly assumes the role of a representative of the German nation and spokesman of 'the forces of German history'. His views are 'typical' by virtue of their mediocrity and lack of distinction, but they are also 'representative' (in something like a literary sense) by virtue of presenting what many of his contemporaries hoped for and feared, but in a stronger, more uncompromising, more radical form than they dared: he is representative by virtue of pressing contemporary thought to the point of no return. This claim to be the Nation's spokesman was frequently reiterated, and several variations of it were offered; in the following example it is reinforced by an allusion to the liturgy for Ash Wednesday (*'memento homo quia pulvis es et in pulverem reverteris'*):

> I have come from the people. In the course of fifteen years I have slowly worked my way up from the people, together with this Movement. No-one has set me to be above this people. I have grown from the people, I have remained in the people, and to the people I shall return. It is my ambition not to know a single statesman in the world who has a better right than I to say that he is a representative of his people!

Now, this claim cannot of course be accepted in the absolute form Hitler gave it. (It is notorious, and part of his appeal in an age searching for a god of some kind, that all his claims were expressed in absolute terms.) But I hope to show good reason for believing that, at certain critical times and suitably qualified, the claim was true, and that what enabled him to make it was no mysterious 'instinct' but his superior political consciousness. The supra-personal vision of world history and of his task in that history was one of the most effective weapons in his political armoury. His appeal to the public, like his conduct of the affairs of the state he adapted to his ends, was nothing if not intensely, incomparably personal.

While the attempt to offer a fuller understanding of the Hitler myth involves no moral revaluation, it does involve a new look at his intellectual equipment. With fuller evidence of his studies in Vienna and Munich now before us, and with the evidence of the table-talk of 1941–42, it becomes clear that (to quote Bullock's phrase in full) to speak of Hitler's 'moral *and intellectual* cretinism' is no longer justified. His knowledge of history ('A man who has no sense of history is like a man who has no hearing or sight'), his architectural knowledge, his readings in the literature of war – all these are rather more extensive than previous biographers had assumed, nor were his sources only cheap pamphlets and newspapers. This is not to suggest that he was capable of disinterested study. The most consequential of his interests, the knowledge of biology and genetics he acquired in Vienna, which coloured his vocabulary and fatally determined his outlook, remained entirely superficial and flawed by false analogies. All his enquiries were geared to concrete political ends, and even his detailed knowledge of the history of architecture was used mainly to surprise and impress his visitors. He liked to stun them into silence by long recitals of divers facts and figures, yet his intellect was not all just memory work. When in 1935 Anthony Eden on a visit in Berlin observed pointedly that the English liked to see international treaties kept, Hitler's instant repartee was apposite in more senses than one:

> Surely that has not always been the case. In 1813 there were treaties which did not allow a German army. Yet I don't remember Wellington at Waterloo saying to Blücher, 'Your army is illegal, please leave the battlefield!'

He liked to hold forth on the history of the medieval emperors, calling it the true glory of the German past, and he evaluated it as shrewdly as any Austrian civil servant of the old school:

> Because of my origin, I am in a wonderful position vis-à-vis the leaders of the other tribes of the German Reich. I can point to the fact that throughout five centuries my own fatherland was a mighty empire with a great imperial city, *but that I didn't hesitate to sacrifice my homeland to the imperial idea.*

The historical understanding that informs this kind of thinking, apart from being embedded in the usual tribal clap-trap, is neither superficial nor cliché-ridden.

This is not an intellectual rehabilitation of Hitler, merely an indication of the kind of knowledge he possessed and pressed into the service of his ambition. The frequent triteness of the historical parallels he used is misleading. His sense for 'the essential in history' was as acute as his sense for 'the deepest aspirations, hopes, fears and sense of destiny' of his contemporaries, and he realized that the one was inseparable from the other. Historicism was the form of knowledge that counted in the age he represented, for it helped to bring its thinking to the point of radical decisions. In all this, then, one is struck by the representativeness of the public and private figure alike, by his grasp of most aspects (other than literature) of the 'culture' of his day.

All representation – whether in the arts or in politics – contains an element of fiction which, exploited for its political effects, becomes a myth, a lie. The nature of Hitler's representativeness changes. Throughout the 'twenties he is absorbing and learning from his encompassing society – not least from the political battles with his communist rivals. Thereafter, perhaps from his address to the Düsseldorf industrialists' club of January 1932 onward, it is he who 'leads' that society and dominates its outlook as well as its *praxis*. To understand the man in his changing situation one is bound to give one's attention to his explicit statements, and more especially to those of his statements in which he appealed to what that society valued most highly, in which *he spoke its language*. But (and here is the second source of a possible misunderstanding) to take his actual language seriously is to invest the object of one's enquiry – the lie – with a measure of dignity it does not deserve. As far as I can see this is inevitable. To give thought to anything is to dignify it. The very act of description elevates. For this reason it is salutary to recall the sheer unpleasantness and deeply unattractive character of the man; to recall the practices that lie behind that complex mythical edifice with its appeal to time-honoured values and societal ideals; to recall that he had men hanged on meathooks while their trousers were being torn off them, and that he watched the scene on a film made for his private viewing; and to recall that life in the concentration camps was part of a system of brutality and oppression kept going by a nation-wide conspiracy of silence. Here there is one point at which the man and the myth coincide. The ultimate aim of one as of the other is to go beyond anything that can be described as political.

There are many aspects of life under National Socialism which are more reminiscent of life in a Central African tribe than in a civilized European state – a life determined by nothing more sophisticated than the battle for survival. In a period of prolonged drought, we read in a recent account of such a tribe, there is 'simply no room . . . for such luxuries as family and sentiment and love. So close to the verge of starvation, such luxuries could mean death, and is it not a singularly foolish luxury to die for someone already dead, or weak, or old? This seemed to strike hard at the assumption that there are such things as basic human values, at the very notion of virtue, of goodness even.' We are surely justified in speaking of 'moral cretinism' where there is a total absence of equity and altruism of any kind, and where the visible signs of deprivation and physical suffering provide almost the only available sources of pleasure and amusement. Among members of that tribe there is clear evidence, in the tales of those few old enough to recall better times, that such a moral and mental outlook is directly caused by material conditions of the utmost harshness, for this is a 'society' whose mental and emotional life is wholly dominated by hunger. Its conditions, which can hardly be called 'social' since they make man into a solitary scavenger, can only be compared with conditions in the concentration camps. It is as well to remind ourselves that one of the aims of the Hitler regime – that aspect of its teaching designed for the initiates – was to create and perpetuate emergency situations in which mental and moral reactions of the kind observed in that tribe on the threshold of death would become not just tolerated but indeed 'natural', the main difference being that such reactions should be directed not by all against all, but by the 'elite' against clearly, 'scientifically' defined groups of people. But this was only a temporary difference. There is little doubt that in the long run the singling out of hostile groups would have failed to deflect the aggressive tendencies of the regime away from itself; in the long run, this society could not have preserved itself from self-destruction.

2 The Authentic Experience

Historical situations (like literary ones) are encounters between tradition and the individual talent. Unlike many social scientists I take it for granted that what is at work on the données of the social world is *an individual*, a single man with the relative and realistically determined freedom that is reflected in his choices and decisions. But can we speak of freedom in Hitler's case? Is he not a man driven by an ineluctable Will, an evil spirit, by the very demon of necessity? Seeing the way he – the demobilized soldier, failed art student and painter of unimpressive landscapes and architectural views – floundered into politics, what freedom did he ever exercise? Like other supreme politicians before him, Hitler had the gift of finding his bearings and making his most effective decisions in situations which had arisen as a result of his irresoluteness, of his half-conscious choosing not to choose. Once such a situation had arisen, he displayed a marked degree of originality in the handling of its political and social aspects (as opposed to the economic, which he always regarded as secondary). This originality seems to me greater than either historians or sociologists are willing to admit; whereas the values to which he appealed and which he professed seem to me a good deal more traditional and more widely accepted than has been thought hitherto – but then, few writers have undertaken the task (which is less than exhilarating) of looking seriously at the system of these values, and at the myth which he created and others helped to cultivate.

His originality consists in a deliberate reversal of the functions normally attributed to personal-existential values on the one hand and social-political values on the other. Hitler's dis-

covery, which others around him made in the immediate
post-war era though none knew how to exploit it to the full, is
astonishingly simple: it is to introduce a conception of personal
authenticity into the public sphere and proclaim it as the chief
value and sanction of politics. What he does is to translate the
notions of genuineness and sincerity and living experience
(designated in German by the word '*Erlebnis*' and its various
compounds) from the private and poetic sphere into the sphere
of public affairs; and to validate this move by the claim that he,
the exceptional individual with his intimate personal experience
of 'the little man's weal and woe', is the Nation's representative by virtue of the genuineness of that experience.

Politics, in the scheme Hitler evolved, is personalized, whereas all impersonal aspects of politics, including its stable institutions and its foundation in the rule of law, are designated
as 'abstract', 'bureaucratic', or 'inauthentic'. This ploy,
Hitler's major contribution to the political theory of fascism,
owes its success to being part of a specifically German situation.
Whereas in other Western countries politics based on the analogy
with private experience comes to be distrusted as arbitrary and
tyrannical, and is superseded by politics based on and regulated
by constitutional and parliamentary devices, German thinking
is apt to distrust these devices as 'mere form' and sham. The
Romantics of the early nineteenth century and after them the
right-wing nationalists of the Second Reich acclaim the analogy
and see in the charismatic personality – the 'genuine' or
'natural' leader – the fulfilment of their political hopes. Once a
self-consciously German ideology is articulated and Weimar
democracy is identified with the Versailles '*Diktat*', those
institutional devices come to be associated with 'the West'
and correspondingly discredited. This is the moment when the
politics of authenticity and of personal experience moves into
the centre of the stage.

Courage and personal resoluteness, vitality and heroism in
adversity, silence and self-discipline – these are qualities which
for men like Marx and Lenin had a certain importance as the

personal attributes of a politician, as means to an ideological end, but it would never have occurred to them to think of such qualities as the main content of their political ideology. For Hitler these personal values are the substantial tenets of the *Weltanschauung* he professes, their cultivation is the proclaimed purpose of his national programme. The notion of the Master Race (if we are to take it seriously) is not really a political conception at all but the hypostatization of certain biological and moral qualities. However, when it is placed within a certain social context, the notion of the Master Race becomes a political factor – though no sooner has it done that, than its political character is denied, for the totalitarian state knows no 'politics', only the undivided Will of the elect. (The partial but disastrous connexion of all this with Nietzsche's thinking lies in the fact that, as he misunderstands, so they misrepresent the political significance of race.) It is true that something like this 'heroic' vision of man was preached by Italian Fascism before Hitler lighted on it. Mussolini proclaimed it as he pressed for Italy's entry into the war in 1915, and so did the egregious d'Annunzio as he set out on his antics in Fiume in 1919. But it is Hitler who gives the heroism its personal stamp, its 'authenticity', and thus adds a religious ingredient – a sort of metaphysical *schmaltz* – to the brew.

Hitler's own character as well as the accidents of his personal history make him virtually unemployable in any stable peace-time society. But in a situation of radical disaffection, may not these deprivations be turned into substantial political assets? He returns from the War without a civilian skill or qualifications, without a job or position of any kind, without property or connexions, without as much as a nationality or a home address. All he has is his Aryan race, his decorations, *and his experience*. None of these things, of course, is unique. What *is* unique is his recognition, heedlessly pursued, that a concept as problematic as race, a confirmation as haphazard as a medal, a validation as specious as private experience publicly exhibited, can become the elements of a new political style. He flounders into politics. Since the Army is the only society whose life he has willingly shared and the barracks (as one of his officers put it) are his only home, he clings to the Army and takes the first job it offers him, that of a political informer and instructor. However, once he recognizes the opportunity that lies before him, his irresoluteness comes to an end.

Hitler's own account is a bit more stylized. The hardest decision he ever took in his life (he tells his generals twenty years later) was his decision to give up his ambition of becoming 'one of the best architects in Germany', and to choose a political career instead. And this decision came to him (he says in *Mein Kampf*) the moment he realized his superlative gift as a public speaker. Yes, but what had he to say? Others beside him spoke out harshly on the subject of the Jews, on the treaties of Brest-Litovsk and Versailles, the betrayal of the German Army within sight of ultimate victory. He too held forth on these topics, for hours on end. But he did more than that. In support of his views he cited, not facts or logic or justice, but the greatest of his assets, his '*Fronterlebnis*'. (Just so, after 1933, he would mythologize *this* story of his humble political beginnings in his '*Parteierzählung*', with which he prefaced every major public speech.) A frightening, unrestrained violence of tone and vocabulary informs even his earliest recorded speeches. And this violence too derives its sanction from the idea of authenticity, from the conveyed conviction that his every utterance is the expression of *this man's genuine feelings*. And are not feelings, unlike the complexities of economics or politics, something Everyman can understand and judge and share?

The conception of an authentic 'inner experience' translated into politics is used in three ways: as a substitute for programme and consistent ideology; as a social symbol and rallying point; and in pseudo-religious terms as a living witness. 'Here is my experience, here are my rock-like convictions, my representative *Erlebnis* of the world', Hitler is saying. 'This is the self-validating source of my likes and hates, my scheme of values which is right because it is yours as well as mine, yours by being mine. I am not a man to politick, or haggle with Fate. To my every decision my whole existence, and thus yours, is committed. Therefore follow me, for there is no other way and I cannot go wrong, the forces of History and Nature (or of the Lord Almighty, or to Fate) are on my side.' This, or something like this, is the motto of Hitler's political message at the beginning of his career; to these sentiments he will continue to appeal until the end, and even in his last will and testament he will invoke this sanction of a personal witness.

The topics to which I shall turn in these pages – Hitler's belief in 'the heroism of the Will', in the superiority of 'the natural' over all rational and institutional criteria, and in the continuity of foreign and domestic politics as well as of war and peace; his recognition of the need for hostile groups, his invocation of an either/or decisiveness, and his appeal to 'absolute sacrifice' and destruction as the ultimate proving-stone of individual men and nations alike – all these are aspects of one coherent fiction, which Hitler's skill, imposed on the circumstances of the age, turns into an effective myth. But what legitimizes the myth and gives it credence is its respectable past in the scheme of traditional values: there is a sense in which the story of Hitler begins where the argument of Lionel Trilling's *Sincerity and Authenticity* concludes. And it it is in Trilling's discussion of Joseph Conrad's *Heart of Darkness* (1899) that we get a glimpse of the moral ambivalence at the root of the modern commitment to authenticity as a self-validating mode of life, and of its transition from the private sphere of sentiment to the public sphere of political action. To be authentic means not so much to be honest about one's self as to be all of a piece. But if the self is all tattered and torn and full of fears? Then it must be made all one, even in the act of exhibiting its wounds. And the myth which makes it so will bear the signs of its origin.

3 The Language of Sacrifice

Traces of reality cling to all myths, and Hitler was not simply the opposite of what his propaganda machinery made him out to be. It is true that, leaving to one side his service in the first World War, he himself was not exactly a 'heroic phenomenon' either in his appearance or in his personal conduct. He never quite dropped the feckless habits of the sort of artistic dilettante whose case-histories fill the pages of *Imago*, Freud's psychoanalytical journal. He shunned exposure to physical danger as well as attendance at the tortures and murders he ordered (though he seems to have watched the film of the trial and execution of the July 1944 conspirators with avid attention). While Ernst Röhm, about to be shot by the SS in a Munich prison, was refusing to kill himself and, frenziedly baring his chest, was asking that Hitler in person should execute the sentence of death he had just passed, Hitler was giving a garden party in the Reich Chancellery to members of his cabinet, their wives and children. The man who planned the Final Solution and set it in train was too squeamish personally to give notice to a cook in his service on finding out that she was Jewish. Not until February or March 1945 did he personally visit a bombed-out German town. And at the point when, with almost the whole Continent of Europe at his feet, his most extravagant aspirations to heroic leadership were fulfilled, he was surrounded by an atmosphere in which, as one of his generals put it, 'nothing was genuine except fear, fear in all hues and shades, an atmosphere of servility, nervousness and lying, which made people almost physically sick'. In sum, it seems fair to say that his personal conduct was as far from the heroic myth he fostered as his physique was from the Nordic racial ideal he frequently extolled and occasionally ridiculed.

But there is another aspect of the heroic myth, which *is* part of the regime's unvarnished reality: its appeal to self-sacrifice and *Götterdämmerung*-like destruction. More than that: the destructive, and ultimately self-destructive, drift of Hitler's cast of mind and of his policies is a reflection of the intellectual temper of his age. The liberal journalist Carl von Ossietzky (who died after imprisonment in Dachau) wrote that among German intellectuals there were 'all too many lovers of every sort of catastrophe, and gourmets of world-political misfortunes'. Franz Werfel, once a member of the Expressionist avant-garde, wrote shortly before his death in Hollywood in August 1945 one of the most succinct characterizations of that spirit of the age to which Hitler – the myth *and* the reality – responded:

> I have come to know many kinds of arrogance, in myself and in others. Yet there is no more consuming, more impudent, more disdainful, more diabolical arrogance than that of the avant-garde artists and radical intellectuals, bursting with the vain passion to be profound and obscure and difficult, and to cause pain: all this I can confirm, since in my youth I myself was of that company for a while. Mocked in amused indignation by a few philistines, we inconsiderable men were the first to bring fuel to the hell-fire in which mankind is now roasting.

But it was by no means only the self-possessed satanists and tawdry 'writers in extremis' of the 'twenties who were stoking the fires of hell to come. Among the conservative writers of the older generation, too, who spoke powerfully of the noble tradition of *Geist* and of literature's national responsibility, the same strangely self-destructive temper – we may here call it 'the sacrifice syndrome' – prevailed. Not even Thomas Mann, far and away the most perceptive of them, seems to have grasped the full significance of this mode of thought when it was presented, not merely as a literary theme, but as a pattern of national values.

In the autumn of 1914 Thomas Mann began his 'intellectual war service with weapon in hand', as he called it – meaning his series of polemical essays in which, throughout the next four years, he was to set out both his position as German intellectual and patriot, and Germany's role in the war. Perhaps the most fascinating of these is *Frederick and the Great Coalition*, written in December 1914 and published early in 1915. The patriotic and homiletic drift of this elegant and complexly ironical essay is unmistakable. The harsh, fanatical character of Prussia's greatest king as well as his diplomatic and military moves are intended to be read 'typologically': August 1914 is a 'repetition or continuation' of 1756; the 'war of preventive aggression' against Belgium is identified with Frederick's invasion of Saxony; Frederick's long years of travail and war, his friendlessness and lack of reliable allies, are put down to his jealous determination that 'Germany' (meaning Prussia) should act out her grim destiny by following his star. His moves are presented as anticipations of Germany's efforts to repudiate the imposition of 'Western' values and to defend her own anti-democratic and anti-Voltairean tradition, if need be by force of arms. Is all this much more than a patriotic tract for the times? The parallel Thomas Mann wishes his readers to draw between the Seven Years' War and the contemporary conflict is as convincing as such parallels usually are; the portrait of Frederick, composed largely of telling anecdotes and familiar quotations, is a literary montage by the author (perhaps also the hero) of *Death in Venice* (which appeared two years earlier) rather than a cool historical assessment; and it is unlikely that Hitler ever heard of the essay, even though in the last years of his life he seems to have read every study of his hero that came his way. Yet whatever may be the value of Mann's essay as history, the aspect under which he presents Frederick, the 'sacrifice syndrome', faithfully anticipates Hitler's own self-stylization and a major aspect of the myth as it will develop in the years to come. And this of course is no coincidence but one more proof of how much broader was the base of Hitler's appeal than those who were to oppose him, including Thomas Mann, realized.

Mann's subtle and sympathetic presentation of the King's mind is difficult to convey, precisely because it is at once sympathetic and riven by paradox. His King of Prussia is a cold monster, a man of the utmost harshness, all his interests and an immense 'Will' turned to one end and one end only, the securing and aggrandizement of that sandy, marshy, godforsaken yet not wholly charmless bit of territory he inherited from his draconic father, Frederick William I. Frederick's originally artistic nature ('I could have been among Germany's first architects', his admirer will tell his captive audience in the *Wolfsschanze*) is consciously sacrificed to the demands of the state, so are Frederick's friends and his every prospect of contentment and ease of life. And so are the precepts of common morality. Driven by 'the demon within', Frederick brushes aside every civilized custom and courtesy and every inconvenient law, too; every treaty and idea of justice that stands in the way of his ambition. *His* ambition? Not really, says Thomas Mann. In 'sacrificing' his philosophical life, epitomized in his friendship with Voltaire, Frederick is not driven by vanity or the desire for military glory or personal power, nor even by the invert's loathing of women and the rule of women, though all these factors are allowed some weight in Mann's analysis of his motives. Bound up with these yet transcending them is Frederick's paramount awareness of the fate in store for his nation: 'He was a victim', Thomas Mann writes, as though the term, *'Opfer'*, were not ambiguous enough without being played upon: 'True, he believed he had sacrificed himself – had sacrificed his youth to his father, his years of manhood to the State. But he was wrong if he believed he could have chosen to do otherwise. He *was* a victim. He had to do injustice and lead a life against Thought' – the thought of Voltaire's Enlightenment – 'he was not allowed to be philosopher but had to be King so that a great nation's earthly mission should be fulfilled.' And he goes on to quote Frederick's Ahasuerus-like

plaint, 'The ox must draw his furrows, the nightingale must
sing, the dolphin must swim, and I – I must make war . . .'
This harshness of person, hardness of fate, and high price
of destiny are what Mann admires and offers his readers for
emulation. Frederick needs his victories, for they alone will
validate his position. Meaning that might is right? Well –
not quite, and yet . . .: 'It was only if success proved that he,
Frederick, was an emissary of Fate, that he was in the right and
always had been in the right.'

This is the train of thought Thomas Mann attributes to his
hero as he sets out on his solitary grim mission to impose his
Will upon Europe. But this argument, too, provides the salient
points of Mann's own assessment of the King, founder and
true representative of the Germany-to-be. 'This nation has a
hard time with itself', Thomas Mann had written (amid much
that had better remain unquoted) when war first broke out;
'it finds itself problematic, there are times when it is a sickness
unto itself, to the point of revulsion. Yet among individuals
and nations alike, those were ever the most valuable who had
the hardest time of all.' The phrase, '*die es am schwersten
hatten*', almost untranslatable in its idiomatic simplicity and
itself not overtaken by irony or criticism in any form, will
remain Thomas Mann's permanent 'moral' device; to receive
its fullest confirmation in *Doctor Faustus* of 1947, his final
reckoning with Hitler's world. Here, as we have seen, the
device serves to designate Frederick's true greatness. And this
greatness, in Thomas Mann's presentation of it, derives, not
from Frederick's diplomatic successes (they were few and un-
stable) or his victories (they were pyrrhic), but from the cost
of the achievement to himself (the cost to others being ignored),
from the size of Frederick's 'self-sacrifice' and the size of his
effort. In sum, a scheme emerges in which *value is commensurate
with the catastrophic nature of a man's existential project.*

This, no longer modified by any critical dialectic, is the
message of *Frederick and the Great Coalition*. But (we shall
ask) is there really a way from this essay in high historical

speculation, to Hitler's world of brutal and primitive power politics? The answer is to be found in the 'sacrifice syndrome'. Its chilling relevance both to the Hitler myth and to the understanding Hitler had of himself is attested throughout hiᴗ public career; there is scarcely a page of the *Table Talk* that does not bear the stamp of it.

Just so, there is no major German writer who does not comment on, and often contribute to, the catastrophe-mindedness of the age and its bitter delight in apocalyptic visions. Hitler's most immediate appeal is of course directed to a less sophisticated level of the populace:

> There are individual people who think they can damage National Socialism by saying, 'Ah yes, but everything [you have achieved] requires sacrifices!' Indeed, my worthy petits bourgeois, our struggle has required unceasing sacrifice. It's only you who haven't experienced it. Perhaps you fancy that our present-day [1936] Germany has become [what it is] because you made no sacrifices! No! Because we knew how to make sacrifices and because we wanted to make them – that is why this Germany has come [into being]. So if somebody tells us, 'The future too will demand sacrifices', then we say, 'Yes, indeed it will!' National Socialism is not a doctrine of inertia but a doctrine of conflict. Not a doctrine of happiness or good luck, but a doctrine of work and a doctrine of struggle, and thus also a doctrine of sacrifice.

No doubt the simple idea of 'sacrifices' for the sake of future material gain is part of the message. But again a fatal ambiguity, exploited by the rhetoric of repetition, informs the word *'Opfer'* – it is as though the German language itself, in its inability to distinguish between 'victim' and 'sacrifice', were an accessary to the ideology. In the presence of his table companions in the *Wolfsschanze* Hitler could on occasion drop all pretence:

> All in all it is surely best for someone who has no heir for his

house to be burned in it with all its contents, as though on a magnificent funeral pyre!

Endlessly the theme is reiterated, from the troglodytic Martin Bormann's pledge 'to perish in King Attila's hall like ye Nibelungs of olde' to Goebbels's ecstatic jubilation, which in 1945 recaptures the diction of the Expressionist plays of the 1920s and his own literary beginnings as a member of that school:

> Under the débris of our shattered cities the last so-called achievements of the middle-class nineteenth century have been finally buried. . . . Together with the monuments of culture there crumble also the last obstacles to the fulfilment of our revolutionary task. Now that everything is in ruins, we are forced to rebuild Europe. In the past, private possessions tied us to bourgeois restraint. Now the bombs, instead of killing all Europeans, have only smashed the prison walls which held them captive. . . . In trying to destroy Europe's future, the enemy has only succeeded in smashing its past; and with that, everything old and outworn has gone.

This is the mixture of truth and lie to which the regime owed its existence, dragging the country all the way to total defeat. What it expresses is the death-wish at the heart of the will to power. The myth had its roots in reality.

Adolf Hitler

00247. HS 756

00247. HS M28413

00247. HS 555

A322 1971

4 Propaganda as Perlocutionary Act

Hitler's will to power is usually seen, in Freudian terms, as the neurotic psyche's compensation for its deprivations, insecurities, and all encompassing fears. Whatever this hypothesis may do to explain the genealogy of the will in the individual, it does nothing to account for its success in the political world. And this success is anything but a matter of inwardness, it is the response the self encounters in the act of asserting itself: 'Men believe in the truth of all that is seen to be strongly believed in', writes Nietzsche. The histrionic self is inseparably linked with its audience, and its link is an unending flow of words. ('*Mein ganzes Leben war nichts als ein ständiges Überreden* – 'My whole life was nothing but constant cajolings!') The histrionic self is indeed 'committed': not, however, to an idea or an ideal, not to anything outside itself, but to the performance of its own act of commitment. 'In all great deceivers a remarkable process is at work, to which they owe their power', writes Nietzsche in his finest *moraliste* vein: 'In the very act of deception with all its preparation, the dreadful voice, expression and gestures, amid their effective scenario they are overcome *by their belief in themselves*; it is this belief which then speaks so persuasively, so miracle-like, to the audience', and is embraced by them.

It is in the political mass meeting that 'the very act of deception' is consummated; and even though here too Hitler had the example of Mussolini's theatrical manifestations before him, the elaborate ritual as well as the function of these meetings within National Socialist practice give them an importance they did not have in Italian Fascism. Several commentators have pointed to the orgiastic atmosphere generated, and contemporary witnesses have described Hitler's state of exhaustion after his big public performances in unmistakably sexual terms.

The first thing to notice about Hitler's speeches on these occasions is how little difference there is between those delivered before February 1933, for the purpose of securing votes in supposedly democratic election campaigns, and those spoken after Hitler's assumption of power and designed to secure popular support for his policies. In each case much the same elements contribute to much the same effect. As often as not the timing of the speech is made to follow closely on some local or national success, and later on a major diplomatic or military victory. The speeches are always held in the late evening; Hitler observes that at any other time of day it is impossible to conjure up the appropriate atmosphere of tension and keyed-up expectation. At the opening stage, and sometimes for more than an hour, he recounts the 'party history' with its recital of all the familiar metamorphoses (unknown soldier into national leader, tiny band of starry-eyed idealists into history's greatest 'Movement', betrayed and deserted fatherland into great and mighty nation). There follows what may be called the element of information: for example, Hitler's decision to stand as presidential candidate; or his decision to take Germany out of the League of Nations, or to press for 'a solution of the Sudeten German problem'. This 'information' is buttressed by a variety of historical, ideological or economic ruminations. Above all, however, it is conveyed within layer upon layer of invective in which a whole network of accusations, recitals of injustices, threats, real and imaginary fears, is personalized as existential attacks directed against the Führer of the German nation and thus against each single member of that nation. The nature of these attacks is carefully calibrated. Their agents are predictable (Jews, Communists, Slavs, the plutocratic, decadent West), the danger they entail must be massive enough to need a great national effort under a resolute leadership to overcome it: in fact it must be all but overwhelming, creating a situation on the stereotype of yes/no, either/or, all/nothing. Finally, the peroration reiterates the leader's iron resolve and his absolute commitment to the nation's future, though the invariable form this prophecy takes is the promise of revenge and the fulfilment of threats.

Here at last myth and reality are one: seen as a whole, the speech is a perlocutionary act. It claims for the present moment a greater national cohesion (a closer '*Volksgemeinschaft*') than Germany has known in all the centuries of her history, and through its very act of affirmation the claim is made good. The true purpose of the meeting is a show of strength, conspiratorial solidarity and nation-wide assent, hedged in by and inseparable from constant reminders of world-wide threats. Solidarity and agreement are *expressed and thus achieved* even before it has become quite clear what precisely the agreement is about. The audience is not being informed, it is made to perform; and its performance 'makes history'. This is the elimination of freedom which Hitler considers essential in mass politics.

It is a matter of some importance that the informational element should indeed be slight; in fact, it may be doubted whether Hitler's great public speeches ever contained anything that had not been disseminated by propaganda of one kind or another well beforehand. To their German audience they say nothing new. And there is good reason for this, since their effect *depends* on an all but complete foreknowledge of their informational content. Anyone who has ever given a public address knows that its most difficult moments are those in which a whole body of new information is being conveyed to the audience. Invariably these are the moments which strain the audience's attention to the utmost and attenuate the link that ties it to the speaker. But there are also other moments, when nothing much is being said that has not been said already

– when the information content is embarrassingly low yet the nexus between speaker and audience creates almost an identity between them. It is at this point – an informational minimum – that the audience is ready to take up the speaker's *parole* and to burst into an affirmation of what he has said: and the strongest affirmation is repetition.

Information, we know, comes to us in the shape of a question-and-answer set: all new information is offered in the form of an answer to a previously uttered – or more often merely implied – question. And dialogue occurs at the point at which the answer comes in turn to figure as the ground of a new question. . . . This is the set taken over by a mass orator like Hitler yet changed almost out of recognition. In the course of this change a political meeting ceases to be an instrument of political enlightenment and deliberation and becomes a weapon of political assertion. Its 'information' is conveyed in a question-and-answer game – a sort of Tinkerbell ploy – which demonstrates, as nothing else can, the unity of speaker and audience, of leader and led. The questions he is asking them may have the form of those partial questions requiring deliberation and choice, 'What do you want?', or Pilate's genuinely half-open question requiring at least a choice, 'Which is it you want?'; but what he is really putting before them are total questions, 'Do you want . . .?', with their entirely predictable Yes or No answers.

D'Annunzio at Fiume:

> 'A chi l'Italia?' [*Answer from the audience:*] 'A noi, a noi, a noi. . . .'

Hitler in 1936:

> 'I put this question to the German people: do you desire that the hatchet between us and France be buried at last, and that there should be peace and understanding? If that is what you wish, then say Yes.' [*Answer from the hall:*] 'Yes.'
> 'And I shall further ask the German people: "Do you desire

that we should oppress the French nation to curtail its rights?"
And it will say, "No, we do not want that!"
'I ask myself: who in fact are these elements that do not want peace, that do not want quiet, that do not want reconciliation, that continue to hound us and that must sow the seed of distrust – who are they really?' [*Answer from the hall:*] 'The Jews!'
'I know' [*applause lasting several minutes; Hitler clearly agrees with the answer, but wishing at this stage to avoid the direct accusation, he repeats the phrase so as to be able to conclude the sentence with a harmless generality:*] 'I know it is not the millions who would have to take up arms if these slanderers had their way and succeeded in their intentions. . . .'

And Goebbels after Stalingrad (February 1944):

'Do you believe with the Führer and with us in the final total victory of the German nation?' [*Answer:*] 'Yes.'
'Do you want total war?' [*Answer:*] 'Yes.'
'Do you want the war, if necessary, to be more total and radical than we can possibly imagine it today?' [*Answer:*] 'Yes.'

The answer to the total question, and thus the amount of deliberation required, is minimal, no more than a Yes or No. And this is all the audience need supply. Indeed, they have come in order to have themselves manoeuvred into a situation in which *this* answer – this Yes or No – is the only answer they *can* supply, morally and physically; where the moral is as close to the physical, the voice and the heat and the smoke, the beer, the Klieg lights, the knuckledusters and the screams and tears, as makes no difference. The procedure of the mass meetings as they developed in the 'twenties is one in which the existential content of the audience's affirmation becomes ever greater whereas the informational content of the speeches diminishes, until at the party rallies at Nuremberg the content drops out altogether and the 'exchange' between the Leader and the masses becomes pure ritual:

[*Hitler:*] 'Deutschland!'
[*Answer:*] 'Sieg Heil!'

'*Ja oder Nein*': three aspects of the relationship of myth to reality are subsumed under this catch-phrase of the public meetings. First, and most obviously, the formula represents Hitler's personal life-style and his intellectual habits. There is no need at this stage to demonstrate that he was a man utterly impatient of subtle situations, incapable of appreciating or thinking in nuances, of taking people as something other than either accomplices or enemies; that he was at all times, from his early days in Vienna to the last days in the bunker under the Reich Chancellery, incapable of conversation, confining himself either to harangues and monologues, or to gloomy silences; that he must at all times structure any public or group of people wholly according to his will or repudiate it if it resisted; and that, on a pattern established in his private relationships, he planned and created one big, overall, 'unitary' national situation in which no private belief and convictions, no acts of courage or charity were allowed to carry any significance except insofar as they contributed to the 'totality' of his regime.

Secondly, the *Yes or No* formula recalls the amount of shared experience and previous indoctrination required to make it meaningful, and the ever more assured expectation of assent, on which Hitler could build from one meeting to the next, from one stage of his career to the next, from one success to the next. The need to reduce all complex problems to single, black-and-white issues is not only repeatedly asserted in *Mein Kampf*, for instance at the point where 'the absolute, single-minded, insolent lie' of Allied propaganda about Germany's responsibility for the First World War is described in terms of unmistakable admiration. The same rhetorical practice is translated into the conduct of politics because Hitler knows that this is the mode of deliverance which this troubled and complex and unfriendly age is waiting for: 'I will reveal to you what it is that has made it possible for me to rise to my position', he tells Bertrand de Jouvenel, 21 February 1936. 'Our problems seemed complicated. The German people didn't know what to do with them. In these circumstances it seemed preferable to leave them to the professional politicians. I however have simplified the problems and have reduced them to the simplest formula. The masses recognized this and followed me.' What is achieved here – by a complete outsider – is the German Romantics' dream of an 'organic national community', a '*Volksgemeinschaft*', but at the price of complete unfreedom.

Finally, the correspondence between Hitler's absolutist outlook and the temper of the age goes much further than he understood or had any need to understand (just as, since he knew no other than the language of his age, he did not know that this was the language he spoke). Its intellectual and literary history shows it to be an age of disinheritance with a longing for the security of tradition, an age of most complex and hazardous and exacting speculation with a longing for deliverance from speculation, an age of catastrophe-mindedness and a bleak 'heroism' with a longing for a 'breakthrough' toward simple resolutions and 'authentic' goals. Hitler had no need to read Spengler's *Decline of the West* to understand its message for the times: 'The history of this age is no longer a witty game, conducted in polite social forms and concerned with a nicely calculated less or more, a game from which one may withdraw at any time. To stand fast or to go under – there is no third way.' At all times, and increasingly as Hitler's career proceeds to its end, the *No* is envisaged as a real possibility, the *Götterdämmerung* pathology which Nietzsche had attacked in Wagner is translated from a private obsession to the *praxis* of national and international politics.

The dominant sense of Hitler's *Yes or No*, then, is not that of a mere rhetorical simplification; its meaning, like the meaning of certain other parts of his ideology, must be sought on three levels. First, it is the catch-phrase of propaganda, and effective as such because it promises deliverance from the complexities of life in a democracy; and this, for twelve brief years and at an unacceptable cost, it in truth achieves. Secondly, it is obviously a lie, since it hides the changes of front and the hesitations, the trimming and tactical adjustments, which characterize Hitler's domestic policies as well as his diplomatic moves. But in a third, final sense, Hitler's *Yes or No* intimates, not just the destructive and self-destructive nature of *his* moves, but the nature of German society's expectations: it intimates, beyond the hope of a *Yes*, the deep longing for a *No*.

5 Nineteenth-century Roots

The age of Napoleon is the age of a new conception of man, whose European name is Romanticism. It places individual man in opposition to a world only now conceived and experienced as the world outside, and it sees man in terms which hitherto had been thought contradictory, as a creature both sentimental and heroic. The value by which this new man lives is neither piety nor virtue, neither loyalty nor constancy nor even the search for scientific truth, but his capacity for experience. Romanticism informs him at one and the same time with a boundless sensitiveness and openness towards ever subtler impressions from the world outside, and a capacity for heroic self-assertion: he lives, in this conception of himself, by his imagination and by his self-determining Will. And under both these aspects – as artist and as man of power – he sees himself, not as the executor of a Divine Will or the servant of an acknowledged authority or the member of a pre-established hierarchy, but as a maker and creator. The Will – not the common will of a body politic but *his* individual solitary will, mythologized to a heroic dimension – is his instrument. He is a maker of his kingdom: the powerful embattled personality we find in Balzac, Dickens or Melville (and German novelists like Gustav Freytag, Otto Ludwig, and C. F. Meyer) imposes its demands upon the world and attempts to fashion the world in its own image. Romantic, Faustian man forms, and in an all but literal sense creates, his own conditions and thus the world.

To this new conception of man the imperatives of traditional morality, whether Christian or Enlightened, do not apply; and, given his assertion of autonomy, it is hard to see that any objective moral scheme, anything but a purely private 'morality', is likely to command his allegiance. His acts are no longer judged in relation to a publicly sanctioned moral code or agreed scheme of public virtues, or by his conformity to a traditionally accepted way of life, or even by the dictates of his conscience (for conscience can never be anything but the inward form of a publicly sanctioned moral code). His acts are judged according to a criterion of immanent, inward coherence: that is, according to the degree to which a man's utterances and actions express his total personality and indicate his capacity for experience. Utterances are seen as actions and actions as poetry, and poetry as the consummation of '*Erlebnis*', of living experience. (The desuetude of rhetoric as a separate and distinct science, or again the supersession of prosody by individual theories of 'organic form', are examples and literary analogies of a process which the nineteenth century saw as a liberation of the experiencing self, and which we have learned to look on more critically.)

Existentialism is the final and most radical form of this heroic Romanticism – most radical because at the farthest remove from the moral and social sanctions of earlier, more stable conceptions of man. In its popular, least technical aspect existentialism is a philosophy for heroic living. Its values are authenticity, commitment, and what for want of a better word we may call personal truth. As such, existentialism from Kierkegaard through Nietzsche to Heidegger and Sartre rejects all values which are not expressive of an individual self and which are not created by that self. 'Let your speculative thinking go no further than your creative Will', says Nietzsche in *Thus Spake Zarathustra*; and: 'Let your self be in the deed, as the mother is in the child.' The self is authenticated by its commitment to its chosen task. The choice, dictated by nothing but the self in circumstances experienced as contingent, is gratuitous. The commitment of the self is authenticated not by the value and worth of its objective – the value of what a man is committed *to* – but by the strength, energy and originality of

the willing self. And personal truth is nothing but the function
of this circular relationship.

The Will, in this conception of what a man is and what he
should do in the world, is dominant. It is the politician's
instrument and, in Schopenhauer's aesthetic philosophy, it is
the object of the artist's will-less creative contemplation.
Nietzsche carries the thought to its radical conclusion: 'Only
as an aesthetic phenomenon is the world and all being justified.' Under this aesthetic dispensation the heroic and the
sentimental are no longer incompatible. To these artist-
politicians, says Nietzsche, belongs the future: artist and political ruler are one: the politician is the artist in another medium.
'Such beings are incalculable, they come like fate without
cause or reason, inconsiderately and without pretext. Suddenly
they are here, like lightning' – the peremptory metaphors from
nature are intended to reinforce the advocacy of spontaneous
experience, to which ordinary morality does not apply – 'like
lightning: too terrible, too sudden, too compelling and too
"different" even to be hated. The work [of such men] is an
instinctive creating and impressing of forms, they are the least
deliberate and the least conscious of all artists . . . What
moves them is the terrible egotism of the artist of the brazen
glance, who knows himself to be justified for all eternity in his
"work" as the mother is justified in her child.' And here is one
such 'artist of the brazen glance' – Mussolini – talking:

> When the masses are like wax in my hands, when I stir their
> faith, or when I mingle with them and am almost crushed
> by them, I feel myself to be a part of them. All the same there
> persists in me a certain feeling of aversion, like that which the
> modeller feels for the clay he is moulding. Does not the sculp-
> tor sometimes smash his block of marble into fragments,
> because he cannot shape it into the vision he has conceived?
> [*And again:*] Lenin is an artist who has worked in men as
> others have worked in marble and metal.

Hitler does not rise to a comparable formulation. But in

following him in his conversations, one is struck by the ease with which he moves, all within a few pages of his *Table Talk*, from one topic to the next: from the gauge of railway tracks to the racial improvement (*'Aufnordung'*) of Berchtesgaden, from a story of how he bought the services of Dr Schacht to the need for changes in the matrimonial law, from musings on what to do with the Jews and on the need to encourage contraception and discourage hygienic measures in Poland and the Ukraine, to the absurdity of building jet engines for aircraft and to his grandiose plans for Linz and the art gallery to be built there after the war. . . . One is struck by the fantastic malleability, the disposability of the world and everything in it in the hands of this *artiste manqué*. His world and his 'creative Will' seem to be co-extensive.

Is this what Nietzsche had in mind? Or did he not rather fail to see the full implications of his vision? I do not know. What is certain is that, for his artist-politician, self-fulfilment and authenticity are one and the same thing. He aspires to the fusion – we have reason to call it a fatal confusion – of aesthetic, ethical and personal values, but goes no further than that. In the resultant ideology, the separation of the private from the public sphere, a commonplace of Western thought since the days of Montaigne, is regarded as inauthentic, and so are all critical distinctions of 'the understanding'. Criticism, reasonableness itself, is decadent. Living experience – *Erlebnis* – is all, and all is *Erlebnis*.

All too ready to speak up fulsomely in praise of literature, literary men are prone to exaggerate its (and their own) importance. What I have here described is a matter of literary history and cultural aspirations and dreams, not the course of European politics in the nineteenth century. True, certain parts of this Romantic vision proved to be readily translatable into political ideology, but what determined this process of translation was 'the ineluctable hardness of political reality', were political not literary considerations. The more firmly entrenched were the institutions of a given society and the older its loyalties, the less effective the vision proved to be outside the imaginative sphere from which it derived. Special circumstances were needed for this essentially literary and poetic vision to have any political effects at all; but these in turn were circumstances it could help to bring about, in Germany more readily than elsewhere in Europe. The circumstances were those of a radical disaffection and anomie.

The beginnings of Hitler's political career coincide with that moment in the history of Germany when her social and institutional ties, and indeed her recently won national coherence, were at their weakest, when the standards and proprieties of her public life were severely undermined and for many invalidated. In this situation, when almost anything seemed possible and almost any alternative preferable, the call for a self-determining, charismatic personality ceased to be a matter of mere literature and took on, almost overnight, the aspect of practical and practicable politics.

There is a sense in which Nietzsche's emphasis on the suddenness, the cataclysmic nature of that process is misleading. It has, as I have suggested, a fairly long history, in which Nietzsche's own writings – at once prophecy and expressions of intent – have an important place. The call for a 'natural' leader, for the abolition of politics in favour of nationalism, of 'civilization' in favour of 'culture', the appeal to Nature, the blood, the iron Will, the appeal to 'Northern', later 'Aryan' values – all these belong to the temper of the Second German Empire. Indeed, there is not a single tenet of the National Socialist Party programme of February 1920 or of its later amendments which was not propagated in the political literature before 1914. Moreover, there was an element of emergency, of impatient waiting for the day, in the atmosphere of Wilhelminian Germany which was noted with alarm by many writers. It was in this spirit of expectancy that the outbreak of the war in August 1914 was greeted by most politicians and intellectuals, among them almost all literary men.

Nevertheless, the moment of defeat and the period of anarchy following the defeat do have about them something of that suddenness, of that 'lightning' quality of which Nietzsche had spoken more than thirty years earlier. It must be remembered that when, in November 1918, the German General Staff with Ludendorff at its head offered its capitulation and sued for peace, with the German armies more than a hundred miles inside enemy territory and not an Allied soldier on German soil, the news came to the vast majority of Germans as unexpectedly as would the news of a natural disaster.

And this emphasis on the suddenness, naturalness and irresistibility of events becomes the style of demagogic politics, it is *the* language of the age. Thus it is not enough to dismiss as 'mere propaganda' the self-advertisement of National Socialism as 'the Movement' in contrast to the Social Democrats' 'System'. It is one among numerous examples of *effective* propaganda: partly because the style of utterance corresponds to the aspirations of those who had reason to hope for gain from a 'sudden' and dramatic change, partly because the Leader's vital energy and capacity for apparently sudden crucial decisions is described, and can be seen, as an outward confirmation of his charisma, his boundless, world-changing Will. The fast drives from one end of Germany to the other (in a supercharged Mercedes, the symbol of speed worshipped by every German schoolboy); the cross-country flights from one party-meeting to the next (heroic days of air transport in an open-cabin Focker-Wulf biplane) – all these are propaganda moves in the service of that myth of a suddenly descending lightning, a myth designed to intimidate by giving to a shrewd political move the aspect of a ubiquitous stroke of fate or a phenomenon of Nature.

6 The Language of Nature

A phenomenon of Nature: even today we are not clear enough
to what extent the language, the thinking and the practice of
fascist movements generally and of National Socialism in
particular were determined by the 'Nature' vocabulary that has
its roots in early nineteenth-century Romanticism, and that
had once been the repository of the most poignant and beautiful lyric poetry in European literature. From those early years
of high spirituality and literary enthusiasm onwards, Romanticism has always implied, more or less clearly, an alternative
to the Christian moral tradition. And in this Goethe concurs
with the Romantic writers from whom he so often dissociated
himself. When he dramatizes the Christian conscience as 'Evil
Spirit', and when *verdammte Unnatur* becomes the worst term
of opprobrium in his vocabulary, we have clearly entered a
moral scheme which has little to do with Christian orthodoxy.
The normative idea of Nature – Nature as a model of human
existence – exercises a profound attraction on Nietzsche; it is
certainly the one scheme of values that is not subject to his
scathing criticism. When coupled with the Romantic dream of
'the one-ness of all things', the idea of Nature comes to
dominate the philosophical and ideological writings of intellectuals on the fringes of the Wilhelminian political establishment. However doubtful the compliment, Goethe and
Nietzsche are the two modern writers most frequently acknowledged by Spengler; and it is no accident that Spengler
builds his entire world-historical megacycle on an analogy with
plant-life taken from Goethe's botanical and morphological
studies, in apparently irrefragable support of an historical de-

terminism which Goethe would certainly have repudiated. The
Romantics had preached the unity of science and poetic inspira-
tion: at the turn of the century the doctrines of race and of
Sozialdarwinismus derive their authority in equal measure from
their 'scientific' pretensions and from their claims to be a true
reflection of the processes of Nature herself. This is the era of
Hitler's formative years in Vienna. *Mein Kampf* is the representative document of that era because (once again) it radi-
calizes and presents in ruthlessly uncompromising manner the
ultimate conclusions of its normative thinking.

Reading the book we become aware to what an extent our
present tangible pollution of nature was preceded by the intellectual pollution of the concept of Nature. The life of
nations, races, cultures and continents (Hitler writes in *Mein
Kampf*) is governed by the same laws of health and sickness as
those governing the life of individuals. States are no more than
artificial means to an end (an echo of *Zarathustra*), the true
'natural' unit is the Nation. Mental, moral, racial and societal
afflictions are all deviations from a natural norm, though some,
like natural catastrophes, may lead to an improvement in the
strain: the chief of these is war. 'The sin against blood and
race' is an infectious disease of the social body in the same way
as syphilis (at all times the object of Hitler's obsessive fear) is
of the physical body, and must be prevented by adequate racial
laws. Education in eugenics must be enforced by commissions
empowered to determine a man's eligibility for a diploma in
citizenship, his right to marriage and to permanent settlement.
(Not until 1942 could these proposals of 1924 be put in train.)
The healthy nation is one in which 'true idealism', which is
in harmony with 'the Will of Nature', follows the 'aristocratic'
principle of natural selection. Accordingly, Nature favours the
man who has 'the Will' to assert himself over others, and the
race which has 'the Will' to displace all others. Hitherto this
'aristocratic' principle was accepted as valid in economics, art,
and culture generally; the time has come to apply it to contemporary politics too. A racially impure state (Austria–Hungary)

that has a diseased heart (Vienna) is bound to have a decadent culture, and this in turn will be reflected in its 'Will to live', its 'Will to defend itself', and its 'Will to resist infection'. The first cause of this state of decadence is a loss of an instinctive understanding of the innate and necessary processes of natural change; it is the failure to recognize where the threat and disease of miscegenation originates – to recognize that the Jew is *Unnatur* incarnate. At the final stage of this process Hitler's apocalyptic imagination sees the Earth as an empty planet, spinning on its way into eternity. The vocabulary of anti-Nature – 'abscesses', 'paralyses', 'bloodstreams carrying the poison into every limb', 'colonies and "cultures" of parasites' and so forth – becomes the chief weapon in the attack on the Jewish influence in German and Aryan life. A reference to various scandals in contemporary Vienna gives Hitler a chance to exploit this imagery to the full: 'As soon as you cut even cautiously into such a cyst, you found, like a maggot in a rotting body, often quite dazzled by the sudden light – a little Jew!'

The popular appeal of this language cannot be doubted. It is true that Hitler's anti-Semitism is not confined to this or any other single vocabulary, and often favours theological conceits, as in the peroration to the second chapter: 'Thus it is that today I believe I am acting according to the intention of the Almighty Creator: by resisting the Jew I am fighting for the work of the Lord!' But from his beginnings in Munich he was surrounded by intellectuals who were, or thought themselves to be, too sophisticated to be taken in by this *Opus Dei* language and (somewhat later) by Hitler's messianic appeal. Yet they shared his habit of deciding social and psychological arguments by racial and biological analogies which to them were made respectable by their antecedents: in the writings of politicians like Georg von Schönerer, cultural polymaths like Houston Stewart Chamberlain (whose *Foundations of the Nineteenth Century* (1898), however, is by no means anti-Semitic), or psychologists like Otto Weininger (whose anti-Semitic *Sex and*

Character was admired by the poet Dietrich Eckart, Hitler's friend and mentor). To these intellectuals, the fascination of the man lay in the wholly unrestrained radicalization of the 'theory of the Organic'.

What the men of the next generation, the heirs of the Wilhelminian theoreticians and ideologists, discover is that there is simply no limit to what can be said in this 'natural', conservative idiom, and that there is an increasingly severe limit to what can be said in criticism of it. These men (splendidly portrayed in the pages of Thomas Mann's *Doctor Faustus*) present the extraordinary spectacle of intellectuals bent on the depreciation and destruction of the intellect: coffee-house philosophers, eternal students and brawling radicals with knuckle-dusters, exalting the life of the instincts and attacking criticism in all its forms as decadent, uncreative and un-German. And again they find their encouragement in Nietzsche's thinking. But where Nietzsche anxiously questions the modern superstition that all knowledge is valuable and all enquiry is justified, and where he tentatively speculates on the idea of an existential entitlement to knowledge, these men reduce his complexities and ambivalences to an exaltation of 'the organic community' (*Volksgemeinschaft*) which, they claim, by its very existence determines what knowledge is valuable and which enquiries are worth pursuing. Men like Martin Heidegger, Gottfried Benn and Josef Nadler (to mention only these few, the most prominent on a depressingly long list) all direct their aggression towards a revival of those 'authentic' values which the modern cosmopolitan world is destroying. And each finds a different haven for these values: Heidegger in a mixture of pre-Socratic ontology (a primacy of *being* and *being-exposed-to* over all forms of social activity) and 'the self-assertion of the German spirit'; Benn in his poetic celebration of chthonic states and primordial drives; and Nadler in a history of German literature presented as a reflection of Germany's tribal, racial and geographical divisions – the work, at any other time, of a harmless crank.

At any other time: what is at issue here is not an evaluation or rejection of Romantic thought but a glance at its consequences. To give it anything like a just appraisal, we should have to emphasize its amorphous, non-systematic nature. We should have to insist, further, that the sheer aggressiveness inseparable from all forms of Fascism is alien to the spirit of nineteenth-century Romantic philosophizing and absent from most, though not all, of its political pronouncements. The point that needs making is an historical one: the Romantic exaltation of the natural being of man and of his Nature-given condition is the intellectual background against which, in the circumstances of lawlessness and anomie prevailing in the 'twenties and early 'thirties, a social *praxis* arises in which men are judged, condemned and eventually done to death, not for what they have done but simply for what they are. This is the triumph of 'ontic' thinking in the modern world. For Fascist ideology is not a regression to the old, pre-1789 apologies for slavery. On the contrary: the primacy of 'natural being' is effectively asserted only when the old institutions with their roots in paternalism and authoritarianism have ceased to provide acceptable forms of social cohesion.

What were the German intellectuals, artists and academics really hoping for when, in 1933, they denied their own past, betrayed their closest friends, and wilfully blinded themselves to the very obvious qualities of their new rulers? Was it really fear of modernity (as Dahrendorf, Habermas, Fest and others have claimed) which caused this greatest defection from reason the West has known in recent centuries? The promise held out to them was of an attractive authoritarian society which would perpetuate the authoritarian mode of their private and professional lives; a society that would be 'non-political' in the sense of freeing them from the need for democratic choices, and that promised them integration with a traditional, anti-urban, rustic, 'natural' community. Few of these men will have demeaned themselves by looking into *Mein Kampf*; fewer still are likely to have penetrated to page 713; but which of them would not have acclaimed the vision of the German community presented there?

> Even at this time our nation has not completely lost its good fundamental elements; only they slumber unawakened in the deep, and many's the time it has been possible to descry, gleaming like summer lightning in a black overcast firmament, virtues which a later Germany will one day remember as the first signs of an incipient recovery. More than once, thousands and thousands of young Germans have come forward with the self-sacrificial resolve freely and joyfully to make a sacrifice of their young lives, just as in 1914, on the altar of their beloved fatherland. Once again millions of men are diligently and industriously at work, as though the ravages of the revolution had never been. *The blacksmith stands again at his anvil, the farmer walks behind his plough, and the scholar sits in his study*, all with the same effort and the same devotion to their duty.

The natural metaphors culminating in the threat of violent change but actually leading to a *status quo ante*; the seemingly pointless reiteration of the religiose notion of 'sacrifice', intimating, perhaps unintentionally, Hitler's belief in the continuity of war and peace; the evocation of a pre-industrial, rustic idyll, reminiscent of the early nineteenth century but also of some of Stefan George's nostalgic solemnities; and, finally, the appeal to the traditional German virtues – all the ingredients of the *völkisch* propaganda which Hitler elsewhere ridicules are here assembled. Of course, not even the German 'scholar in his study', however lacking in a sense of humour, could possibly have believed in this as an authentic picture of Germany AD 1926. Yet at the point where belief petered out, ambition and expectations of an altogether more mundane kind took over. These Hitler could gratify with spoils or the promise of spoils, and with power or the promise of power. For he shared, and radicalized, that belief which had grown alongside the Romantic idolatry of Nature and in which that idolatry culminates – the belief in 'the Will'. What he was unable to do, at any time and in any of his functions, was to protect the individual against the tyranny of 'natural' differences. And so like greater men and better thinkers before him, he mythologized that which he could not change.

7 Hitler's Ideology of the Will

The language of 'the Will' informs Hitler's speeches and writings throughout his entire public career. All who met him and all who have written about him agree that this is the vocabulary to which he resorted whenever the authority behind his orders and decisions was in question. 'My absolute Will' is the concept in which most of his political arguments were grounded and in which they culminated, the *fiat* he offered not only to his adherents and collaborators but to the whole German nation as a mystical token of success. This, assuredly, is what he believed in. And, in the years of his ascendancy at all events, an overwhelming majority of Germans in all walks of life shared his belief. They were the large mass of the people, 'the German Nation', of which Hans Frank tells us in his memoirs (written during the year preceding his execution in 1946) that it 'excluded at all times a number of Germans – certainly upward of a million – who, in spite of Hitler's successes and achievements, never in any way owed their allegiance to him; just as' – and it is this second estimate of Frank's which makes the first at least plausible – 'just as this same concept of "the German nation" must also be understood to exclude a number of Germans – again, upward of a million – who, in spite of all his failures, were undeterred in acknowledging their obligation to the Führer and remained loyal to him to the end.'

Hitler's deadly seriousness, his singlemindedness and his commitment all issue from this notion of 'my adamant Will'. The origin of this notion and of its vocabulary in Schopenhauer and Nietzsche is a commonplace in the history of ideas. Now, although it is very unlikely that Hitler ever read Schopenhauer at all extensively (in spite of repeatedly claiming that 'in

the trenches I read and re-read the little volumes until they
fell apart'); although, unlike Mussolini, he almost certainly
knew no more of Nietzsche's work than a few catch-phrases
like 'the Will to Power' and 'only he who lives dangerously
lives fully'; and although he was familiar with the tenets of
Sozialdarwinismus only through the pamphleteering literature
that made the rounds of the Viennese cafés, working-men's
hostels and lending libraries, it is clear that by the time he
wrote *Mein Kampf* he had fully recognized the personal and
political value of this vocabulary of 'the Will', and had decided
to make it his own. Konrad Heiden observes that after Hitler
was released from 'honourable detention' in the Landsberg
fortress he gave up sporting the horsewhip of crocodile hide he
had always carried when walking the streets of post-war revolutionary Munich: the outlook and vocabulary that went with
that whip remained unchanged to the end. If he was constant
in anything, it was in the assertion of 'my constant Will'.

We are speaking of an historical era when, in Central
Europe at all events, no one who was not born to the exercise
of political power could hope to enter politics without laying
claim to a coherent *Weltanschauung*. To a man of Hitler's
background and ambitions, of course, more than one ideology
was available. And we know from the early chapters of *Mein
Kampf* that during his stay in Vienna he took a good deal of
interest – certainly superficial but not at first hostile – in the
political literature of socialism and in the activities of the
Austrian trades unions, at that time the most active of Continental Europe. Very soon, however (he tells us), he set his mind
against any form of socialism as it was debated and practised
around him. Why? Was it really because, 'after some initial
hesitation and scrupulous misgivings', he 'unmasked' socialism
and the unions as integral parts of 'the Jewish world conspiracy'? But at that time (he also tells us) he wasn't conscious
of ever having met any Jews, even though we now know that his
mother was operated on by a Jewish doctor in Linz, with whom
he was on very friendly terms. His rationalization (if that is the

right word) that he soon turned against socialism because 'the Aryan mind' is instinctively repelled by anything 'Jewish' came a good deal later. What divided him from socialism was the most tenaciously held and desperate of social attitudes, the petit-bourgeois fear of *déclassement*. Whatever may be fictitious about the description he gives of himself sitting in isolation from his mates on a building site and drinking his bottle of milk, it conveys this attitude accurately enough. What then was the alternative? If the urge to self-assertion and the feverish, consuming desire for power, together with the fear of the social abyss to which his failure to succeed as an 'artist' had exposed him, were the dominant motives of his early 'struggle', then his adoption of the 'ideology of the Will' was indeed 'instinctive', in the sense of not being a matter of a clear, conscious choice at all: it emerged from the dawning recognition that this ideology alone would answer his innermost need since it alone was identical with his innermost motives.

Marxist socialists as different from each other as Rosa Luxemburg and Bertolt Brecht have spoken of the strenuous intellectual discipline, the rigorous process of learning they had to undergo in order to become familiar with the doctrine and its mode of thinking. Although in later years Hitler liked to boast that he had read all the 500 volumes of a Viennese public library at one go, the indications are that his studies were conducted at a fairly low intellectual level, at least in the sense that they led, instantly and in every case, to outright acceptance or outright rejection. Of the kind of critical effort which the study of Marxism involves and which requires at least some degree of openness of mind and some suspension of personal interest, he was not capable. Moreover, the 'ideology of the Will', being explicitly and in its very tenets hostile to rational criticism, vaunts this absence of disinterested intellectual openness, and makes of it a major value. An anti-rational and anti-critical element is constitutive of its structure. Between the man and his doctrine a pre-established harmony obtains.

The ideology he concocted was an intensely personal thing,

authenticated by being identical with what he was, or rather
with the image, the *persona* he fashioned from his ambitions
and superimposed upon his fears; which is one of the reasons
why, when his career came to an end, there was nothing to hand
on. Yet it was not just a hand-to-mouth contrivance but a fully
considered ideology for all that: a framework of ideas proclaimed for the sake of acquiring and maintaining political
power, and practices tactically modified in the light of the
changing political situation. His *Weltanschauung* showed
marked affinities with French and Italian fascism on the one
hand, and local (German and Austrian) antecedents on the
other; and it had a distinct, recognizable style of its own. Its
elements were the common intellectual property of the age:
traditional Austrian religious anti-Semitism intellectualized
and focused into a racial and social doctrine by means of arguments derived from social Darwinism; ill-digested bits of
Nietzsche, Schopenhauer, and Wagner, H. S. Chamberlain,
Paul de Lagarde, and the fantastic Lanz von Liebenfels,
propagator of the 'Ostara' cult and the swastika; perhaps some
Le Bon, Gobineau, and Sorel, acquired almost certainly at
second hand – all of this being re-activated (and de Lagarde
probably added) in Hitler's mind after the First World War by
his friend, the poet Dietrich Eckart. 'There is a tide in the
affairs of men . . .': Hitler's task at the outset of his career as
a politician consisted in radicalizing this far from original
mixture after having first perceived that a situation had arisen
which permitted such radicalizing and encouraged its translation from pamphlets into practical politics. The intellectual
task (and let me stress that, in spite of what has here been said
about his intellectual habits, it was nothing less) did not consist
in rationalizing the personal traits of self-assertion and fear that
carried him into the political arena. It consisted rather in articu-
lating them in a form that would be publicly acceptable while
at the same time retaining and fully displaying the signs of a
personal commitment and passion. National Socialism is his
creation. It presents to the world of the 'twenties the image of a

movement in which public and political values are privatized
and personalized, whereas its actual day-to-day practice aims
in the opposite direction, toward a politicization of all values,
including the most private and personal: this is the formal
structure of the ideology he concocted. In several important
respects more comprehensive than any tyranny known to
history, it is of a piece with the products of Kafka's prophetic
imagination: a single man's vision is elevated to a law valid for
all men, private arbitrariness to a system of political rules: 'You
had worked your way up alone, by your own energies,' Kafka
writes in that famous 'Letter to his Father' which so mon-
strously, so splendidly exceeds its biographical occasion,

> therefore you had an unbounded confidence in your opinion.
> . . . From your armchair you ruled the world. Your opinion
> was right, every other opinion was crazy, unbalanced, *me-
> schugge*, not normal. And with all this your self-confidence was
> so immense that you had no need to be consistent at all and yet
> never ceased to be in the right. Sometimes it happened that
> you had no opinion whatsoever about something – therefore
> all possible opinions on that matter were bound to be wrong,
> without exception. You could, for instance, run down the
> Czechs, and then the Germans, and then the Jews – not only
> selectively but wholesale, in every respect – until at last nobody
> was left but yourself. You assumed for me that mysteriousness
> which belongs to all tyrants, whose right is founded, not in
> thought but in their persons.

This is the right Hitler claims in the turgid diction of *Mein
Kampf*:

> From among the host of millions of men, who as individuals
> more or less clearly and definitely sense these truths or even
> grasp them, *one man* must step forward in order with apodictic
> force to form granite principles from the wavering world of the
> imaginings of the broad masses and to take up the struggle for
> the sole correctness of those principles, until from the shifting
> waves of a free world of ideas there rises up a brazen cliff of a
> united commitment in faith and will alike.

The general right to such an activity is founded in necessity,
the personal right in success.

Kafka's anticipations are certainly surprising, even if we don't
think of him as living on some island of the anti-Semites'
imagination. In pointing to them, however, we should add that
he has not a word of warning or of advice on how to resist the
solipsistic evil he so clearly descries. Something of his bemused,
suicidal passivity, too, belongs to Hitler's world.

If every one of the beliefs with which Hitler has been credited
should turn out to be sham, of his belief in 'the Will' there can
be no doubt. By the criteria of this chimeric belief he chose his
henchmen, his military and political leaders. This was true at
all times and in all situations, yet the later stages of the Second
World War provide some of the most striking recorded examples of this faith.

In the face of the almost complete encirclement of the Stalingrad army he tells Zeitzler, his Chief of Army General Staff,
towards the end of December 1942: 'Stalingrad must simply be
held. It must. It is a key position.' Twenty-four hours later,
after receiving Göring's assurance that the troops will be fully
supplied from the air (what in fact reached them were con-
signments of contraceptives and packages of broadsheets
announcing the imminent defeat of the Russian forces) and in
the certain knowledge that, unless the Sixth Army and its
allies are allowed to retreat, the fate of more than a quarter of
a million men will be sealed: "Then Stalingrad must be held!
It is senseless to talk any further of the Sixth Army's breaking
through [the Russian lines]. It would lose all its heavy arms and
have no fighting power. The Sixth Army remains at Stalingrad!' Of Field-Marshal von Kluge's failure to hold the
advance of General Patton's Third Army (15 August, 1944):
'Success failed to come only because Kluge *did not want*
success.' A few days later, during one of the countless conferences with his generals (who cravenly participated in the ritual

of those endless *Lagebesprechungen*, in the course of which they hardly ever dared to contradict Hitler's most unrealistic estimates or to oppose his fantastic plans): 'It has been my task, especially since 1941, in no circumstances ever to lose my nerve but on the contrary, wherever a collapse occurs, to find ways and means to repair the affair somehow.' Again, with his characteristic mixture of 'inflexible determination' and self-pity: 'For five years I have been separated from the rest of the world. I haven't been to the theatre, I haven't heard a concert, I haven't seen a film. I live for one task only: to lead this fight. Because I know that if there is not an iron will behind it [*wenn nicht eine eiserne Willensnatur dahintersitzt*], this fight cannot be won.' Again, after the first Ardennes offensive (18 December 1944), in an outburst that is characteristic of the blatantly personal way in which he determines all strategic and political issues: 'There is one thing I must stress, gentlemen. I have been in this business [*in diesem Geschäft*] for eleven years, and during those eleven years I have never heard anybody report: Now we are completely ready. Our situation is after all not different from that of the Russians in 1941 and 1942. . . . The question is . . . whether *Germany has the will* to remain in existence or whether she is to be destroyed. . . . *For me* there is nothing new in this situation. I have been in very much worse ones. I mention this only because I want you to understand why I pursue my goal with such fanaticism and why nothing can wear me down.'

But are these more than hectic assertions without substance, and hysterical, often childish adjurations? Even a worn-out recording, full of crackles and blurred sounds, played in the privacy of one's sitting-room, conveys abundantly the rhetorical force of his speeches. One has to listen to the astonishing fervour, the heedless *Pathos* with which Hitler concludes his first speech of the War (1 September 1939) –

If we form a community closely bound by sacred oath, ready for every decision, never willing to capitulate, then *our Will* shall be master of every *affliction* [*dann wird unser Wille jeder Not Herr werden*]. I close with the credo [*Bekenntnis*] which I spoke when I first took up my struggle for power in the Reich. This is what I said: If *our Will* is so strong that no *affliction* can subdue it, then shall *our Will* and our German state overcome every *affliction* and triumph over it.

– one has only to attend to that note of abandonment to violence with which '*unser Wille*' is repeated and each time placed in counterpoint to the passionate rise-and-fall of '*Not*' (a word, like '*Bekenntnis*', brim-full with religious connotations), one has to follow with a minimum of empathy the liturgical rising double note of that '*niemals*', in order to realize that the sequence carries absolute conviction, and fully and unreservedly conveys the speaker's commitment to the cause he shares with his public. The peroration, like the whole speech, is dominated by the two leitmotifs of '*Wille*' and '*Not*'. It may not, on the printed page, amount to more than a wordy tautology. But its real strength, like the strength of most of Hitler's speeches, derives from the certain expectation of being understood – understood in the precise terms of the ideology to which this vocabulary belongs, even by those who on occasion are critical of him. And this rapport, Hitler clearly realizes, can only be achieved by the spoken word. To be sure, the delivery eschews – indeed is incapable of – any great variations. It is emphatic and vehement without any of the complex histrionic effects of a Goebbels speech; the intonation I have described is confined to a narrow range of tones, and the actual rhetorical ploys all tend toward an effect not far short of the monotonous. But this overall effect, too, helps to create and sustain the impression of sincerity, of the authentic 'voice of the people' which says what they all would want to say in the manner they are all familiar with and share.

There are other, subtler ways in which the ideology is transmitted. One of them, which seems to have no obvious equivalent in English, is the frequent use Hitler makes both in his public speeches and in his recorded 'conversations' of the simple word, '*ruhig*'. Its primary lexical meaning – 'calmly', 'quietly' – conveys little or nothing of its peculiar force. In translating phrases like *Ich kann ruhig behaupten, daß* . . . or *So habe ich mich ruhig entschlossen* . . . one wavers between omitting it altogether – 'I can assert that . . .' – or over-emphasizing it – 'And so without fear of contradiction I have decided . . .'; in other contexts – *sie sollen ruhig einmal versuchen* – something like 'let them just try' comes nearer to the nuance. What all these uses of that little word convey (it is too common and too unemphatic to have been consciously chosen by the speaker) is more than calm assurance, more than a harshly cynical certitude of being in an unassailable position of power: it is the strength of a dominant, all-encompassing, unshakable Will.

Hitler's confidence in his power to use his 'will' in order to sway individual people in the course of a personal encounter has often been described. That he was capable of mustering this confidence all the way to the end is attested by one of his private secretaries, who worked for him throughout the twelve years of his rule. She is describing an occasion in March 1945, when Gauleiter Forster of Danzig came to Berlin to speak to Hitler. (Forster, we know from his public speeches as well as from Rauschning's memoirs, was as tough as any of his colleagues.)

Forster walked through my office, in complete despair at what was happening. He revealed to me that 1100 Russian tanks were closing in on Danzig, that the Wehrmacht had no more than four Tiger tanks to oppose them, and that they didn't even have any petrol. Forster was determined not to hide his view of things and to represent to [Hitler] the entire disastrous reality of the situation. . . . 'You can rely on it [Forster told her], I will tell him everything, even at the risk of his throwing me out.' How great was my surprise when he came out of his interview with Hitler a totally changed man. 'The Führer has promised me new divisions for Danzig' he said. Seeing my sceptical smile, he added: 'Of course, I wouldn't know where he could find them. But he has told me he will save Danzig, and so the matter is beyond any doubt.' I was truly disappointed at what Forster said. . . . Undoubtedly it was Hitler's fatal suggestive power that had worked upon him.

And if this was the reaction of a party boss, there were soldiers who turned out to be equally impressionable. In the same month, March 1945, Field Marshal Ernst Busch (described as a serious professional officer of the old school) arrived in the bunker under the Reich Chancellery, 'in dirty field uniform, angry, worn out and indignant, determined at long last to give [Hitler] a piece of his mind'. An hour before, Busch had left his troops well to the west of the Oder and seen the conditions under which they were retreating – their only aim now was to gain the safety of an American prisoner-of-war camp. Yet Busch too emerged from the interview reassured by the (presumably secret) measures Hitler had described to him, and convinced that final German victory was merely a matter of time.

Such dramatic encounters have often been cited as examples of Hitler's charismatic psyche, and exploited for propaganda purposes. But much has also been made of these supposedly occult powers by writers who viewed his career with alarm, yet sought to explain it in demonic or satanic terms. The atmosphere of the German 'twenties, with its numerous apocalyptic sects and extravagant chiliasms, many of them based on misinterpretations of Dostoyevsky, favoured such 'demonic' explanations. They were all too readily seized on by artists and intellectuals who in any event did not scruple to perpetuate the traditional fatalistic view of history and to belittle the role of reason in contemporary politics. In this atmosphere the term '*Vernunftrepublikaner*' was coined to describe the attitude of those who supported the Republic 'merely' by rational arguments, without committing themselves to it emotionally, 'heart and soul'. In a culture dominated by the idea of 'total' commitment as an absolute value, anything short of such a commitment was readily condemned as defective and provisional.

8 'There is no such thing as the Will'

Thomas Mann was one of those who readily understood and criticized this absolutist expectation of politics and saw the dangers of a charismatic conception of political leadership. His novella *Mario and the Magician* (1930) sets out the predicament of the liberal mind in the grip of the demagogue's will at the same time as it shows his ambivalent relationship with the masses. It does this more accurately and more searchingly than any other work of fiction I know. Yet even here, in a story whose intention is obviously anti-fascist, analysis is foreshortened by a characteristic obscurity.

The story is set in a seaside resort in Mussolini's Italy, the splendidly evoked atmosphere of xenophobia, provincial nationalism and mass-hysteria points also unmistakably to Hitler's Munich. Its action centres on an evening of 'magical' entertainment; it is recounted by a narrator who, while distancing himself from its absurd and horrifying events, is yet almost as much their victim as are his less sophisticated fellow spectators. In charge of the proceedings is the *artiste* Cipolla,

> a man whose age it was hard to determine but by no means young, with a sharp, ravaged face, piercing eyes and a compressed mouth, a small black waxed moustache and a so-called imperial in the hollow between lip and chin . . . Cipolla had in his whole appearance much of the historic type of mountebank and charlatan; his very clothes emphasized it, pretentious as they were, for in places they were pulled tight and in others they fell in absurdly loose folds. Something was wrong with his figure, both fore and aft, which was to become plain later on. But I must emphasize that there was not a trace of personal jocularity,

let alone clownishness, in his pose, his expression or his behaviour.

Cipolla, the classical Nietzschean-Freudian type of 'the under-privileged' who by his 'art' compensates for his vital and emotional deprivations, is a travelling conjurer and 'scientific hypnotist'. Gradually he comes to dominate an audience composed of Italian and foreign summer visitors and the local populace of hotel keepers, waiters and fishermen. As the evening proceeds, most of them, including an aristocratic gentleman from Rome, are drawn into the act. One is made to dance, another is turned into a rigid mummy, a third mistakes Cipolla for his own girl-friend and implants a kiss on his sweaty grey cheek. At the height of the saturnalia the stage is filled with will-less marionettes, dancing, leering, contorted, stuttering, all firmly held by the Magician's leading strings, to be suddenly released by a crack of his riding crop. The eagerness with which they offer themselves to him is matched by the almost sexual satisfaction he experiences in making them perform their abject tasks to the dictate of his will. Describing Hitler's comparable exertions during the Nuremberg party rallies, Hans Frank slavishly echoes his master's wordiness: 'But then, he gave his every last ounce of energy to stand up to the monstrous hardships of those days.' Cipolla's endless patter ('parla benissimo', say the Italians admiringly), his emotional need of 'the people' and his self-pity at having to suffer with his victims and bear their shame for them (*qui tollit peccata mundi*) – all these are masterly insights into the complex psychological and social situation, both on the level of the action itself and also in terms of the historical allegory; and so is the murder with which the story ends. As in one of Hieronymus Bosch's hellish scenes, the grotesque is in the service of poetic truth. Yet there is something of a flaw in Thomas Mann's story.

A few members of the audience, including the gentleman from Rome, strenuously set their minds against doing the Magician's bidding. Yet they too, we are told, are subjected to his ravaging will, at least as much as all those who are eager to obey his ever more humiliating orders. In fact, what Cipolla tells these reluctant victims (and the narrator corroborates his claim) is that all *they* can do is to will *not* to do what he wills them to do, and from 'willing not to' (the narrator again agrees) it is but a short step to 'willing nothing, to not willing at all', and therefore to doing what *he* wills them to do. . . . Now it is generally agreed that hypnosis cannot conduce to wholly uncharacteristic action. The most it can do is to 'suggest' mediating situations, in the context of which the subject is made to perform an act he would normally refuse to do, but only if he is 'predisposed', that is, by being hypnotically deceived about the true nature of the situation (as when a man is made to shoot at another because he has been made to imagine himself in a jungle, threatened by a tiger). But what Thomas Mann insists on (and what the Schopenhauerian sophistry about 'willing not to = not willing at all' is meant to underline) is an unmediated antagonism, a head-on collision of wills. And it is more than doubtful whether in such a situation, where 'you shall do this' constitutes a wholly uncharacteristic action and is opposed by 'I will not', hypnotic effects of the kind described can ever take place. Here simple country folk and the more sophisticated alike are said to be wholly at the mercy of a demonic, irresistible will whose demands run counter to their moral habits (whereas in the sordid reality of the Hofbräuhaus it was not the magic of the Leader's will which brought the occasional opponent to heel but the knuckle-dusters and lead-filled truncheons of the SA). What the story thus implies is in a sense the opposite of Thomas Mann's guiding intention: it is the audience's complete powerlessness in the demagogue's hands, their literal acceptance of his claim to be a magician. And the political implications of *that*, in terms of fatalism and personal responsibility, are depressingly obvious.

Of greater political importance than Hitler's supposedly hypnotic powers in individual encounters was his perfectly realistic

expectation of being understood by the masses and of deriving
political support from his appeal to that understanding. A
striking instance of this occurs in his last speech on the German
radio (30 January 1945). The speech adds nothing substantial
to the ideology itself. What it does is to lay bare the basis
which the ideology has helped to create and from which in turn
it operates throughout the twenty-five years of his political
career. The peroration recalls the vocabulary of that first war
speech from which I quoted:

> As we form such a community bound by sacred oath [*eine so
> verschworene Gemeinschaft*], we have the right to stand before
> the Almighty and ask Him for His grace and His blessing. For
> this is the utmost any nation can do: when each man fights who
> can fight, and each man works who can work, and when all
> together are prepared to sacrifice and all are filled with the one
> thought of safeguarding the freedom, the honour, and thus the
> future of life. However grave the crisis may be at this moment,
> nevertheless it will be finally overcome *by our unalterable will*
> [*durch unseren unabänderlichen Willen*], our readiness to sacri-
> fice, and by our abilities. . . .

What is here asserted is an expectation not merely of passive
understanding or agreement but of a nation-wide conspiracy
and connivance. Moreover, the understanding to which he
appeals seems to distinguish between 'our unalterable will' and
'our readiness to sacrifice' – between 'the Will' and its means.
But are his words more than a string of clichés, unthinkingly
uttered? It seems so. On 20 May 1943 he is (as so often)
berating his generals for failing to do what they regard as
impossible. When they tell him that the Hermann-Göring
Division cannot be moved from Sicily to the mainland in time to
anticipate the Allied invasion, he explodes: 'It's not the ferries
that are decisive. What is decisive is the Will!'

There is perhaps no need to add that this ideology, too,
determines Hitler's conception of the state and his view of
history. The state (we are told in a memorandum of the
Ministry of the Interior, 1935), is no longer a juridical body

governed by 'several will-forming agencies', it has become *der Führerstaat* governed by 'one will only' – a will which 'is the law' and thus in a sense makes all laws redundant; the principle of *Führerwille* (Hans Frank argued in a speech before the 'Academy for German Law' on 18 June 1938) replaced a 'formal written constitution'. And Hitler's admiration for Frederick the Great (whose portrait was with him in the bunker to the last and 'whose final victory' he believed 'was due to nothing but his strength of soul'), for Mussolini, Stalin and Lloyd George (*dans cette galère*) is due to his understanding of them as *Willensmenschen*, as 'fanatics of the Will', just as his contempt for the Western democracies derives from his dealings with their 'weak-willed', 'decadent' politicians.

It seems, then, that 'the Will' is for Hitler what, in German popular mythology, it was for Schopenhauer and Nietzsche: the agent of a law of nature and of history, an all-encompassing metaphysical principle; in short, creator of the world and all that is in it. This certainly is the mythology whose language he uses and to which he unreservedly appeals. And numerous historians, English as well as German, have accepted Hitler's claim (the sincerity of which we have no reason to doubt) that his possession of a superior 'Will' is the key to his successes. Even Alan Bullock, who can hardly be accused of wishing to contribute to the Hitler myth, lists 'the strength of will which underlay all his hesitations, opportunism, and temperamental outbursts' as one of the aspects of Hitler's 'unusual consistency of purpose'. However, before we too accept this interpretation, we had better consider what sense (if any) may be made of it.

Kant, whose view on such matters is a good deal plainer than some of his commentators have made out, bases his deduction of the Categorical Imperative on a thoroughly realistic description of what it is we do when we use our will in a given concrete situation. Far from being some disembodied cosmic principle, the human will is, in his account, a disposition of the mind whereby a man is enabled to attain a certain end. More specifically, it is a capacity not only to conceive that end but at the same time also to consider – to evaluate and choose – the means towards attaining it. A consideration of those means – of their appropriateness to the end in view – is for Kant, not the function of some other human faculty accompanying the will and thus giving it some 'pure', transcendental status of its own, but an integral part of our exercise of the will. (What he calls 'the pure will' still includes a choice of the means, though in that case the admissible means are of a special kind.) So insistent is Kant on the undivided nature of this exercise that he regards the proposition which so describes it as analytical: 'He who wills an end, wills also (to the extent that reason has a decisive influence upon his actions) those indispensably necessary means that are in his power.'

It is clear – indeed, it may be thought painfully obvious – that whatever may be the sources of the 'ideology of the Will', Kant's writings are not the place to look for them. But is it not equally obvious that these sources will be found in Nietzsche, in his notorious preoccupation with 'the Will to Power'? After all, every book Nietzsche published and every posthumously edited collection of notes has something to say on the topic, so much so that an account of his entire work could be written *sub specie voluntatis*. And it is certainly true that there are many occasions when Nietzsche argues as though 'the Will' were just such a disembodied, independent metaphysical principle as Hitler seems to have in mind, an unmoved mover that lies behind the empirical world and explains men's activities in the world, something like Hegel's 'Spirit' whose realization is the universal history of mankind. In other words, there are many passages where Nietzsche seems to be taking over the Schopenhauerian cosmic vision of 'the Will' and merely changing Schopenhauer's negative evaluation of it into a detailed and often hysterical affirmation. But of course Nietzsche is not content to extrapolate – albeit affirmatively – from the earlier

philosopher's system, here too he lives up to his reputation as
the most critical of modern philosophers.

In Schopenhauer's work, certainly, this critical vein is absent.
'The Will', in his systematic presentation of it, is *the* universal
principle, which precedes – logically, and also in time – the
human and the natural world; it is that of which the world and
everything in it are 'objectivizations'; it cannot be ascertained
by reason or proved by the scientific understanding because it
is antecedent to reason and understanding, and because anyway proof itself is only possible *in* the objectivized world,
whereas 'the Will' is the foundation and origin of the world.
(This argument, which Nietzsche also uses, is very far from
being a mere logical quibble: it will in fact be one of the constitutive elements of the politicized 'ideology of the Will', that
is, of fascism in its various forms.) And although much of
Schopenhauer's main work, *The World as Will and Idea*, including the entire second volume, is taken up with illustrating
and drawing inferences from this *a priori* insight, the insight
itself – 'the world is my Will' – is absolute and unqualified. And
this is so, Schopenhauer tells us, even though a full understanding of this proposition cannot be obtained in this world.
The world, which is 'Will through and through', can only be
perceived as such (he argues) from the vantage point of 'the
world as idea'. This may be described as the world *sub specie
contemplationis*, postulated as a higher metaphysical reality.
As we ascend to its fullest apprehension, it becomes increasingly
alien to what we are and what we strive for as social and political
beings in the world we share with others. 'The world as idea',
Schopenhauer tells us, is the haven of the philosopher, the
artist, and the saint; 'the world as idea', history tells us, is the
haven of the disaffected 'non-political' intellectuals.

There are occasions, as I have said, when Nietzsche too
accepts this Schopenhauerian account of the Will, and when he
does little more than bring the detailed implications of it up to
date. His inversion of Schopenhauer's negative evaluation
doesn't, in itself, amount to a criticism of the system or of its

overriding metaphysical claim. However, unlike Schopenhauer, Nietzsche is not a system-builder. The very forms of his utterance – from the briefest aphorisms and sentences to extended reflections and short essays – bear witness to an unparalleled intellectual energy which knows no arrest. These genres have their serious drawback too, but as weapons of anti-systematic, anti-ideological criticism they have never been improved on. No sooner does he settle on a sustained mode of enquiry than he turns round to question, criticize, and demolish it, suspecting every 'truth' of being merely an easy way out, subjecting every opinion including his own to what he calls 'my evil eye', to the most searching scrutiny he is able to muster. And this is true even in the last phase of his philosophizing, in those last months before his mental collapse and the onset of those long years of insanity from which he never recovered. In that last winter of 1888 he writes many of the reflections and jottings which are intended for a systematic philosophical treatise, to be called 'The Will to Power', a book he never wrote. But just as, in his earlier books, the danger of allowing the notion of 'the Will' to burgeon into an absolute had been held in check by an unabating concern to find out what it is we actually do when we impose our 'will' on another person, what motives, means, and ends we bring into play, so here too, in these late notes and speculations, the mind at the end of its tether is still a profoundly critical mind. Leapfrog-fashion, the critical self-consciousness overtakes each of its previous positions. Thus, under the heading 'Weakness of the Will', he writes:

This is a metaphor that can mislead. For there is no such thing as the Will, and consequently neither a strong nor a weak will. The multiplicity and dissociation of motives, the lack of system among them, result in 'the weak will'; their coordination under the rule of a single motive results in 'the strong will'; – in the former case there is an oscillating and a lack of gravity, in the latter, precision and clarity of direction.

There is a Hobbesian realism about this and similar passages; whatever may be Nietzsche's intellectual sins, he is not taken in by his own abstractions.

'There is no such thing as the Will'? Obviously, both in common discourse and in philosophy the word has a meaning of some kind. It denotes a wanting which is 'neither a [mere] wishing nor hoping nor the feeling of desire'; a something that 'cannot be said to exist in a man who does nothing towards getting what he wants. The primitive sign of [this] wanting is *trying to get*' or, better still, *trying to change*. The conclusions of contemporary analytical philosophy are really in agreement with Kant's commonsense observation that 'he who wills an end, wills also' – to the extent that he is in his right mind – 'those indispensably necessary means that are in his power.' Or, to put the matter in a more familiar idiom, 'Where there's a will there's a way,' since the will is itself part of the way.

This does not seem to be Hitler's view, for if it were, he would not again and again speak of his own and other people's Will as a thing separate and distinct from its means. What he wishes to 'bequeath to history' (he returns to this thought several times in the *Table Talk*) is the notion that his 'adamant Will' was betrayed by the unworthy means at his disposal – by scheming generals, treacherous and cowardly officers, incompetent ministers and bureaucrats, defeatist 'critics', and finally (in his testament) by the German nation itself: betrayed, in short, by men of 'weak will' who were unable to match his own capacity for the ultimate exertion and sacrifice. Clearly, what he is doing in such statements is to anticipate defeat and write his apologia in advance. But what enabled him to make the distinction in the first place? What has he in mind when he claims that the Army, or the generals, or the German nation, have the means but not the Will to ultimate victory? Why (to return to that earlier quotation from his last public address) does he distinguish between 'our unalterable will' on the one hand, and 'our abilities', 'our readiness for the last sacrifice', on the other? And if all this is 'mere rhetoric, mere propaganda', why does it take *this* form? The short answer is: because it fulfils a religious need, which the propaganda machinery is designed to articulate.

Between propaganda and the ideology of the Will there is a connexion of a special kind. What they have in common is, once again, their perlocutionary character. For if we take it that propaganda is the recommendation of some thing or action on inadequate grounds, we can now see that where the Will is recommended as a thing absolute and disembodied – as that which is not – there the recommendation itself becomes what Kant had called 'the indispensably necessary means' towards bringing about the desired end. On these grounds alone, therefore, propaganda turns out to be, not a fortuitous adjunct of Hitler's ideology (and of the ideology of National Socialism which, if not identical, is at all times brought into line with it), but an integral, constitutive part of it. The structure of this situation resembles nothing so much as a rudimentary poetic structure. Take away the propaganda from what it recommends, and what is left is, not a political programme without its means of realization, but a content rendered defective by an absence of form, an inconsequential nothing.

All propaganda is aimed at, and answers the expectations of, a specific audience; and the language of the mythology of the Will is, as I have suggested, the characteristic language of the audience, the time and place Hitler sets out to conquer. There is no need to labour the point that this is not necessarily the language of all political propaganda. During the 1972 German national election the chief candidate (Willy Brandt) repeatedly exhorted his audiences to ignore 'the personalities' of the contestants and to consider the parliamentary records and the programmes of their parties only, while his rival (Rainer Barzel) was described in *The Times* as follows: 'He is almost an image-maker's model of a modern politician – smooth, charming, articulate, self-controlled, ambitious, ruthless, and unpredictable.' Some of these adjectives may be relevant to the Hitler-image of the 'twenties and 'thirties too, but it is obvious that, seen as a whole, this image of the 1970s belongs to a very different age and is shaped by very different expectations.

The hallmark of the age of Hitler – its historicity – is hardness: 'I do not merely imagine that I am the hardest man the German nation has had for many decades, perhaps centuries, but I also possess the greatest authority' (8 November 1940). In attempting to explain the expectations of the age of Hitler, we must go beyond the sort of historical reasons I have suggested earlier, if only because the more cogent these reasons are, the less they allow for the possibility of freedom of contradiction, for the chances of change. What we are looking for at this point is an explanation of why this language of hardness had the appeal it had, why the ideology of the 'absolute Will' provided the dominant scheme of values. And the answer that suggests itself is: because it and apparently it alone satisfied, albeit in a monstrous fashion, a religious need.

'I will do such things – / What they are, yet I know not; but they shall be / The terrors of the earth.' It is obvious that the more 'absolute' the Will becomes, and therefore the further removed from all concrete means, the more ineffectual it will be, and the more its assertion will resemble childish tantrums. This is not the way Hitler is likely to see himself. No sense of the ridiculous prevents him from using the absolutization of his Will as a means of drawing attention to that self whose gratification, protection and assertion are the substantial grounds of his every decision and every political move. On the contrary: at the point where the self is so imperiously asserted a curious reversal, from complete subjectivity and arbitrariness to what looks like its opposite, is said to take place. In declaring 'the Will' absolute, the ideologist makes a show of replacing the subjective self by an objective principle; 'the Will' is now to be seen as a cosmic 'law' *and* as an element of a religious faith. It is scientific too: I have already suggested that 'the

Will' is given its place in the fascist ideology within the framework of *Sozialdarwinismus* as that agency of Nature which acts in the social and political sphere with the same absolute validity as the principle of natural selection does among the species of animals; and this doctrine of 'the Will' is one of the many points at which National Socialism coincides with other forms of fascism.

But above all 'the Will' becomes a pseudo-*religious* concept: in speaking of himself as one sent by History, or again as the agent of cosmic forces or natural laws, Hitler comes close to Christ's affirmation, 'I can of mine own self do nothing: as I hear, I judge; and my judgement is just: because I seek not mine own will, but the will of the Father which hath sent me' (John v. 30), and we shall see good reason for thinking that he was eminently conscious of the blasphemy. Endowed with a transcendent authority and a providential sanction (for it is part of the propaganda to present the leader as one chosen by Fate, or Providence), the Will becomes the object of that dedication to the absolute which had been characteristic of German Protestant thinking and which in happier ages had found worthier though not necessarily less heterodox objects.

9 The Language of Prophecy

From the time of Heine and Nietzsche onwards German literary and philosophical thinking is apt to find expression in apocalyptic statements and prophecies of doom. Though they occasionally strike a note of moral warning, these are hardly prophecies in the biblical sense. What they contain, however, are undertones of intent. When (to choose the most obvious example) Spengler foretells the advent of a new breed of men, the Engineers and Technicians, and greets them as the heirs of 'Faustian man' and the fulfillers of European destiny, he is at the same time facilitating that advent by declaring that all alternatives are hopelessly unrealistic, mere daydreams of an 'unworldly idealism'. When Ernst Jünger, following in Spengler's footsteps, describes the coming of 'the Worker' or 'Technocrat', he too couples his utopia with a recommendation for the speedy dispatch of *bürgerlich* individualism, socialist progressivism and the like. The obvious thing to say about these and similar prophecies in the present context is that they are words, mere words on a page, unsupported by action or even, before 1918, a clear prospect of action. This is equally true of Nietzsche. He too is far from squeamish in his choice of metaphors. When that stentorian *persona* of Nietzsche's, the fiction called Zarathustra, addresses his disciples, he advises them not to try to halt the process of contemporary decay (the choice of the biological metaphor is significant of the supposedly ineluctable character of the process). On the contrary, they are to hasten the demise of 'all that is today' by *choosing* to speed it on its way down; or, to put it in Zarathustra's own elegant words, 'Whatever falls – it should be kicked, too!' Yet these are mere metaphors woven into fictions. However gravely Nietzsche inveighs against the intellectual habit of 'mere hypothesizing', against non-committal speculating, many of his own metaphors are conceived and elaborated in that experimental and badly 'literary' area of experience where they are not confronted with events in the social world. The feel of that world, and of the future in which his prophecies will be enacted, often eludes him. The only thing that is not metaphorical is the prophetic self, is Nietzsche, the bearer of a message of doom.

With Hitler it is the message that is non-metaphorical. There is a metaphor, here too, but it concerns not the action but the speaker. He is not really a 'prophet' at all, not even in the secularized 'literary' sense. He hides behind the metaphor of 'the prophet', turning the fiction into an active political myth; his declaration of intent becomes an action programme:

> In the course of my life I have often been a prophet, and I was mostly laughed at. During the time of my struggle for power it was the Jewish people first and foremost who received with mere derision my prophecies that I would assume the leadership of the state and thus of the whole nation, and that I would then find a solution to the Jewish problem, together with many other problems. I believe that in the meantime the hoots of laughter have choked in the throats of German Jewry. Today I will once again turn prophet: if international financial Jewry within and outside Europe should succeed once more in dragging the nations into a war, the result will be, not the Bolshevization of the world and thereby the victory of Jewry, but the annihilation of the Jewish races in Europe.

The statement must be understood in its full context. It is made at the end of January 1939, halfway between the Munich agreement and the occupation of Prague, during one of the peak periods of Hitler's popularity. It is addressed to a public that knows, if not as a matter of certainty then of overwhelming probability, that there will be a war; addressed by one who knows that they know, and is adept at maintaining this open conspiracy. This public can be expected to delight in the vast terms employed ('international . . . Europe . . . the world'), because it has been accustomed to this global vocabulary by previous party pronouncements. The 885 National Socialist deputies assembled in the Kroll Oper, meeting for the first time since their election ten months earlier to listen to this giant oration of two-and-a-half hours, are of course not Hitler's real public at all. His real public are the millions at their private radio receivers and in the assembly-rooms and restaurants all over Germany. They are unlikely to have read any of Spengler's or Jünger's sophisticated and wordy literary 'prophecies'. But there does exist a bridge between the 'serious' literature and the mind of the people. It is supplied by the barrage of articles from Dr Goebbels, his 'press chief' Dr Dietrich, and their host of collaborators.

Moreover, this global vocabulary is not the only thing Hitler's public takes in its stride. By now it also readily accepts the peculiar logic of Hitler's anti-Semitism, according to which, without a word of explanation, 'international financial interests' are seen as being not at odds with 'Bolshevization' but identical with it. And the public accepts this for no other reason than that it has been told that the two are identical; for no other reason than that on numerous previous occasions these have been declared to be the twin aspects of the Jewish bid for world power and hence for the extinction of Germany, or Nordic man, or the Aryan race. Suitably dramatized and frequently repeated, this double-pronged attack has the advantage, unique among *all* political programmes available at the time, of uniting what was once the moderate Left and the entire Centre and nationalist Right by creating a single common enemy – the only enemy against whom the entire political spectrum save the extreme Left can make common cause. The ploy may seem obvious, yet it amounts to a major act of the political imagination. Nobody thought of it before.

The logical conclusion of this is to identify 'international Jewry' with the totality of Germany's enemies, that is, of those who can be expected to oppose Germany's territorial demands. This again is an act of the political imagination, which a few months later will be confirmed by Sir Nevile Henderson, who (if correctly reported) tells the Führer that there is no ill will against Germany among the English people, and that all hostility has its origin 'among Jews and anti-Nazis'. This attribution of all anti-German sentiments to a world-wide Jewish intrigue scarcely corresponds to the reality of international politics, in spite of Henderson's assurance; but this, at least for the time being, in no way detracts from its domestic effectiveness. The propagandist principle employed is already mentioned in *Mein Kampf:* 'It is part of the great leader's genius to let it always appear that even widely separated enemies belong to a single category only, since among weak and vacillating characters the awareness of different enemies leads all too easily to the beginning of a doubt of the justice of their own case.'

Hitler's 'prophecy', then, builds on this complex of shared and implicitly understood hopes and fears – fears rather than hopes – which is constitutive of the *Volksgemeinschaft* as a community of expectations. The 'prophecy' reads like a threat, yet it is also a demand for conformity. The assertion it implies is not only, 'The war I am about to unleash is one in which not the Jews our enemies but we shall be victorious', but, 'This war, in which our victory is the same as the annihilation of the Jews, is an inseparable part of my programme, in which domestic "tasks" are continuous with international "tasks", and will receive a single, continuous solution'; and furthermore, 'The annihilation of the Jew our common enemy is the reward and deliverance I offer you for following me into this war.'

Like the use of 'Nature', like the '*Yes or No*' scheme, the prophecy that is not really a prophecy at all displays the characteristic pattern according to which the leader and his party conduct major aspects of their domestic policy and propaganda. The election that is really an acclamation, the plebiscite that is really the confirmation of a decision already taken and largely implemented, the policy based on 'the healthy

feeling of the People' that is really based on an expectation of
assent from fear, the party conference that is really a military
display, and above all the party address that is really a quasi-
religious ritual of mutual renewal – all these are adaptations of
the procedures of liberal social democracy towards totalitarian
ends.

The part played by modern (or rather not so very modern)
technology in all this is certainly considerable. Without radio,
the private receiving set as well as the public loudspeaker
system, without the stop press in black and red and the speedy
printing of up-to-the-minute broadsheets in large numbers,
without the transport of large numbers of men by train, truck
and car, these adaptations would not be possible. The success
of a Nuremberg party rally (for which 400 trains were mobilized) undoubtedly depends in no small measure on the organ-
izing ability of a man like Albert Speer, and on his particular
gift of exploiting some of the more spectacular inventions of
the time. One readily agrees with Speer when he writes that
the most memorable thing he ever designed was that 'cathedral
built of ice' which so impressed the British Ambassador – a
huge area covering the entire Zeppelinfeld on the outskirts of
Nuremberg, bounded by the beams of 130 flak searchlights
which formed a canopy of lights at a height of 24,000 feet.
But the role of technology, which in any event would have
been available to Hitler's enemies, should not be exaggerated.
Unlike propaganda, it could never be more than a means, that
part of the medium that was not the message. Speer thought
otherwise. When, in his defence at Nuremberg, he claims that
'the criminal events of those years' were to be explained by the
fact that 'Hitler was the first to be able to avail himself of the
means of modern technology', an opinion Speer repeated,
uncritically though at greater length, twenty years later, his
misunderstanding is not arbitrary. Like those who thought to
explain the Third Reich by pointing to some impersonal and
supposedly irresistible 'forces of history', Speer is appealing
to some equally impersonal and equally irresistible 'forces of

modern technology' to explain what were in fact deliberate personal decisions and moves of political intrigue with clearly conceived ends. (Some of these ends were to be achieved in very different circumstances and long after the collapse of the National Socialist state, but that is another story.)

This technological mystification, which has its origins in Spengler, was not part of Hitler's propaganda; unlike the myth of historicism it was too sophisticated for his purpose, perhaps even for his understanding. (He was singularly accurate in gauging the point at which an opinion, an idea or a practice would cease to be subservient to his ends, and he was quick to suppress it as soon as it reached that point.) But this myth, too, could be turned into a bogey, against which the 'anti-material-istic' and 'natural' aspects of party ideology offered protection. The background of Speer's argument is familiar enough: lack of moral scruples, lust for power, greed for authority, the sadism of 'absolute' command, and vanity are acknowledged, but then again at least partly disguised, behind talk of 'the automatism of progress' and 'terrorization by technology', where before they had been disguised behind the fatalism of 'historical forces'. What is perhaps unexpected is that the ideo-logical rationalizations with which Speer and others like him assuaged their bad conscience were gratuitous. Like so many of his fellow-intellectuals, he was not under pressure to offer active support to the party ideology, he was improving on it and going beyond it on his own initiative and of his own free will. To be an intellectual in National Socialist Germany, it appears, was to toe the party line even where there wasn't one, and to make it up as one went along.

Hitler's 'prophecy' of 30 January 1939 came true, and was publicly known to be coming true. On at least two subsequent occasions he refers back to it, to prove to his audience that he is 'not one to engage in hasty prophecies', that he is as good as his word. These statements seem to be no longer strictly propaganda (the advocacy of a future course of action) but the naked display and boast of power. Yet where, between advocacy and boast, and between boast and threat, is a line to be drawn? Hannah Arendt warns against overestimating the power that propaganda can have over people, by arguing that it 'is indeed part and parcel of "psychological warfare"; but terror is more. Terror continues to be used by totalitarian regimes even when its psychological aims are achieved . . . Where the rule of terror is brought to perfection, as in concentration camps, propaganda disappears entirely . . .' Miss Arendt's sequence, however, presupposes a stability of 'psychological aims' such as National Socialism at all events never achieved, and never really intended to achieve. Moreover, the distinctions which she mentions are those that the regime successfully obliterated. A spectrum of regimented *praxis* stretches from the camp fires with their seventeenth-century part songs sung by bright-eyed youths with guitar accompaniment, through the mass meetings well backed by the truncheons and knuckle-dusters of the SA, to the physical terror of the labour camps with their degrading treatment and psychic deprivations administered under the motto, 'Work Makes Free'. The extermination camps are at the dark end of this spectrum. Here, as Miss Arendt says, all propaganda has disappeared. They are 'the solution of the Jewish problem' of which Hitler has so often spoken. His words are 'prophetic' only because he can round up his victims at any time to make them come true, yet the millions who support his actions do so because they have been assured, and indeed can see, that his words are self-fulfilling, 'prophetic'. This is the fullest meaning of propaganda as a performative statement.

Thus Hitler establishes a firm continuity between persuasion, propaganda, intimidation and terror, between words and deeds, and this continuity is the characteristic *praxis* of his regime. Facing this continuity, the citizen of the Third Reich has allowed himself to be placed in a situation in which he must choose: acclamation or brutal suppression, Yes or No. The religious insinuation is unmistakable.

10 The Religious Expectation
and its Ritual

Hitler's claim to be the redeemer of the Reich (identified by
the party ideologists with the medieval *rîche*) and the true
spokesman of Germany has all the *Pathos* of a religious conviction; putting to good use his own Austrian origins, he
places himself at the centre of a series of rituals in which the
Southern mentality blends with that of the North. The irritable
reaching-out for metaphysical absolutes of which I have spoken
is of course a German and Lutheran phenomenon. (Freud, the
only Austrian among modern mythologists, has some scathing
comments to make on this particular discontent.) Hitler and the
Party respond to it by blending the impersonal ethos of the
Frederician tattoo with elements of a highly personalized
Austrian and Catholic liturgy. Hence the fixtures of the party
calendar, organized to keep the faithful in close and constant
touch with the activities of the regime.

The feasts of the party year are related to the feasts of the
Christian calendar in much the same way as these were to the
seasonal celebrations of the pagan era. The year begins on 30
January with the anniversary of Hitler's accession to power in
1933. On that day each year 'the Nation' is presented with a
lengthy account of 'what I took over and what I have done with
the power entrusted to me', and the day ends with a public
ceremony, broadcast by radio from every street corner in the
land, when those eighteen-year-olds who have proved their
qualities of leadership in the *Hitler Jugend* are sworn in as full
members of the Party. On 24 February the 'annunciation' of
the 'immutable' party programme of twenty-five points in the

Hofbräuhaus in 1920 is commemorated. This had been the first mass meeting Hitler ever addressed. Year after year until 1943 he liked to look back on the beginnings of his career as a public speaker, addressing the Old Guard in the simple, sentimental language of an old boys' reunion, though this again, like every other ceremony, received nation-wide coverage. Here Hitler presents himself as 'the truest executor of the Party's sacred heritage'. The movement's modest beginnings are contrasted with the great opposition it has had to overcome, and during the War these past successes are invoked as a guarantee of its, and Germany's, future victory. 18 March, the national day of mourning consecrated to the memory of the dead of the First World War, is celebrated in the Kroll Oper in Berlin with a performance of the second movement of Beethoven's Third Symphony – a solemn 'cultural' occasion attended by all foreign diplomats. The Führer's birthday is celebrated on 20 April (the pictures and *objets d'art* he receives as presents are duly passed on to the museum in Linz, which he hoped after the War to turn into the greatest art gallery of Europe); the day culminates in a parade of the *Wehrmacht* through the Brandenburger Tor, designed as a display of Germany's growing military power. Next the May Day celebrations: their purpose is to emphasize the Party's solidarity with the workers (its 'socialist' component) and Hitler's part in the creation of the welfare state.

The high point of the year was the all-German Party rally, supposedly modelled on the old German *Thing* or assembly, which from 1926 onwards occupied the first full week in September, and from 1927 to 1938 took place in Nuremberg; the average number of those attending was half a million, reaching a record 950,000 in 1938. 'Here all centred on the Party and its Leader', writes Hans Frank, 'here he received general absolution for the year that had passed since the last rally, and full general power for the coming year. . . . In that week-long hymn of jubilation, colours, lights, music and festivities nobody thought "ideologically", "programmatically", or "objectively-politically".' Parades of soldiers with fixed bayonets in lines of twelve, SS men with spread-eagle standards, the *Kraft durch Freude* battalions presenting gleaming shovels; manifestations and appeals, 140,000 political leaders marching past the solitary figure of the Führer, congresses and conferences and resolutions. . . . Each year was a sort of 'Anno Santo', and each year this gigantic gathering ('No country in Europe – it may even be said, no country in the world, could duplicate its significance' wrote the enthusiastic correspondent of the New York *Times*) was conducted under a different device: in 1933 it was 'the *Reichsparteitag* of victory', in 1934 it was 'unity and strength', 1935 was 'the rally of freedom', 1936 of 'honour and freedom', 1937 was 'the *Reichsparteitag* of work', 1938 'the day of Greater Germany'; the rally of 1939, called predictably 'the rally of peace', was cancelled and the hundreds of trains prepared for it were used for the mobilization of troops. All 'positive' sections of the Party and of the State sent their delegates to these rallies: the old comrades representing the glorious past (on another occasion Hitler called them 'my hunchbacked ancients'), the SA, SS, the farmers' and labour organizations standing for the embattled present, the *Hitler Jugend* for the eternal future; tens of thousands of women paraded before their beloved Führer and were told that the ultimate purpose of the National Socialist state was 'the German child' (though admittedly *das deutsche Kind* sounds a bit less fatuous): brought up with appropriate rigour, 'he will be woman's veritable safeguard and shield'. Within the framework of this entirely political rally the Army conducted its annual manoeuvres, incidentally demonstrating its inferior position and uneasy relationship with the Party.

As the homilies addressed to a gathering of pilgrims are concerned to chastise the sinners present and prepare them for the spiritual regeneration in the life to come, so the slogans and main speeches of the Nuremberg rallies were designed to emphasize that the building of the Reich was far from complete, that the old Adam still stirred and Satan himself was far from vanquished, that the Party was a living organism, ever discontented with the present and in the service of tomorrow – the thorn in the flesh of the Reich and the harbinger of the classless millennium. If the *Reichsparteitag* was informed by the spirit of expectancy and hope, the next feast in the party calendar, at the end of September, was the day of thanksgiving, 'the Reich's harvest festival', when 50,000 farmers and peasants in ancient folk costumes ('the beautiful, strong, healthy-hard men of our *Landvolk*') trooped to the Bückeberg and there erected a giant Germanic crown-like wheatsheaf. And finally, exactly a week after All Saints and All Souls, the dead of the *Putsch* – the 'blood baptism' – of 1923 were commemorated. On 8 November the survivors, decorated with their 'Blood Order' and including as the only woman Sister Pia, the nurse who had attended to the wounded, met for their traditional gathering in the Münchner Bürgerbräukeller, to listen to Hitler's memorial address dedicated to 'the sixteen martyrs of the National Socialist movement'; and on 9 November the march to the Feldherrnhalle was repeated in the precise order of 1923, along a road flanked by pylons of burning torches, to the accompaniment of funereal music, tolling bells, and the slow recital of the names of all those killed or mortally wounded since 1919 in the service of the Party. And again the solemn *Kitsch* went out over every public transmitter in the country.

The main function of the Party year was of course to provide occasions for displays of Hitler's rhetoric. The factual content of his ceremonial speeches is even lower than usual, their aim is to work up support for decisions already taken and often already announced. What is remarkable about these speeches are the set passages they contain, passages whose function and form are purely homiletic. Hitler's address to the Party's political leaders at the 1936 Nuremberg Rally ('Honour and Freedom'), centred on a sustained identification with Christ the Redeemer, offers a particularly rich example. The setting is described by a correspondent in the New York *Times* (12 September 1936):

As he appeared there shone upward from a hidden circle of 150 army searchlights behind the grandstands as many spears of light to the central point above. It was the same device employed at the closing ceremony of the Olympic Games, but it was greatly improved and infinitely larger.

In this bright light Hitler walked down the steps through the group awaiting him and slowly a procession with him at the head marched across the field to the tribune. The thunderous cheers quite drowned the music of the massed bands playing him in.

He ascended the tribune and stood there waiting until there was complete silence. Then suddenly there appeared far in the distance a mass of advancing red color. It was the 25,000 banners of Nazi organizations in all parts of Germany.

The color bearers marched with them across the rear of the brown columns on the field. Then they came forward, six abreast in the narrower lanes and twenty abreast in the wide center aisle, so there was presented the spectacle of a great tide of crimson seeping through the lanes between the solid blocs of brown.

Simultaneously the minor searchlights along the pillared rim above the grandstands were turned down on the field, lighting up the gilded eagles on the standards, so the flood of red was flecked with gold. The effect was indescribably beautiful.

The only thing the author of this period piece has no eye for is the grotesquerie of the scene. The man with the spontaneous speech habits of the Austrian lower middle classes (*'Ihnen pressiert's wohl recht sehr?!'*) is addressing 140,000 political functionaries in a solemn declamatory style superimposed on the intimately personal language of Luther's New Testament. What is enacted here is a situation of total immanence, where nobody believes in anything; or rather, where few if any believe in the man before them but all, including Hitler himself, fully believe in the image they have created. What his rhetoric appeals to is not their personal religious experience but their readiness to take part in the religious image-making, to connive at his self-dramatization as a messianic figure:

How deeply we feel once more in this hour the miracle that has brought us together! Once you heard the voice of a man, and it spoke to your hearts, it awakened you, and you followed that voice. Year in year out you followed it, without even having seen the speaker; you only heard a voice and followed it.

Now that we meet here, we are all filled with the wonder of this gathering. Not every one of you can see me and I do not see each one of you. But I feel you, and you feel me! It is faith in our nation that has made us little people great, that has made us poor people rich, that has made us wavering, fearful, timid people brave and confident; that has made us erring wanderers clear-sighted and has brought us together!

So you have come this day from your little villages, your market towns, your cities, from mines and factories, or leaving the plough, to this city. You come out of the little world of your daily struggle for life, and of your struggle for Germany and for our nation, to experience this feeling for once: Now we are together, we are with him and he is with us, and now we are Germany!

An astonishing montage of biblical texts is put in the service of this act of self-dramatization. After an initial allusion to the voice crying in the wilderness (Luke iii. 4), Christ's Epiphany (John xx. 19–31) is presented, with its exhortation to transcending faith, 'blessed are they that have not seen, yet have believed'. The next passage ('Not every one of you . . .') continues the messianic parallel by alluding to John xvi. 16–17, 'A little while, and ye shall not see me: and again a little while, and ye shall see me'; and so does the subsequent enumeration ('us little people . . . us poor people . . .') with its allusion to Luke vii. 22, 'how that the blind see, the lame walk, . . . to the poor the gospel is preached'. The last paragraph opens with Hitler's favourite antithesis on the theme of 'your little lives . . . my great mission'; the topos of the 'little villages' has no direct parallel in the English Bible but relates to Luther's rendering of Micah v. 1 (and Matthew ii. 6), 'And thou, Bethlehem, which art little among the towns of Judah . . . '. The final clarion call, 'We are with him and he is with us!' takes up the earlier 'I feel you and you feel me!', again in Luther's version of John xiv. 3, 'I will come again and take you unto me, so that ye shall be where I am'. And the Johannine allusion is joined by a reference to some of the most famous and familiar lines of German medieval mystical love poetry, *'du bist mîn, ich bin dîn | des solt du gewis sin'* : Tristan wooing Isolde, Christ the Bridegroom wooing the Church, Hitler wooing the communicant members of the nation. . . .

11   A Society Longing for 'Transcendence'

'Je suis athée, mais je suis catholique': Charles Maurras's remark has an aphoristic sophistication (a concern with form, not with self) of which Hitler was not capable, yet it applies to him too. He was brought up in Catholic schools, liked to recall his boyhood impressions as a server at Mass and his early ambition to become an abbot. He never publicly renounced his membership of the Church or ceased to pay his dues. He professed a cynical admiration for the Catholic hierarchy (not least after the Concordat of 1933), its world-wide organization, its educational policies and its pomp and circumstance, whereas he had nothing but contempt for 'the soiled collars and stained frock coats' of the Lutheran clergy. Above all he admired the Church's practice of recruiting her priests from all classes of society, and aimed at a similarly broad basis in the hierarchy of the Party. The anti-Semitic element in Austrian and Bavarian Catholicism provided him with a 'religious' legitimation of his own obsessive hatred of the Jews – indeed, his need of 'a visible enemy' corresponds to the need, expressed by certain sections of the Church, to disclaim her own Jewish origins. In his conversations he likes to indulge in a certain prurience of the confessional, and he undoubtedly 'believes' in sin. When he confines his notion of sin to the sexual and excludes from it all political and social crimes (except 'Jewish' usury), he is in fact following characteristic trends in the popular theology of trans-Alpine Catholicism of the period. As against this, there is his occasional coarse abuse of the Catholic clergy and the physical persecution of many individual priests;

and there are his plans (once the War is won) for the total liquidation of all religious bodies. In a secret address in 1937 he spoke of 'the hard inward struggle' it cost him 'to free [himself] from the religious ideas of [his] childhood, . . . whereas now', he added, 'I feel as fresh as a foal in a meadow'. This is because his studies have proved to him conclusively 'the fallacy of all religions', and have led him to accept the laws of Social Darwinism as absolutely determining the life of individual men and races alike.

The picture we get from these more or less contradictory opinions is characteristic of the many thousands of his contemporaries throughout Central Europe who, on migrating from their native province into the total alienation of the big city, lose their religious faith and seek to replace it by a 'scientific' *Weltanschauung* of one kind of another. The 'religious' *raisonnements* I have briefly mentioned might be those of a minor character in a naturalistic play by Gerhart Hauptmann or Karl Anzengruber. They are utterly banal and commonplace. They provide a foil for the messianic self-dramatization I have described, but they do not explain it.

What lifts Hitler out of the sphere of the banal and commonplace (and makes Karl Kraus's observations on the banality of evil misleading) is his wholly political perception of a religious need in contemporary German society, and his growing confidence of being able to exploit that need for his own ends.

True, the passage in which this political perception is expressed (in the second volume of *Mein Kampf*) is so involuted as to be barely intelligible. The empty assertions, the helpless repetitions and pretentious pleonasms – which I have not spared the reader and which make the passage sound like some tasteless parody of a twentieth-century Doktor Teufelsdröckh – belong among the stock devices of a speaker addressing a popular audience on a 'philosophical' topic. Yet the main point of the argument – to the effect that men's ideals correspond to

their vital needs – emerges clearly enough. More is wanted
(Hitler writes) than a general definition of religion, for

> it does not lead to that [practical] effectiveness which emerges
> from an inward religious longing at the moment when out of
> the purely metaphysical, unbounded world of ideas a clearly
> bounded faith forms itself. Assuredly, this faith is not an end
> in itself, but only a means to an end; yet it is the indispensably
> necessary means which alone makes it possible to attain the
> end. This end, however, is not only concerned with ideas,
> but taken in the last analysis it is also eminently practical.
> For indeed one must be clear that the highest ideals always
> correspond to the deepest vital necessity [*Lebensnotwendig-
> keit*], just as the nobility of beauty at its most sublime in the
> last analysis lies only in what is logically most purposeful
> [*im logisch Zweckmäßigsten*]. In helping to raise man from the
> level of mere animal survival, faith really contributes to the
> securing and safeguarding of man's existence. Take away
> from present mankind its religious–dogmatic principles which
> are upheld by its education and whose practical significance is
> that of ethical-moral principles, by abolishing religious educa-
> tion and without replacing it by something equivalent,

– which of course is where the Party, its 'dogmas' and its ritual
come in –

> and the result facing you will be a grave shock to the founda-
> tions of mankind's existence. One may therefore state that not
> only does man live to serve higher ideals but that, conversely,
> these higher ideals also provide the presupposition of his
> existence as man. So the circle closes.

This is the mode of writing of an age. In its turgid form the
passage points to the social-Darwinist and materialist thinking
of men like Ernst Haeckel, Ludwig Büchner, and the historian
Alexander von Müller, whose lectures at Munich University
Hitler attended in the Spring of 1918; it shows familiarity with
contemporary neo-classicist aesthetics, perhaps with the writings of the Viennese architect Adolf Loos; and the argument

which asserts a reciprocal relationship between 'higher ideals' and 'vital necessity' belongs to the ambience of Nietzsche's *Genealogy of Morals*. But whereas Nietzsche argues from his diagnosis of man's exposed condition to man's grave responsibility for his own future, Hitler is using the same diagnosis as one of several legitimizations of his own political ambitions. My earlier claim that Hitler's knowledge of Nietzsche, unlike Mussolini's, was probably confined to a few tags and *idées reçues* still stands. Nietzsche, more than any other thinker, understood the situation which Hitler exploited. In response to this situation Hitler's messianic image came into being, embodying the religiosity Nietzsche despised. Its creation is the political act of an Austrian Catholic, but by virtue of its claim to absoluteness the image finds its place in a German rather than an Austrian context.

Let us look at the world for which *Mein Kampf* was written. Faced with grave economic crises, waves of mass unemployment and little consistent support from the Western powers, the new republican regime does its undistinguished best to placate the right wing at the expense of the left by a variety of new constitutional, political and economic measures (the legal system is least affected). Not all of these measures fail – we shall see that the National Socialists will adopt several of them and claim them as their own. But they are administered half-heartedly by a civil service, police and judiciary who are largely reactionary. Consciously disloyal to the democratic regime, which they associate with the 'fulfilment policy of Versailles', the officials of the new state are in fact bent on its destruction. The most active men in this society are also the most gravely disaffected. The majority of them are without political affiliation, others come from the nationalist Right, others again from the disillusioned Left. Unwilling to renounce the warlike spirit of the trenches and of the *Nachkrieg* (the military skirmishes of the Freikorps), these are men who see their own social failures as a national calamity; and writers like Spengler and

Ernst Jünger tell them that their failure has world-historical significance. What they now seek is a religious solution – religious in the sense of being total and absolute and an object of faith rather than of prudential thinking. Since they are seeking a single, 'total' thing, their 'idealism' appears wholly compatible with material satisfactions. What they are looking for is in fact not a solution but a salvation – not however as an alternative to and an unwordly substitute for material concerns and demands, but as the subsuming and validation of such demands.

And they find the embodiment of that salvation in the messianic leader. The more total and 'religious' or (to use one of Hitler's favourite terms) 'fanatical' the demands he makes on them and the more uncompromising his call for the warlike virtues of obedience, hardness and self-sacrifice, the more certain they are that his claim to a god-given authority and to the 'historic' nature of his mission is authentic, that he is the true Messiah. In a situation largely bereft of communally valid religious dogmas and of socially binding institutions – a situation of spiritual chaos and material deprivation – his messianic creed is experienced as anachronistic – at one and the same time backward-looking *and* utopian. The more it diverges from the status quo, which is the direct source of disaffection, the more the messianic image becomes an object of faith and a powerful force of social integration.

Ernst Nolte's extended description and analysis of fascism (1963) culminates in the claim that in each of its three forms (Action française, Italian fascism, German National Socialism) it constitutes an onslaught on the idea of 'transcendence'. By transcendence Nolte means man's theoretical (e.g. philosophical or theological) capacity to conceive of an idea or a goal that stands over against his defective and humdrum condition, as well as man's ability to direct his *praxis* by such an idea or goal: it is to be 'a reaching-out of thought beyond all that is given and all that can be given, in the direction of an absolute whole; it is every kind of going-beyond that frees man from the constraint of the everyday, and enables him . . . to experience the world as one whole.' Hence thinkers from Parmenides to Hegel, Marx and Max Weber, for all the difference between the goals they envisage, are seen as practitioners of 'transcendence' thus defined, whereas Charles Maurras, Mussolini and Hitler are presented as its implacable enemies. It is a disappointing conclusion to a remarkable book. As far as Hitler is concerned the statement is in need of considerable qualification, for which Nolte's own treatment of National Socialism supplies the material. Hitler's onslaught on 'the world as one whole' – on the idea of our common humanity – is the successful thing it is precisely because it is conducted under the image and in the language of transcendence, as the answer to a religious longing and demand. Of course Nolte would agree that it is the *wrong* answer, but his essentially antinomian argument does not provide the grounds for calling it wrong. Why should the gigantic dream of destruction, which Hitler not only dreamed but attempted to put into practice, *not* be seen as a project to transcend the human condition in the direction of a (racially pure) whole, and to free men from 'the constraint of the everyday'? Everything in such an argument (it would seem) will depend on the way that 'whole' is conceived, but when it comes to deciding whether the metaphysically valid 'whole' is to be 'matter or spirit, cosmos or chaos, a god or a devil', Nolte is astonishingly indifferent. The burden of his argument is too much on the 'going beyond', and too little on the moral and political safeguards with which that 'going beyond' must be connected if it is not to degenerate into a negative utopia. His argument has a precedent. In a diary note of 1943, published in 1949, Ernst Jünger criticized National Socialism for being the wrong, 'a-metaphysical solution'. One can think of more radical objections.

12   The Indifference to Liberty

In positing a perverted religious need as the ground in which
the appeal of 'the Führer's Will' was founded, I don't wish to
belittle the more mundane explanations and analyses which
have helped to form our picture of the 'thirties. For the dominant group of German voters between 1929 and 1933 the promise
of economic stability on the one hand and of a 'total' reorganiza-
tion – a 'rebirth' – of German society on the other formed
undoubtedly the most important because the most concrete
attraction, even though the two things, being obviously incompatible, were soon disrupting the precarious unity of the party
and, after 1933, of the state. Fear of a communist revolution
and socialist reforms, dislike of a weak parliamentary system,
German middle-class conformism and love of 'order' at all
costs – indeed the whole syndrome of an outdated paternalist
system (*der Obrigkeitsstaat*) – were exploited to the full; and
again the contradiction between the promise (to the industrialists and the patricians in the *Volkspartei*) to do nothing that
would undermine the old authoritarian structure and the conception of a totalitarian state informed by the *Führerprinzip*
was successfully camouflaged by party propaganda. Different
social groups were attracted by the promise of full employment
on the one hand and strict control of labour and low wages on
the other, by the revanchist attitude towards 'the crime of
Versailles', economic autarky, or again the old dream of a
'Greater Germany' beyond the confines of Bismarck's Reich.
But, however varied their ends, there was one thing which every
social and political group that voted Hitler into power as well
as some that opposed him, chief among them the Communists,

were prepared to forgo, and that was political liberty under the law; one thing that every group (except the Jehovah's Witnesses) was ready to sacrifice, and that was freedom of individual conscience. Hitler himself knew how to exploit this defective concern. At the height of his power he proclaims that the readiness to forgo freedom is the sign of a truly cultured nation; adding that 'the more primitive men are, the more strongly do they feel every restriction of their personal freedom as an act of undue coercion'.

So complete was the absence of any strong feelings on the subject of civil liberties that even today, in a very different situation, few if any historians of the Third Reich remark on it. All other aspects of the regime have received their full treatment: its social composition, the form and content of its legislation, its ideological tenets and contradictions, its rule of terror and the bureaucracy that made it possible; the internal tactics and foreign-political moves of its ruler and his conduct of the War . . . whereas the underlying violation of every conceivable idea of freedom – conceivable in Western terms but also in the terms of Germany's own liberal tradition – has received little comment.

Yet it is surely noteworthy that in the 'thirties such feelings were absent not only among the ideologists of the regime and its fellow-travellers on the Right, but also among its opponents. On 23 March 1933 there took place in the Reichstag what was to be the last genuine public debate in Germany for the next thirteen years. Hitler, elected Chancellor on 5 March with 43.9% of the votes (and 288 deputies in a Reichstag of 647, as opposed to the Social Democrats' 120 and the Communists' 81), was asking for a law granting full powers for the next four years to himself and his cabinet (which at that point and for several months to come did not have a National Socialist majority). The Communists having been prevented from taking up their mandates by the simple device of being thrown into gaol or detained in 'protective custody', the only speaker to oppose Hitler in the debate was Otto Wels, leader of the Social

Democratic parliamentary party. With the SA baying in the
streets outside, several SPD deputies beaten up or arrested on
their way to the Chamber, and the situation of terror which
Hitler had allowed to build up in the previous three weeks, for
Wels to have spoken up at all was an act of remarkable personal
courage; but his speech was remarkable for little else. In
opposing the Enabling Law for which Hitler was asking, Wels
once briefly appeals to the constitution and to its guarantee of
freedom under the law – that is all. For the rest, his speech
makes melancholy reading. He in no way opposes Hitler's
plans for economic autarky and rearmament, he is eager to
associate himself with Hitler's gesture of good will towards 'our
brother nation, Austria'. He too pours scorn on the socialist
opposition that was at that time assembling in Prague (and
which he himself was to join before the year was out). He
refers to the destruction of the freedom of the press, but instantly qualifies his remarks by deploring the 'exaggerations'
of foreign newspaper reports on the state of Germany. The
Social Democrats (he assures his audience) have always been
and still are every bit as patriotic as the National Socialists. The
Social Democrats were 'the first to deny the untruth of German war guilt', the first to protest against the injustices of the
reparations, the first to defend the honour of the German nation
before the tribunal of Europe; the Social Democrats have the
economic interests of all classes just as much at heart as the
National Socialists, 'our achievements in the rebuilding of the
state and of the economy and in the liberation of the occupied
territories will stand the test of history . . .'. Both Hitler and
Wels were of course speaking to a far wider audience than the
Reichstag, and neither was saying anything this audience
didn't already know. That Hitler would be asking for absolute
power was as predictable as that the Social Democrats would
oppose the demand and fail to present a united front in doing
so. Was it already too late? There is a sense – the sense of
Hitler's 'thirties – in which Wels had lost the verbal battle even
before Hitler, under the field-glasses of Göring, president of

the Reichstag, rose to make his reply. For at *this* game, which
Hitler had played for the past thirteen years, he knew he could
not be beaten. It has been said that this was one of the very few
occasions in Hitler's career when, without a prepared script, he
engaged in the give-and-take of a real parliamentary debate.
Whoever thinks him incapable of debating skills need only
read his reply. It is certainly, as Bullock says, ungenerous, but
it does not fail to take issue with the points Wels had made.
From the notes he had made during Wels's address Hitler
constructs a rhetorical edifice which, in its skill of repartee,
sarcastic litotes, anaphora and half-a-dozen other tricks from
the orator's bag, compares with Mark Antony's funeral oration.
In addressing the German public at large, both Wels and Hitler
are speaking the language of nationalism – the one haltingly and
ending on a note of despair, the other with the assurance of
victory *which was as yet not his*, a victory which this speech
(and half-a-dozen similar ones delivered in those crucial six
weeks) would secure for him. The outcome is never in doubt.
The Centre Party having been squared before the debate,
Hitler gets his Enabling Law with a comfortable majority (441
to 94). And Wels? Anxious to safeguard his credentials as a
patriot, he no more thinks of appealing to international working-
class solidarity than did his predecessors in the notorious war-
credits debate of 4 August 1914. To say that the language
of political liberty is not available to him is to recognize
the extent to which Hitler and his party had succeeded in
discrediting all alternative solutions to the crisis. Opposition
from now on will be reduced to the anguish of individual
protests.

The fate of the Centre Party, without whose block vote
Hitler's majority would have been in doubt, was to be similar
though less honourable. Two days after the debate, one of its
members is wondering whether it is likely that Hitler will fulfil
the promises which secured him its support:

Is it morally and politically justified to grant such unprecedented full powers to a government whose very instincts are so different from what we might hope for? The Centre has always been the party of law and constitution, and of freedom too. What is happening now has nothing to do with law or freedom or the constitution. . . .

And therefore?

Just as in 1919 we calmly and resolutely boarded the Social Democratic ship, so in 1933 we can board the ship of National Socialism and try to help steer it. . . . If we are successful in this great venture, everybody will applaud the conduct of the parliamentary party – just as they did after 1919, when our collaboration with the Social Democrats preserved the country from Bolshevism. Today, too, all we can hope for is that this alliance with the National Socialists will preserve us from Communism, Bolshevism and anarchy! This is now the most important thing. *Prius vivere, deinde philosophari* is what one ought to be saying: first banish the danger of Communism, the rest is bound to follow.

What is significant about this and similar orations at the obsequies of the democratic process is of course the wholly mistaken evaluation of the National Socialist Party's future conduct, as though its thirteen years of politicking had provided a shred of evidence that, once in power, it would behave differently. But in this false evaluation there is also an element of wilful blindness, or rather an alarming readiness to allow the National Socialists to hide behind a façade of legal technicalities. They themselves indicated as plainly as may be what the Party's intention was. They turned every invocation of legality into a farce, played out before an audience which connived at the subversion of its own institutions: 'We are entering the Reichstag', Goebbels proclaimed in 1928, 'in order that we may arm ourselves with the weapons of democracy from its own arsenal. We shall become Reichstag deputies in order that the Weimar ideology should itself help us to destroy it. If democracy is so stupid as to reward us for this disservice [*für diesen Bärendienst*] with free fares and parliamentary pay, then that is its own business. We are content to use all legal means to revolutionize the present state of affairs. Mussolini too went into parliament. Let no one think that parliamentarianism is our Damascus. We come as enemies! Like the wolf falling upon a herd of sheep, that's how we come.' What, in the face of such candid pronouncements, made those disastrous misjudgements possible was by no means only fear of socialism or communism. Equally important was the general lack of concern for those laws which guaranteed both personal and political freedom, and the independence of parliament. These were the laws which, in one emergency situation after another, were the first to be suspended. High expectations of what politics could offer by way of spiritual renewal – expectations which we know to be incompatible with parliamentary democracy – went hand in hand with a consistent neglect of the most rudimentary political safeguards. A high legalism towering over a weak democratic structure – that was the prevailing ethos of the German states throughout the nineteenth century, and the heritage that National Socialism was putting to its use.

What Hitler was offering, however, seemed to satisfy a whole spectrum of expectations and hopes – national, political, economic and social, cultural and even religious. . . . He certainly appeared to believe in the state as a source of national cohesion and 'positive' politics. Only libertarians could have found nothing acceptable in his programme or in his promises; such men existed but they had no political following.

13 Three Wise Men

This neglect of liberal principles was not confined to the politicians. It was also to be found among intellectuals who might have been expected to understand that the regime threatened everything they stood for: as the following three examples will show, freedom was not one of the values they were worried about.

Writing about 'the spiritual situation of the age', the philosopher Karl Jaspers describes its danger as that of a mass-society ruled by 'anonymous powers'. His book was published in one of the most popular paper-back editions on the German market in 1931 and revised in a sixth edition in 1932, yet about the party that was then making its final bid for power it says not a single word. Bolshevism and 'the mechanical dialectics of Marxism', atheism, bureaucracy, even homosexuality and psychoanalysis are listed as the factors leading to the alienation of modern man and to the collapse of human values. 'Man in his present situation' is incapable of responsible political decisions (the argument is repeated, somewhat worse for wear, thirty years later by Herbert Marcuse); democracy means mob rule, egalitarianism, and hatred of excellence. Political education as a possible remedy is not mentioned. Instead, we are told that what is needed is a spiritual aristocracy and 'genuine leaders' who are capable of 'being themselves'. They are contrasted with 'those who, though knowing no cause other than their own, feel an inner emptiness and are thus attempting to escape from themselves'. These qualities which Jaspers deplores, together with their opposite, *'das Selbstsein des Menschen'*, are conceived as purely private character traits. What they have to do with any realistic attempt to solve the socio-political predicament of the age remains unexplained. While the possibility of solving the crisis by making the leadership subject to constitutional limitations is wholly ignored, control through public opinion is rejected as destructive of the idea of the state. The whole sphere of politics is merely the ground of an unrelenting battle between 'the leader' and 'the masses', it and the social life of the age are dominated by the bogey of technology. (An earlier formulation of this theory is to be found in Ortega y Gasset; we have seen its most recent version in Albert Speer's autobiography.) With Jaspers's repeated emphasis on 'the self-being of man' we are back at the theory of authenticity. The form Jaspers gives to his version of the theory is of course wholly unaggressive and non-violent: the remedies he offers are to be found not in personal or collective heroism but in the purely private sphere of spiritual recollection (*Selbstbesinnung des Geistes*). Yet by stamping political and prudential thinking as inauthentic and by denying to the institutionalizing of group conflicts the dignity of serious thought, Jaspers – like Heidegger and countless others before him – implicitly advocates an attitude of political quietism and conformism. And freedom? 'Man's history is a vain attempt to be free', and his freedom lies in his acceptance of this failure (*Scheitern*). Alternatively, freedom is present 'in the interstices of the giant apparatus of modern technology' – that is, once again as a purely private value, to which the rule of law is irrelevant, which is to be attained adventitiously and in the greatest possible seclusion from 'the spiritual situation of the age'. Jaspers's book has a wrong – and in the circumstances disastrous – sort of timelessness about it: barring its idiosyncratic philosophical terminology, it could have been written by Jung-Stilling a hundred and thirty years earlier.

In Freud's *Civilization and its Discontents*, the same situation is viewed in rather less exalted and apparently more realistic terms. As a piece of social criticism, the book represents no advance on that thin essay of 1915, *Zeitgemäßes über Krieg und*

Frieden, in which Freud had analysed the warlike conflict of nations as though it were a brawl between aggressive individuals called 'the German', 'the Austrian', 'the Frenchman', 'the Englishman', and 'the Russian', caused by the fact that each had a different *Kinderstube*. In *Civilization and its Discontents* he, like Jaspers, offers an account of the contemporary world in terms of the conflict of 'individual *versus* the masses', and has next to nothing to say about the actual arrangements of the 'civilization' on whose psychic genealogy he speculates. Freud too believes that men are incapable of freedom and frightened of it. He too sees ontogenetic and phylogenetic changes as identical, the private sphere as identical with the public. Indeed, outside the ranks of religious reformers the fallacy that you have to change individuals before you can change their social arrangements has had no more powerful advocate. He views attempts at social reform with a dose of irony and a gentle but unremitting pessimism, and sees 'the psychological misery of the masses' – with a glance at Russia, but also at America – as the greatest contemporary danger. In the course of explaining this 'psychological misery', the very basis of modern socio-political life is denied: 'This danger is at its most acute where social ties are produced mainly by an identification of the members [of a given society] with each other', Freud tells us, because in such a situation 'leader-individuals do not attain the importance they should have when such mass-formations occur'. What importance *should* they have? Freud doesn't say. The *aperçu* about 'the psychological misery of the masses' leads on to the celebrated discussion of 'the death instinct', which is related back to some mythological *Urvater*. But what happens after that prehistorical 'event', and whether in some historical periods and some cultural situations this 'instinct' operates more powerfully than in others – why indeed *this* is the age of 'discontent' – we aren't told. The idea that historical and institutional thinking might be critically examined in its own terms, rather than as a symptom of individual or collective neuroses, is never considered. For 1930, the year when the

Führerindividualität won 11.4 million votes, Freud's observations on the state of the world that surrounded him strike one as less than perceptive.

C. G. Jung's notorious essay of March 1936 has at least the advantage of being concerned with an actual feature of National Socialism, namely the propagation of pre-Christian Germanic mythology and ritual. This was the 'religion' in which some of the party intellectuals, at least during the first years of the regime, saw the National-Socialist answer to Christianity. The resuscitation of the Wotan cult had been part of the *völkisch* ideology of the last years of the Wilhelminian era. Traces of 'the German Faith' are to be found in Ernst Bertram's Nietzsche book of 1918, and of course Alfred Rosenberg's *Mythus des zwanzigsten Jahrhunderts* (1930) contains long and rambling chapters devoted to it. Hitler was not insensitive to the absurdity of the cult and repudiated it, being anxious to postpone a confrontation with the Catholic clergy (who had attacked Rosenberg's book), or at least to choose his own grounds of battle. He argued against this sectarianism in the opening sections of the second volume of *Mein Kampf* (1925), ignored Rosenberg's book, and took the line (at least in his public pronouncements) that the *Weltanschauung* of the Party involved no rivalry or conflict with either of the established Christian denominations. (His ultimate plans, revealed in the *Table Talk*, were different.) C. G. Jung's essay addresses itself to the chief foundation document of 'the German Faith', Wilhelm Hauer's *Deutsche Gottschau: Grundzüge eines Deutschen Glaubens*, written in the autumn of 1933. The book is a good deal less aggressive than Rosenberg's; its anti-Semitism is discreetly muted; Christianity is not so much the enemy of the Aryan-Germanic tradition as rather irrelevant to it. The work of a well-known Indologist, the book has a scholarly air about it, is rich in literary and liturgical quotations, and full of exercises in comparative mythology (thus the story of the

Purusha tree in the Rigvedas is traced to the tree Yggdrasil in the *Edda*, which is related with the Platonic myth, which in turn is related to the German oak, and so to an image in Jakob Böhme . . .). Also, Hauer's book contains no direct exhortations to political activity or indeed to action of any kind, and its passionate style is all in the service of its religious message. The Christian tradition, we are told, is alien to all that's best in German religious thinking, in German philosophy and poetry; Meister Eckhart, Goethe and Hegel are the prophets of a vision of German humanity that must be freed from Levantine accretions. The Christianization of Germany hasn't really taken (a belief which Hauer shares with Heinrich Heine, though one doubts whether he would have thanked the poet for his revelations). German culture is the true heir of 'Indo-Germanic' spirituality, of which Plato and Plotinus are the authentic representatives; its gospels are the old Nordic myths. The true god of the Germans is either nameless or else it is Wotan the Usurper ('*der Ergreifer*' – the epithet which Nietzsche had applied to the god Dionysos). It is a god of opposites and contradictions – of rebirth and decline, of good and evil, transcendent and immanent, a dispenser of 'the blessing of sin'. All the strong virtues, such as nobility and true manly piety, justice, belief in fate and capacity for sacrifice, are said to have existed long before Semitic Christianity, as quintessentially Germanic virtues they are the '*Urphänomene*' of the 'god-vision' to which the book exhorts the populus (Hauer also wrote a treatise 'for theologians and religious philosophers' which, being neither, I have not examined). Coming somewhat closer to his own day, the author proclaims that man's revolt against the gods–personified in Prometheus, Faust, Nietzsche's Superman, and 'German atheism'· – springs from a faith in 'the inviolability of the noble man's will'. This contemporary revolt is 'fundamentally' a religious attitude, for it is 'the breakthrough of man to his livingly-immediate selfhood, the sole ground from which a genuine and adequate faith may arise. . . .' Obviously, it would be as tedious to extend this list of euphoric assertions as to attempt to refute them. The salient point of the book is simple enough. It is that the rebirth of 'the German Faith' is at hand, for the nascent Reich and its Leader have created the appropriate conditions in which this 'faith' may at last become 'an historical reality'.

This claim Jung's essay takes entirely seriously and enjoins its readers to accept as sincere and valid. The religious dimension of National Socialism is for Jung not a matter of propaganda but the psychic *donnée* of contemporary Germany; and those who, looking at the regime, once again speak of *furor teutonicus* are merely 'psychologizing' a genuine 'archetypal' religious manifestation. Hauer's book, so the Swiss sage tells us, 'cannot be read without profound emotion', for it is 'the tragic and truly heroic attempt of a conscientious scholar who, as a member of the German nation and unaware of what has befallen him, has been called by the inaudible voice of the Usurper [= *Wotan der Ergreifer*] and seized by him' – indeed Hitler himself has been thus 'seized' and must communicate his ecstasy to the people. Jung is anxious to make sure that what he says should not be understood merely metaphorically: 'There are representatives of the German Faith movement who, both intellectually and in human terms, are fully in a position not merely to *believe* but also to *know* that the god of the Germans is Wotan and not the universal God of the Christians. This is not a thing to be ashamed of but a tragic experience.' (Here again, in the phrase '*tragisches Erlebnis*' applied to a nation, the ontogenetic fallacy is revealed.) And so to Jung's conclusion, which is once again a denial of the possibility of freedom: 'We outsiders [i.e. the Swiss] judge the contemporary German too much as though he were one who may be held responsible for what he does; perhaps it would be more correct to regard him at least as one who passively endures [*als Erleidenden*].' Some of the 'German Faithful' at any rate must have been gratified by the ally they had gained, seeing that a good many Party officials (apart from Himmler) were rather sarcastic about their antics.

What is it that causes this Swiss patrician of liberal sentiments, who had recently visited Germany and met some of the
leaders of the regime (including Dr Goebbels), to discover
in this hotchpotch of mythological bits-and-pieces a genuine
religious faith, the modern German analogue to Christianity?
Is it his own theory of archetypes which makes him attribute
the same non-moral, purely functional value to very different
psychic phenomena, so long as they display a certain emotional
vigour, a certain psychic energy? Whether this ghastly misunderstanding is entailed by Jungian theory, I am unable to
say; others have certainly arrived at similar evaluations of
'German paganism' without any reference to that theory. What
is at work here is that 'dynamic' fallacy, according to which all
psychic energy is *ipso facto* positive, all 'movement' is a sign of
vigour, all vigour is divine, and all divinity dynamic. So
numerous are the affinities of this fallacy with the view that
authenticity is the supreme value and with the 'religious' element in what I have called the ideology of the Will, that we may
speak of three aspects of one and the same thing. And the thing
itself is the chief metaphysical tenet of fascism.

14 Institutional Patterns

In the absence of a stable liberal tradition, in the face of the glaring ineptitudes of liberal and Social Democratic politicians and worse mistakes on the part of the Communists, the disaffected of all groups and classes were united by a demand for a charismatic leader who would 'express all their deepest aspirations, hopes, fears and sense of destiny' – this is the scenario Freud may have had in mind when he spoke of 'the misery of the masses', and Jaspers and Jung had undoubtedly in mind when they spoke of 'the threat of anonymous powers'. What constituted that 'idealism' and 'religious fervour' extolled by party propagandists and admired by impressionable foreign observers was devotion not to the reality but to the image of a Leader of god-like status. His closest collaborators did all they could to foster the cult: Gauleiter Joseph Wagner called him 'the greatest artist of all times'; the labour-leader Robert Ley claimed he was 'the only man in history who never errs'; Hess called him (probably quite sincerely) 'pure reason in human form', while Himmler contented himself with saying that 'from its earliest beginnings Aryan humanity has not produced anything to compare with him'. But it would be misleading to think that this image of a paragon of all the virtues was merely the fabrication of a few intellectuals in the Party's propaganda bureaux or in Goebbels's ministry. *Der Führer* was as much an image created by the masses as it was imposed on them – as much a heroic norm as an embodiment of their self-understanding. The complex process at work here is one that Hitler himself does not describe. He devotes many pages of *Mein Kampf* to the subject of public oratory and mass meetings generally, and to his mastery of the art of persuasion in particular; his description of the public speaker as one who is involved in something like an aggressive sexual relationship with his audience has often been quoted. He loves to expatiate on the way the audience 'carries' the speaker, and we have numerous accounts of his habit of nervously and haltingly feeling his way into the mood of a meeting, until he in turn 'carries' them to the triumphal climax. What he does not discuss is his absolute need of them: the self-generated response of the mass-audience (fortified by a strategically placed claque of mobsters) rises to the point at which that audience 'spontaneously' – not in a hysteria of fear but, on the contrary, in a hysteria of power that comes from self-identification with power – takes over and 'makes' the leader in its own image. Presumably this part of the process only dawned on him as he perfected his technique. Yet the basis of this mutual identification of speaker and audience is already to be found in the stylized sketches for a self-portrait in the pages of *Mein Kampf*. It is the portrait of 'the unknown soldier', *das arme Frontschwein*, 'the poor devil of a private', one who, though he is about to become his people's leader and redeemer, will not forget that he once was – that he still is – one of their own kind: 'I, together with the Duce, am the only head of government in Europe who knows the war as it really was, I mean for the front-line crock.' Who but he knows 'where the shoe pinches', knows 'the little man' and feels with him in his troubles, *qui tollit peccata mundi*! The self-assertion of the leader's undivided personality is matched by the devotion of his followers' undivided belief. How strong and persistent this devotion was may be gauged from the fact that until the middle of the War the most heinous crimes of the regime – the concentration camps, the killing of the congenitally insane and of the members of 'inferior races', described in a statutory law for the Government General of Poland as 'rabble' [= '*Gesindel*'], but also corruption and intrigues in the Party and in the civil service – were all known and excused by broad circles of the population in the professed belief (voiced by Hans Frank) that 'the Führer does not know', and that *the knowledge of these deeds must be kept from him.* 'At no time did Hitler, whom I saw in the Chancellery on 22 April 1945 for the last time, ever say a single word about the killing of Jews', writes the astonishing von Ribbentrop. 'Therefore I cannot even now [1946] believe that the Führer ordered the killing of Jews, but I assume that he was faced by Himmler with a *fait accompli*'. Here, too, propaganda is not merely an instrument but a constitutive part of political action.

My emphasis on the perverted religious status of this image of the charismatic leader and his absolute Will is not intended to obscure or deny the insights of classical sociologists. Durkheim's formal definition of collective disaffection remains valid, but it requires some modification. 'Anomie' is seen by him as 'a state where large numbers of individuals are to a serious degree lacking in the kind of integration with stable institutional patterns which is essential to their own personal stability and to the smooth functioning of the social system'. This defines very accurately the failure of the Weimar Republic. What Hitler and the Party were offering, however, was something different from what is envisaged in Durkheim's theory. The institutional patterns they proposed and eventually established were in no important sense stable – neither in intention nor in fact nor in the propaganda. The protean character of these patterns is one of the few instances where image and reality coincided. It is true that 'the Führer's Will' was extolled as utterly self-consistent; that he claimed to have completed his development as a political thinker before his thirtieth year – that is, well before he entered the political arena – and therefore had no need ever to change his mind about his goals; that the party programme of 24 February 1920 was declared to be unalterable even though some of its tenets, especially those that were closest to the eclectic 'socialism' of early party members like Gottfried Feder and Gregor Strasser, were at first played down and later

completely ignored; and that much play was made with the notion
of 'the Millennial Reich', though Hitler himself does not seem to
have used the phrase. In these respects, then, we see the familiar
discrepancy between fact and propagandist fiction. But to an
overwhelming extent both party propaganda and party practice
alike were concerned to establish a system of government and
administration that should not be a 'system' at all but should
remain fluid and 'dynamic'. *'Es war immer was los'* – 'there was
always something going on' – is the phrase on the lips of people
who, in Germany today, try to convey the atmosphere of the
Third Reich to those who did not experience it.

The 'institutional patterns' of the regime, chief among them
the 'leadership principle', *were not intended* to be stable. The
number of new laws and administrative regulations passed by
the new regime in its first six months must be unparalleled in
the constitutional history of any country. Not that they were
considered binding: any of them could be reversed by Hitler's
own direct decision (though not without a snappy phrase,
'führer-unmittelbare Entscheidung', being coined for the purpose). Laws were passed *post facto*, administrative posts
created after their holders were appointed, several institutions
(among them the Reichstag) continued in existence after they
ceased to have any function, though (again, characteristically)
there seems to have been no organization whose existence was
not confirmed by a public pronouncement of some kind. In
sum, whenever possible *'Adolphe Légalité'* remained faithful to
that system of pseudo-legality which had helped him to come
to power in the first place, at the same time taking special
pleasure in disparaging 'the whole legalistic mentality' (*'die
ganze Paragraphenreiterei'*) as static and sterile.

The frequent changes in domestic policy and in the distribu-
tion of power among rival professional and party groups; the
vagaries of spheres of administrative and legal competence,
magnified by pathetic attempts to resuscitate their Carolingian
nomenclature; the attempt, also vaguely medieval, to replace
'the un-Germanic conflict of classes' by a 'symbiosis of the

estates'; the unclarity in the relationship between party and state, between state and government; the mutual interdependence of industry, government, civil service and army *and* their tug-of-war with each other; the rivalries between police, auxiliary police, secret police, and the *Sicherheitsdienst* (which sometimes meant that the longer a gaol sentence passed by an ordinary court, the greater the chances of the prisoner's survival); the projected and never completed, never wholly abandoned changes in the constitution of the Reich and in the status of individual *Länder* – these are some aspects of that *controlled institutional chaos*, which was the characteristic form of National Socialist government.

The 'divide and rule' policy that has often been attributed to Hitler must not be understood to imply a rule above conflicting opinions, for none were tolerated. The characteristic procedure, initiated well before 1933, may best be described as 'annex and rule'. It consisted in the reduplication of all professional, commercial and industrial organizations, and of all branches of the civil service, by creating parallel National Socialist institutions; and these then either completely displaced their non-political or democratic rivals, or allowed them no more than a shadowy and purely formal existence. By 1933 or 1934 the students, lawyers, trade unionists, farmers, doctors, and even members of the German automobile club, were faced with the choice of either entering the new National Socialist organizations or losing their corporate representation. Those professional and non-party organizations (other than the Churches) which were not forcibly dissolved had their independence destroyed by being integrated into the party structure, or at least co-ordinated with it.

15 The Spirit of National Socialist Law

Hitler's and the Party's attitude toward the various professions was determined by a series of prudential guesses and manoeuvres: how far and how fast could they revolutionize these groups without endangering that minimum of social stability needed for the running of the State? Some – like the university students and teachers and the writers – could be trusted to do Hitler's and the leadership's work without coercion and with a minimum of bribing. Others, like the industrialists and economic experts, had to be treated circumspectly; the most prominent ones had frequently to be allowed to remain outside the party or to buy themselves out by generous contributions to its winter welfare fund. Others again, like the farmers and the Ruhr workers, continued to be the objects of powerful propaganda and had to be bought by concessions and special material rewards. The armed forces were left a semblance of independence, their loyalty and their material interests alike being ostensibly tied to the State rather than the Party, to Hitler as Supreme Commander rather than 'Führer'. Sculptors and painters and film makers and the whole theatrical profession were subjected to radical changes in the party line around 1936, and they responded to a mixed carrot-and-whip treatment. As for the Churches, it was found best to conclude a temporary truce with them, to interfere as little as possible with their internal organization and to accede to their strongest representations – it seems beyond any doubt that if the Churches had opposed the persecution of the Jews as they opposed the killing of the congenitally insane and sick, there would have been no 'Final Solution'. By and large it seems to have been the scientists who were best able to protect their professional interest while making least concessions to the regime. On the other hand in the crucial months in the spring of 1933 the country's most eminent philosopher, its most brilliant international lawyer and its most interesting poet – Martin Heidegger, Carl Schmitt and Gottfried Benn – were the regime's most enthusiastic supporters. Once again, what makes the collaboration of these intellectuals so dishonourable is its entirely voluntary character – is the fact that they went out of their way, freely and often without being subjected to any pressure, to offer support and intellectual credentials to a leadership which did not want them, and which missed no opportunity for showing its utmost contempt for such support. It may be worth recalling the Nietzschean conundrum, whereby intellectuals like Dr Goebbels do blatantly what other intellectuals, like Benn and Heidegger, do more covertly: that is, construct complex intellectual arguments in contempt of the life of the mind.

This was especially true of the legal profession, which had dominated German public life and the civil service for more than a century. This dominance Hitler had mocked when he triumphantly told the workers in a Berlin armaments factory, 10 December 1940: 'For the first time in our history we have a state which, in filling its positions, has done away with all social prejudices, not only in civilian life. I myself am the best document in proof of this. I am not even a lawyer – just think what that means! And yet I am your Leader!' Yet however much Hitler abused and humiliated the lawyers, believing that he could do without them altogether, they could always be relied upon to provide the rationale of their own debasement. By the time Hitler ceased to be greatly interested in his role as leader of the Party and head of government and assumed the function of Supreme Commander, the 'leadership principle' had become the maxim of the process of controlled chaos: because the principle embodied that conception of 'dynamism' on which party propaganda was centred, but also because it promised the greatest material rewards, with impunity, to

those groups and individuals capable of maximum self-assertion. Given the organizational problems of what, in spite of
appearances to the contrary, remained in several respects a
European state, this principle had to be legalized in some form
or other. And it is clear that any legal system which set out,
often *post facto*, to articulate and give objective validity to this
practice of self-assertion and the 'dynamism' it embodied,
would have to be very different from the traditional German
code of law, the *Bürgerliches Gesetzbuch.* However, before
looking more closely at 'the leadership principle', it may be
useful to consider the legal spirit the Party attempted to put
into practice. For it is here, more clearly perhaps than in any
other area of national life, that the regime's characteristic
mixture of a little truth and a great lie, of arbitrary motivation
and popular appeal, may be discerned. The Party's legal
machinery, which will remain notorious as long as there is
such a thing as European history, dominated and very soon
swamped the supposedly non-political 'positivist' law courts
and the public security organizations of the Weimar Republic;
here the 'annex and rule' procedure was at its most effective.
But that was not enough. Since this was a German revolution,
the resultant lawlessness was by no means unprincipled.

Hitler's own personal contempt for all lawyers was no doubt
based on his experiences during the later years of the Weimar
Republic, when he was defended by Hans Frank in several
hundred legal actions, and when he discovered that a mere
formal acknowledgement of the law gave him all the licence he
needed for destroying its substance. In the *Wolfsschanze*
monologues, his wholesale attacks degenerate into indiscriminate abuse:

> . . . I shall not rest until every German sees that it is shameful
> to be a lawyer. . . .
> Therefore he ['the Chief'] declared today clearly and unam-
> biguously that anyone who is a lawyer must either be mentally
> defective by nature, or else is bound to become so in time. . . .
> But alas, the lawyers are every bit as international as the crim-

inals, only not so clever, which is why the trial [of van der Lubbe] dragged on for weeks and ended in a ridiculous verdict. . . .

Besides, to spend a life-time defending malefactors could really not be described as a decent occupation . . . If in previous ages it was the actor who was buried in the knacker's yard, then today it is the lawyer who deserves such a burial. Nobody is more akin to the criminal than the lawyer, and also as regards their international character there is no difference between them. No reasonable human being ever understood the legal theories which the lawyers have excogitated for themselves, often of course under the influence of Jews. In the end the whole bulk of today's legal theory comes down to nothing other than a huge system for avoiding responsibility. [Hitler said he] would therefore do everything to make the study of law as contemptible as possible. It was not a study that educated men for life, men who were capable of guaranteeing that the natural legal order would be upheld in the State. It was solely an education for irresponsibility. He would see to it that the legal administration should be reduced to a real elite of judges, a mere 10%. The whole swindle of juries would be done away with . . . What he needed by way of judges were men who were deeply convinced that the law should not safeguard the individual *against* the State, but that the law should first and foremost see to it that Germany will not perish.

Is it not both pretentious and absurd to speak of a 'spirit of national socialist law' where all that is discernible are personal and political interferences of the most arbitrary kind? Yet it is an arbitrariness which, for some time and in some areas, was felt to be a liberation, an immense simplification of abstruse legal technicalities, a return to natural justice. Legislation took on the shape of a nightmare, yet for some it had a fairy-tale quality. Overnight and quite literally, the Queen of Hearts' 'Off with their heads!' became law.

In 1938, a number of armed robberies occurred on the *Autobahnen*. On 22 June – all in a single day – Hitler personally formulated, put before the compliant Reichstag, and promulgated a law, retroactive to 1 January 1938, consisting of a single sentence, to wit: 'Anyone setting a motor trap with criminal intent will be punished by death.' Equally laconic was the 'Law in Defence of the State' of 3 July 1934, which declared, also in a sentence, that yesterday's massacres (or rather 'the measures taken against the acts of high treason of 30 June, 1 and 2 July 1934') were legal. On the day following the Reichstag fire of 27 February 1933 a law was passed against 'Communist acts of violence', whereby seven articles of the constitution were suspended, and a number of crimes, including arson, previously punishable by life sentence, were declared capital crimes; as though this were not enough, on 29 March a further law, known as *lex van der Lubbe*, was formulated in such a way as to antedate the validity of the law of 28 February, in order to 'legalize' the execution of the young Dutch communist convicted of the crime. The complex anti-Jewish legislation begins with the laws of 15 September 1935, one of which restates Point Four of the Party Programme of 1920 by declaring citizenship of the Reich to be a matter of 'German and related blood', entailing by a single stroke the disfranchisement of Jews and Gipsies and Poles resident in the Reich; a second law of the same day renders illegal both marriage and extra-marital sexual intercourse between Jews and Germans. These and further anti-Jewish laws – among them the compulsory adoption of 'Israel' and 'Sara' as first names (17 August 1938), confiscation of property (e.g. 3 December 1938), the wearing of the Star of David (1 September 1941), and the gradual disablement of Jews in all legal matters – were all formulated so as to follow clearly and 'naturally' from the axiomatically given idea of race. The radicalization of all forms of punishment and the immense increase in the number of offences liable to capital punishment once war broke out, as well as the setting up of the notorious People's Courts (1934), correspond to the two rough-and-ready legal rules which underlie those observations of Hitler's with which I began: simplification of procedure and concern with the welfare of 'the People' as conceived by the Party rather than with the liberty of the individual.

The German lawyers' attitude to National Socialist legislation was often one of compromise, occasionally leading to courageous attempts to do justice under the protection of the prevailing system yet in defiance of it; the career of Karl Sack, the Chief Army Judge, who was executed in the last month of the War, is a splendid and rare example of this. But most lawyers were not content with compromise and felt the need to adopt a more positive attitude. Once again we witness the humiliating spectacle of demands by the Party to have its lawlessness legalized being acceded to at a time when opposition to those demands would have checked the Party's road to power; once again we see the characteristically German situation in which the craven belief in historical inevitability is rationalized in a theory – a theory which not only validates and *absolves* but also *precedes* practice. These men – the fathers of today's generation of protesting students – are not Chicago shysters. They are ponderous professional men of the Central European middle classes, scholarly and intellectual, heirs to a tradition of literal-mindedness rather than fairness, but also of honesty, thoughtfulness and integrity. How (we shall ask) can such men put their minds at the service of so primitive, so transparently arbitrary a conception of law and legality?

Six months before Hitler's take-over, in September 1932, a conference of German jurists discussed the question whether the liberal reform of the penal system initiated in the early years of the Weimar Republic should be continued. One of the speakers, a law professor at the University of Vienna, argued strongly against further liberalization, and against 'the point of view according to which the latest political events, which are merely the effects of new spiritual forces, have nothing to do with the reform of the penal system. I consider this point of view untenable . . . What is at work today are very powerful popular movements with very definite aims, which seek to penetrate everything – economic thinking, intellectual culture, the State and the law. The fundamental outlook of the young movement is that the law generally and criminal law in particular are no more than the means for furthering and cultivating the German national community,' which is defined as a 'community of men united by a common ancestry and a common cultural inheritance'. In this new and supposedly irrevocable situation, 'the starting point of legislation is not the freedom of the individual but the weal of the whole'; and the legal profession's 'paramount task is to avoid the dilemma, all too common nowadays, between justice and morality. . . . The basis of imprisonment is the guilt of the single responsible individual in falling behind the demands a people may make on him; punishment is retribution.' A return to ancient Germanic legal thinking is enjoined, and so is the extirpation of all foreign (Jewish) ideas. The highest legal maxim as well as the ultimate sanction is the old (and frequently contested) notion of 'natural law', brought up to date in the concept of *'gesundes Volksempfinden'* (sound national feeling): 'There is no authority and ultimate source of law other than the conscience of the Nation itself', writes Roland Freisler in his commentary on the Nuremberg laws, echoing Hans Frank who, in 1929, as Hitler's defending counsel, informed a court of law that 'justice must be that which makes the whole Nation prosper, injustice must be that which harms the whole Nation'; and since the Führer is the keeper of the Nation's conscience, *his word is law*. 'It is the first time in the history of the People', Hans Frank tells the assembled members of Munich University, 'that love of the Führer has become a concept in law'. And in June 1938, now holding the splendid title of *Reichsrechtsführer*, Frank proclaims: 'Whether the Führer does or does not govern according to a formal written constitution is not a fundamental legal issue. Only the question whether the Führer through his activity safeguards the life of the Nation is the fundamental legal issue of our time.' This sovereignty of 'the Führer's Will' is confirmed in the law of 26 April 1942, which consists entirely of a verbatim passage from Hitler's address to the Reichstag, and specifically mentions that he is not 'bound by existing legal regulations'.

The old German legislative practice, which even in the Weimar Republic had led to a notoriously right-wing bias in the courts, remains unchanged. The judges are no more than civil servants sworn to the constitution and the government of the Reich; the making of laws is entirely removed from the judiciary, it is in the hands of the Reichstag, which in practice means in the hands of Hitler, Frank, Lammers, Bormann and a small circle of associates; and there is of course no free expression of public opinion. In this situation what makes the notion of 'the sound feeling of the People' so attractive is that it offers to repair the remoteness and 'abstractness' of the law. It offers to replace the complexity of stable and in some respects rigid legal generalities by law that prides itself on being just by virtue of being subjective and by repudiating any notion of fundamental equality. The *a priori* of justice is to be a natural *in*equality based on genetic, that is biological and psychological, differences: hence the idea of '*Willensstrafrecht*', law which relies to an unprecedented extent on the criteria of a man's intention and 'will' in determining the gravity of his offence. The deliberate loosening of the rules governing factual evidence, the vast increase in the number of indictable offences, the provision that punishment depends not on the gravity of the act objectively assessed but on the 'psychological character type' to which the offender is said to belong and on the national political situation in which the offence took place, the toleration of indisputably illegal acts (such as the pogroms of the *Reichskristallnacht* of 9 November 1938) as long as these accord with 'the sound feeling of the People' – all these practices combine to create the myth of a law that is uniquely capable of identifying and justly evaluating the authentic subjectivity of the offender, that which he 'really' is, and of meting out punishment accordingly.

Just as the truth of philosophical doctrine or physics or history is assured by the German character of those professing the subjects concerned, so the nexus between legality and justice is assured by the German character of the judge who cannot, in his subjectivity, express anything other than the proper popular sentiment. Now he no longer hides behind the statute book, all he has to do is to hearken to the *vox populi* within him. The old Germanic idea of justice as retribution was revived, presumably as part of the Wagnerian Nibelungen syndrome. A favourite of Schopenhauer's, the concept of retributive justice was intended to replace social-democratic ideas of remedial penology; yet the fact is that a number of extensive reforms in the juvenile courts were introduced by Franz Gürtner, Minister of Justice until 1941, which have been acknowledged and taken over by the legislators of the Federal Republic. Side by side with this progressive treatment of young offenders went the barbaric laws of 4 October 1939 and 6 November 1943, according to which offenders aged 16 (in the case of the first law) and 14 (in the case of the second) could be deemed to have reached the mental and moral age of 18 and thus become liable to the death penalty. In these as in all other cases, the sentence depended on the judge's assessment of the offender's 'criminal attitude of mind', on the specifically anti-social (*volksfeindlich*) nature of the offence, and on the 'national' or rather military situation of the time. Here was punishment in accordance with the act *and* its intention, including the total life-story and character of the offender, and it seemed to have a positive existential value attached to it. Like the Lutheran priority of faith and intention over works and achievement, like the Kantian imperative whose moral criterion is not the act but the good will behind the act, this kind of justice purported to take into consideration the most intimate personal circumstances of the offender, the punishment fitting not merely the crime but the criminal too – it is this idea of a 'personalized' justice and its glimmer of formal similarity with the Protestant-Kantian ethic that made for its plausibility and invited assent.

The truth, of course, was quite different. If there was a similarity in form, the difference in substance made National

Socialist law a travesty of the Kantian ethos, and the claim to Protestant antecedents a sham. In reality the judges were even more political than before, in the simple sense of supporting the interests of their boss, the state, that is, Hitler, to the extent of letting themselves be forced into a position where they allowed the police to predetermine their verdicts. Earlier attempts of the judiciary to control the activities of the various branches of the police and to place them under the control of the law were subverted and turned into their opposite. Nor is this surprising, seeing that such attempts were made in the name of 'the National Socialist conception of law and order'. When, in 1935, Hans Frank's deputy in the League of National Socialist Jurists declared that the Gestapo's refusal to allow its prisoners legal representation was 'in contradiction of the Nordic nations' natural feeling of justice', he was of course being hoist with his own petard. He was appealing to the same amorphous and indefinable notion of 'sound national feeling' which his League had declared to be the cornerstone of the new conception of Justice. This was the fatal heritage of Nietzsche's and Schopenhauer's paradoxes. It was Nietzsche who had once proclaimed that life stands above all rational processes and cannot be defined by its ancillary, reason, because reason must be subordinated to, and placed in the service of, its master, life; and it was Schopenhauer before him who had insisted on the ineffable nature of 'the Will' as the ultimate ground of all life and reason alike, as that which cannot be encompassed by reason, its derivative. What neither Schopenhauer nor Nietzsche dreamed of was that this paradox, the exploitation of which lies at the heart of all forms of fascism, would one day be resolved quite simply by brutal force. What was 'the natural feeling of justice'? What was 'the sound feeling of the People'? What was truly, authentically German? Who would so much as ask the question, unless he were a stranger to the community? In the end only those who sent men to the block and the gallows and the gas chambers knew the answer.

It is true that the subservience of the regular courts to the police did not become complete until the second half of the War. Thus it was not until 30 June 1943, after the assassination of Reinhard Heydrich, that the chief of the Reich Security Office informed its officials that legal proceedings, as opposed to summary 'trials' by the Gestapo, were to take place only at the discretion of the police 'when this appeared desirable for reasons of the political atmosphere' prevailing at the time, and only 'if it has been ascertained through previous enquiry that the court will pronounce sentence of death'. But this directive was anticipated three years earlier by a letter (dated 29 July 1940) of the chief public prosecutor of the People's Courts to the Reich Minister of Justice, containing the following passage:

> 'Unless otherwise instructed, I shall in future proceed as follows: in all cases of acquittal or when sentence has expired during the period of imprisonment awaiting trial, I shall, as a matter of principle and in agreement with the President of the People's Court, hand the persons concerned to the Gestapo. Whenever acquittal is consequent upon proof of innocence, I shall inform the Gestapo before disposal takes place, and I shall enquire whether this procedure is to be dispensed with. If however the Gestapo considers protective custody appropriate, I shall arrange for disposal to take place forthwith.'

But while it is true that the war brought with it a number of draconic measures, one must repudiate the suggestion made by numerous writers that National Socialist justice, and indeed the regime as a whole, did not show its true face until . . . whatever post-dating the writer thinks appropriate to his particular argument or special plea. In a sense the activities of the courts were peripheral to the dispensing of justice, for the real power of the judiciary lay in the hands of the Gestapo, whose members were appointed not by the Ministry of Justice but by the Ministry of the Interior. And the Gestapo, far from being a product of the regime in its last stages, was instituted by a law of 26 April 1933. The full extent of its activities, its rights to arrest and interrogate without warrant and to detain in 'protective custody' for any length of time; its right to inflict any form of punishment without being accountable to anyone other than its own state-appointed officials; and its responsibility for the execution of the regime's racial policies – all this was made public by a law of 10 February 1936, which also confirmed the Gestapo's responsibility in the setting up and administration of the concentration camps.

National Socialist law is not, as the law is in Dickens, 'an ass': that is, extravagant, purblind, a pomposity remote from the true interests of the litigants and the community at large. It is, as Hitler unwittingly suggests, itself criminal. It is the exercise of objective-seeming power in support of purely arbitrary and subjective decisions, its true character in no way hidden but emphasized by the mock-formality of its wordings. It is the law as it informs Franz Kafka's unfinished novel, *The Trial* (1914–15).

'Someone must have falsely denounced Josef K., for without having done anything wrong he was arrested one morning', runs its famous first sentence; and from this opening to Josef K.'s execution at the end, neither he nor anyone else in the novel ever asks the obvious question as to what this very ordinary bachelor of thirty is supposed to be guilty of. Similarly, the jurisdiction, composition, and indeed the legality of 'the Court' that is supposed to be trying him remain indeterminate. The reason for Josef K.'s peculiar arrest and protracted involvement in 'the trial', which quickly becomes '*his* trial', is never formulated. And when he protests, 'But I am innocent, it is a mistake. Besides, how can a man be guilty? Surely we're all human beings here, one like the other', the only answer he receives is, 'That is right, but that's the way the guilty are wont to talk.' The implication is that Josef K. is guilty because of what he is rather than because of anything he has done. In this sense, as concerning not an *offence by* his person but the total *existence of* his person, the verdict eventually passed on him will be absolute, as from a divinity – it will be sentence of death – but this will not give it a wider, more objective validity: the verdict will be not 'true' but 'necessary'. The effect of 'the trial' is total: involvement in its proceedings stamps Josef K. as with a blemish or a disease ('You have a trial', people whisper sympathetically), many people he meets once it is under way see him as an outcast and won't shake hands with him, and he himself soon comes to share their revulsion: 'If you want to keep your boarding house clean', he tells his landlady, 'I'm the first person you ought to give notice to!' His entire family comes to be involved in the malignant, sinister affair from which, it soon transpires, no complete discharge is ever possible. Certainly, as Josef K. soon finds out, 'the question of my innocence doesn't simplify the matter', for there is neither a stable code of law nor acquittal. To be involved in this trial is the same as losing it – 'Why, do you think we would summons someone who hasn't done anything?' is not a quotation from *The Trial* but the reply of a Gestapo official to a question by a Jewish woman who is about to be delivered to her death. The reversal of the ordinary functions of judiciary and police characteristic of every totalitarian regime is reflected in the view put to Josef K., that 'the verdict doesn't come all at once, the proceedings gradually merge into the verdict'.

What does Josef K. ever learn of the actual law according to which this farce of a trial is to be conducted? What little he learns comes to him in a complexly ambiguous tale-within-the-tale, the parable of 'the Man before the Law'. After waiting uncomplainingly for a whole life-time at the outermost gates guarded by one of the Law's lowliest keepers, 'the Man from the Country' is allowed his one question: ' "All men are intent on the Law", said the man, "Why is it that in all those many years no one other than myself ever asked to enter?" The Keeper realizes that the man is finished and, so as to reach him while he can still hear, he shouts at him: "Nobody else could gain admission here because this entry was intended only for you. I shall now go and shut it".' This is the consummation of National Socialist justice, the *lex van der Lubbe*, the law that is 'attracted' (as Kafka says) or rather created by the offence and fits only the one man whose life it will take, whom it is specially and exclusively designed to destroy 'like a dog'.

Yet even this isn't the full story of the topical parallel. We notice with growing surprise that Kafka's evaluation of this 'law', and of its courts and procedures, is very far from clear and unambiguous. Its prisoners, we read, are distinguished by a special kind of beauty, the signs of an election of some kind. Josef K. is free to leave the law's sphere of competence and doesn't. More than once does he speak as though he were proud of the complexity of 'his' trial, impatient of other men's attempts to solve his difficulties for him. Finally, it seems as if only under the impact of the invisible persecution was Josef K.'s dim life given a meaning it had lacked before, as if his 'arrest' amounted to some strange validation. But this is a situation to which I shall refer again – the moment when the desperate victim behaves as if what held him captive was something other, something more than the tormentor's might masquerading as right. True, Josef K. utters his sentence of protest: 'The lie has become the order of the world.' But that is said at the point where he has missed his chance (it is not the only one he is given) of stepping out of the jurisdiction of the Court. For the rest he is all too eager to comply with what he thinks is expected of him. Why is his attitude at the prospect of his execution so unresisting? Why is he so ready to help 'the authorities' in their terrible preparations? 'True, he couldn't help them completely, he couldn't take all the work of the authorities upon himself, the responsibility for that last failure' – his refusal to commit suicide – 'lay with him who had denied him the last bit of necessary strength . . .' Why should he, too, connive at the substitution of might for right? Does he, in his hour of death, agree that he has no right, no right to live? ' "Like a dog!" he said, and it was as if the shame should survive him': the shame, it seems ultimately, not of being in the wrong, but of being alone and weak, or rather of being in the wrong because he is alone and weak.

16 The Leadership Principle

Turning now to 'the leadership principle' which National Socialist law was intended to protect and further, we are once again struck by the readiness of leaders and led alike to forgo all libertarian claims. In this situation a characteristically German rule of thumb became operative, to the effect that any number of considerations – patriotic, racial, pseudo-theological and *weltanschaulich*, but also considerations of social and material welfare – were at all times more vital and more important than the concern for freedom and liberty under the law. But this was no new rule. In one form or another it had been operative in Germany since the time of Napoleon.

The application of the 'leadership principle' was not restricted to members of the Party. It is no accident that a very full formulation of it occurs in one of the most effective of Hitler's speeches, addressed to the 'leaders of industry' in their club at Düsseldorf (27 January 1932). The basic principle of life (he tells them) is war, which, translated into social terms, means 'absolute supremacy of the value of personality'. Private property can only be justified 'logically, . . . morally and ethically' by recognizing that

> 'the performance [*Leistung*] of different people varies. Only then can I state: because the performance of people varies, therefore the results of that performance vary. But if the results of the performance of different people vary, it is appropriate that the management of the results of that performance should remain in the hands of those who stand in a relationship approximately corresponding to their performance. It would be illogical to transfer the management of the

results of that performance (which is thus tied to a particular
personality) to the next best man who is only capable of an
inferior performance, or to the generality of men who by the
very fact of their inferior achievement have proved themselves
incapable of that management. . . . It is nonsense to build
economic life on the idea of achievement and the value of
personality, and thus in practice on the authority of personality,
and at the same time to deny this authority of personality in
politics and to replace it by the law of the greater number, that
is, by democracy.'

The speech covers thirty-two closely-printed pages. It is clear
from the enthusiastic cheering which interrupted its delivery
that this kind of logic and the 'world-historical philosophizing'
which garnished it were not beyond the mental capacity of
Hitler's audience. I have quoted from it at length to suggest that
its tone had nothing in common with Hitler's beer-cellar
harangues. How perfect was his rapport with his patrician hosts
may be seen from the fact that the speech, like all those delivered between 1930 and 1933, avoids any overt attack on the
Jews. (Not that the industrialists liked Jews, but no doubt they
worried lest anti-Semitism should get a bad name.) Its one
covert anti-Semitic remark is contained in a tendentious
misquotation from the Roman historian, Theodor Mommsen;
Hitler could safely assume that Mommsen's observation on
the Jews as 'the ferment' of the nations of Europe would be
familiar to his audience not in its original form but in the
corrupted version in which it appears in countless anti-
Semitic pamphlets of the preceding twenty-five years.

What the speech has in common with Hitler's less restrained
harangues is that it tells the audience all that they want to hear
and hardly anything that they didn't already know. His task
with respect to the industrialists and bankers is quite simply to
sell them the 'leadership principle' as that which they have been
practising all along and which they share with the Party and its
Weltanschauung. His means are appropriate to this end. Nothing violent by way of propaganda is needed to get their collabor-

ation on these grounds alone, especially if the more fastidious among his listeners can be assured that, having established a generous fighting fund (the purpose for which the meeting was convened), they don't actually have to join the Party itself. Beyond that, the speech contains the assurance that it is National Socialism that has saved Germany from a Bolshevik revolution, and some promises – entirely vague at this stage – that a renewal of the national spirit will solve all economic and social problems. But the strongest applause is reserved for his attacks on the Weimar Republic and its attempt to *legislate* against the crisis, for the passages in which he spells out the difference between 'a system which attempts to save a nation only by means of regulations' and 'a new spiritual attitude [which] will revitalize the nation inwardly and lead it from being a dead object of the legislative machinery as a living factor back into life'. What matters (he tells them) is not the dead letter of the law but 'the political formation of the Will of the whole nation'. By the time Hitler found it expedient, in his negotiations with Hindenburg and the Conservatives, to emphasize the legality of his own bid for power, the insidious party propaganda had done its work: the view (known commonly as *'Taktik und Prinzip'*) that this was merely a tactical manoeuvre in the service of a paramount national principle had by then become a 'secret' shared by millions.

While in his dealing with industrialists Hitler stressed the local equivalent of 'rugged individualism', the propaganda directed toward the working classes extolled the virtues of collective solidarity in the face of common national tasks. And so successful were the regime's claims on behalf of its economic policy that even today the originality of that policy is exaggerated and its full cost to the working class largely ignored. The *Autobahn* projects were no invention of National Socialism and had in fact been begun in the late 'twenties. The *Kraft durch Freude* movement was an imitation of Mussolini's *Dopo lavore* (it was first called *Nach der Arbeit*), and in any event it had been anticipated by a voluntary labour corps which in 1932 was a quarter-of-a-million strong. Even a major aspect of Hitler's and Darré's agricultural policy, the compulsory reduction of interests on agricultural mortgages, had been introduced in September 1932. The idea of the *Volkswagen* scheme came from Henry Ford's missionary zeal on behalf of his Model T. (Ford's anti-Semitic explanation of the Bolshevik world conspiracy was an added recommendation.) And of course the policy of full employment was from its beginnings tied to the re-armament programme (a fact which alone makes nonsense of A. J. P. Taylor's thesis that Hitler did not intend war). The policies adopted to secure full employment were not particularly National Socialist in character, for the simple reason that, apart from a few isolated tenets (like hostility to 'anonymous' capital and large department stores), the Party had no economic policy. The main instrument adopted, an ingenious invention of Dr Schacht, was a system of government credit vouchers (amounting to 16% of the national product) which enabled heavy industry to expand its production and by investing in research and new production methods to offset the effects of the government's policy of economic 'autarky'. There was nothing original about any of these schemes except their more or less directly war-like purpose. What made them work now (where they had not worked before) was a confidence and euphoria which the Weimar Republic had been incapable of generating. But this confidence and euphoria, too, though not identical with the war-like purpose, were inseparable from it.

And the workers? State *dirigisme* involved conscription and compulsory service in the labour corps, and supposedly 'total' direction of labour, especially into agriculture; it involved dissolution of the trades unions and confiscation of their funds, and their replacement by a 'united labour front organization'; denial of the right to strike and to collective bargaining and, as an especial humiliation, the re-introduction of the old *Arbeitsbuch* which had been abolished in the 1840s. While it proved impossible to repeal the old labour laws (the pride of German legislation in the 1880s), industrial disputes were outlawed by being declared inimical to the 'German concepts of social conscience and honour'. Under these concepts (as the 'Führer of the Reich Estate of German Industry', Krupp von Bohlen und Halbach remarked) the interests of workers and employers alike are subsumed in their 'high purpose of creating a true national community'. And with these utterly vague and arbitrary notions of 'social conscience and honour', we are back at the 'idealistic', 'anti-materialistic', 'authentic' scheme of essentially private values with which the propaganda machinery trimmed all its measures and answered all expectations: 'There is no such thing as a commercial balance of expenditure and profit. There is only a national balance of being and not-being.'

17 Conservative Opposition and the True Antagonist

Full employment with low wages, a welfare state with subsidized housing and elaborate recreational schemes, the highest degree of social mobility ever experienced in Germany, a sense of unity and national purpose – these were the benefits the first four-year plan brought to the workers. Not all swallowed the bait. There were the many who opposed the regime by acts of industrial sabotage, who succeeded in building up Communist and Social Democratic underground networks, established contact with foreign workers or prisoners of war, or languished in concentration camps. They are more typical of the German opposition than the conservative conspirators of July 1944; their numbers are in the ten thousands, and they acted on many occasions in the 'thirties and throughout the early stages of the War, certainly well before national defeat was imminent. But they were isolated. The extent of their isolation in a sea of hostility and fear is hard to imagine today, though it is occasionally intimated in their letters and diaries – together with their nobility of outlook and their lack of political realism. Apart from the Communists in the *Rote Kapelle* group, who worked for Soviet Russia, they had no clearly defined political purpose, and little by way of an indigenous tradition of non-conformism, let alone civil disobedience, to which they could effectively appeal.

The conservatives, with Carl Goerdeler, former Mayor of Leipzig, at their head, were in a similar position. They failed to understand (as some German historians still fail to understand) the nature and extent of the hostility the regime had unloosed in the West as well as in Russia; they too believed in the possibility of separate negotiations with the West. How else is one to explain the fact that Goerdeler's peace plans of 1943 envisaged a Greater Germany which would include Austria and Alto Adige, the Sudeten area, East and West Prussia, Poznań and all of Silesia, Poland to be compensated for her losses by a union with Lithuania and by German protection against Russia? How else is one to explain Goerdeler's proposals (in a document written in 1941), for a Jewish legislation which would avoid the strictly 'racial' measures of the Nuremberg laws but at the same time accept the premise on which these laws were based? The personal heroism and capacity for self-sacrifice of such men as Goerdeler or von Hassell is unimpaired by their anachronistic attitude to European and German social questions alike, yet the fact is that their political (though not their moral) thinking is circumscribed by the thinking of those whom they opposed. In one important respect at least their war-aims were identical with those of Hitler's regime. They too hoped to come to an agreement with the West on their own terms, and to improve those terms by offering the West military help against Russia. Few if any members of the Conservative resistance seem to have had any doubts about the realism of these expectations; few if any seem even to have understood that to people outside Germany their plans were all but indistinguishable from the plans of their worst enemies.

The list of names of the conspirators sounds like a doomsday roll call from the Almanach de Gotha: Stauffenberg, Guttenberg, Redwitz, Witzleben, Dohna, York, von Wartenburg, Moltke, Schwerin, von Schwanenwald, Trott zu Solz, Kleist, Lynar, Schulenberg. . . . The twentieth of July 1944 marks not only the failure of a political plot but the end of the Prussian tradition and of Prussia herself as a political force in Europe.

The isolation of these groups and individuals, their total lack of support from their fellow-countrymen, is in a sense more tragic than the terrible fate they suffered at the hands of their executioners. Their aims were for the most part utopian and their expectations illusory. When the Catholic student conspirators of 'The White Rose', Hans Scholl and his sister Sophie and their friends, were arrested for distributing subversive pamphlets (which they had showered in broad daylight into the stair-well of the main building of Munich University), they seemed sure that their action would be supported by their fellow-students. 'What does our death matter,' Sophie Scholl said to a fellow-prisoner on the morning of her execution, 22 February 1943, 'if thousands will be stirred and awakened by what we have done? The students are bound to revolt!' The opposite was the case. That same evening a demonstration organized by the official students' union was attended by more than 3,000 students eager to express their loyalty to the government. (The majority were medics on study leave from the Russian front, and they had reason to wish to be in good standing with the party officials.) The figure of 3,000 is mentioned by the *Reichsstudentenführer* in charge of the union and may well be exaggerated. His report as a whole, however, is fully borne out by the account of one of the students present: 'That demonstration in the *auditorium maximum* is one of the most terrible memories I have of those days', she writes. 'Hundreds of students shouted and stamped their feet to greet the beadle of the University who had denounced [Hans and Sophie Scholl]. He received their ovations standing and with open arms.'

As examples of moral heroism and of that 'reasonable service' of which St Paul speaks ('I beseech you therefore, brethren . . . that ye present your bodies a living sacrifice, holy, acceptable to God, which is your reasonable service'), the actions of 'The White Rose' are unsurpassed in European history and worthy of our highest admiration. Considered as a political act in defiance of a political system, however, the conspiracy was conceived on a level of moral utopia, executed with a heedless enthusiasm, and attended by no tangible results: and in these respects 'The White Rose' was characteristic of other groups and individuals who met with a similarly terrible fate.

Hitler's true antagonist – his moral anti-self – is not to be found among the military leaders or the landed aristocracy with their illustrious names, all of whom shared with him some political aim or patriotic fear; nor yet among the clergy of the established Churches, whose martyrs chose self-sacrifice rather than resistance; nor among the Jews, most of whom were his helpless victims, forsaken by God and all men. To find his true antagonist we must look for a Nobody like himself, one who, sharing his social experience, yet lived and died on the other side of the moral fence: his name is Johann Georg Elser. It is not a name honoured in the literature of resistance. In Bullock's biography of Hitler, Elser is mentioned as an obscure figure in an implausible Gestapo intrigue, a cat's-paw betrayed by his masters. The truth is very different. Were it not for the accidental survival of a bundle of Gestapo archives, his name would even now be buried in complete oblivion.

Johann Georg was born out of wedlock on 4 January 1903 in the village of Hermaringen in Württemberg. His father, the smallholder and timber merchant L. Elser of Königsbronn, married Georg's mother and legitimized him a year later; three girls and another boy were born during the next ten years. Georg did well at the elementary school at Königsbronn and passed its eight forms without effort, though he received no encouragement from home and had no expectation of higher studies; his favourite subjects were drawing and geometry. From the days of early adolescence he quarrelled with his father, yet there was never a complete breach between them. The father had always been an alcoholic; after the First War he fell into debt, mortgaged and finally sold the business as well as portions of his timbered land. Money was tight, yet no member of the family ever suffered grave material hardship. The father's bouts of drunkenness brought the boy close to his mother – this is the familial pattern described in *Mein Kampf*, where the supposedly sociological observation has the ring of an autobiographical disclosure. With other members of his family Georg was on more distant terms. Though he always remained in touch with his sisters, visiting them and their families when they married and left Königsbronn, these were practical rather than sentimental relationships – a small network of standbys during hard times – which reflected the formality and lack of intimacy characteristic of family relations among the German working classes. Moreover, these relationships reflect Georg Elser's own natural reserve, his tendency to keep to himself and share his thoughts with no-one. Yet he was not a solitary, although he was slow-spoken and deliberate in his manner; on occasion he could be gregarious enough. There was something old-fashioned about him.

But then, there was also something old-fashioned about the social world in which he grew up. In the summer of 1917 he left school and by the autumn of that year he had found an apprenticeship as a turner in a local iron factory, continuing with weekly lessons at trade-school. He learned a good deal about the treatment of crude metals, but working in the foundry began to affect his health, and so he left after two years, to be apprenticed to a carpenter. He passed his journeyman's examination as cabinet-maker with the highest marks of his class in the spring of 1922 (henceforth he called himself *Kunsttischler*). Carpentry and metal work were not only his daily bread but also his passionate hobby. In the cellar of his family home (where he was still living at the time) he had assembled a well-equipped workshop where he built and repaired furniture, locks and clockwork machinery. In 1925 he left Königsbronn, walking alone the hundred miles or so to the Dornier aircraft works near Friedrichshafen, where he worked in the propeller department, and then to Constance where, together with a fellow-carpenter from Königsbronn, he found employment in a clock factory. Here he worked on and off for the next seven years, building wooden housings for the clock mechanisms which were bought ready-made from Swiss manufacturers. He had brief periods of unemployment when the firm went bankrupt and was taken over by new owners; for a few months he took a job across the border in a Swiss clock factory.

The fellow worker who persuaded him to leave Dornier's for Constance was a keen clarinet player; Georg Elser took lessons on the zither, and they both joined the dance band of the patriotic *Trachtenverein Oberrheinthaler* (a sort of German equivalent of the Country Morris Dancers' Club). Apart from his comrades at work he had no close male friends, though with his wavy dark hair, pale grey eyes, regular intelligent features and light build he was very popular with the girls. He had a number of mistresses – a milliner's assistant, a waitress, several landladies; it seems that these were quiet, undramatic affairs. By Mathilde N. he had a son for whom he was forced to pay maintenance, deducted by court order from his earnings, even after Mathilde N. married. He never saw the boy again after his sixth month, but he intended to take him from his mother and look after him one day.

Although Georg Elser had no interest whatever in ideological or intellectual matters – it seems that all his reading was confined to newspapers and trade journals – he was interested in practical politics. As an adolescent he had been a member of a timber-workers' trade union, in all national elections before 1933 he voted Communist, and in 1928 or 1929 he joined the *Roter Frontkämpferbund*, a militant *KPD* group founded in 1924. He seems to have been an indifferent member of the group, for he held no office in it and bought no uniform, and apart from acquiring a party badge, paying his dues for a couple of years and attending three or four *RFK* meetings, he made a good deal less use of his membership than he did of the *Trachtenverein*: 'I was never interested in the programme of the *KPD*', he testified later. 'The only thing ever mentioned during the meetings was that there should be higher wages, that the government should provide better housing, and things of that kind. The fact that it was they [the *KPD*] who formulated these demands was enough to give me a Communist orientation.'

The slump did not hit Georg Elser as badly as it did millions of others. He worked in clock factories in various towns on

Lake Constance, then returned for a period to Königsbronn. Whenever he was out of a job, he earned his food and lodgings (and, in the true fashion of Hans Sachs's comedies, a place in his landlady's bed) in return for making or repairing pieces of furniture to private orders. After 1933, it seems, his political contacts ceased; he became a member of a zither-club instead and took lessons on the double bass. There is not a shred of evidence to suggest that he had contact with underground organizations of any kind. Once only did he appear in a court of law – when an affair with the wife of one of his customers ended in divorce proceedings and he was cited as co-respondent. Towards the end of 1936 he took an unskilled labourer's job in an armament factory in Heidenheim; by next summer he had worked his way up to a fairly responsible post in the firm's dispatch department, where he was in charge of checking, packing and dispatching rifle and small cannon ammunition and fusing devices. This is the point at which this ordinary life, uninteresting and yet fascinating in its ordinariness, culminates: for here it was, some time in the autumn of 1938, that Georg Elser decided to assassinate Hitler. This, at all events, is what he confessed to the Gestapo, at times under torture, during their investigation; I shall return to the question of the credibility of their protocols.

Why did Georg Elser decide on this deed? What caused this Nobody – who said of himself, 'I was always known as a very quiet person', of whom the *Völkischer Beobachter* wrote that 'he had nothing of the obvious physiognomy of the criminal' and that in his presence 'one completely forgot that one stood before a satanic monster' – to· attempt this act single-handed and without anyone's knowledge, setting about its preparation systematically and with all the care and foresight of a devoted German master craftsman?

Around the time of the Munich agreement he considered the purchase of a·radio set and took it home on approval. He listened to a few German broadcasts from Moscow and London, but after a fortnight decided to return the set (it cost 200

Reichsmark, the equivalent of five weeks' wages after deductions). It therefore seems that foreign propaganda played as little part in his thinking as did any clandestine conspiracy. What moved him were personal and political considerations of the simplest, most commonplace kind – considerations shared no doubt by millions of others, but in their minds outweighed by other arguments.

For one thing, the Munich agreement deeply perturbed him. He was sure it would lead to war 'because Germany would make further demands on other countries and incorporate them', and he said so to several fellow workmen, who agreed. ('It was clear to me from the first moment', Hitler said a year later to his generals, 'that I could not be satisfied with the Sudeten German territory. It was only a partial solution. My decision to march into Bohemia was made. Then came the establishment of the Protectorate, and with that the basis for the conquest of Poland was laid . . .') Elser also felt that industrial wages were not high enough (as late as 1938 they were still below the 1929 level), and that the various deductions made by the state were unjust. There was, too, 'a certain amount of compulsion – for instance, a worker is not allowed to change his place of work, because of the *Hitler Jugend* he is not master of his own children, and also as regards his religion he can no longer be so free in his activities'. These were some of the reasons – he could not remember any others – which made him think that 'the workers were furious with the government' [*daß deswegen die Arbeiterschaft gegen die Regierung eine Wut hat*], and that something ought to be done to change things. Yes, he had discussed some of these matters with colleagues in the factory and with people he did not know in trains and restaurants, but 'with the best will in the world' he could not remember their names, if he ever knew them. No, he never spoke to anybody of his plans, and he was sure he never used the phrase 'something must be done' when talking to other people.

But still we ask: why did he feel the act had to be done *by him*? We are dealing with a man of simple moral and political ideas, of whom we know that he was stubborn and courageous enough not to salute the swastika flag and to leave the room as soon as the radio was transmitting one of Hitler's speeches, a man who had no interest in abstract thought and to whom 'doing something' meant above all doing something with his hands. His work was the one thing he felt passionate about; several people after the War testified to his perfectionism, his accuracy and meticulous attention to detail. Does it not follow that the decision to place his skill – the only precious thing he had – at the service of the act must have come to him as soon as he had concluded that 'something must be done'? There is nothing fanatical, let alone pathological or 'hierostratic' about his resolution or his conduct at any time. Only psycho-historians (that is, analysts whose patients are dead), indifferent to human freedom, think it necessary to postulate more 'profound' (meaning more disreputable) reasons to explain why it happens that a man is possessed of a very sensitive feeling for the rights that are his due and therefore for the limits of the State's right to interfere with them. Elser told his interrogators that he had never been 'against National Socialism', and at least this much seems true, that he never considered politics abstractly, in terms of -isms. But he felt that 'conditions in Germany could only be altered by disposing of the present leadership', meaning Hitler, Göring and Goebbels, and that once these 'high-ups' were out of the way, they would be replaced by more moderate men who would make no demands on other countries and improve the lot of the working classes. Assassination of 'the highest Leadership' (he obviously feared to refer to Hitler by name) would prevent greater bloodshed; that was the rationale of the deed he planned. 'If they catch me, I thought, why then I must take the punishment upon myself.'

And so, in the autumn of 1938, while most of the country was rejoicing over the 'return' of the Sudeten Germans to a country their ancestors had left five centuries before, Georg

Elser began thinking about ways of implementing his decision. He began by appropriating explosives from the Waldenmaier armament factory where he worked – a simple matter for one in his position of trust. (By the time he left their employment in the following year he had accumulated some 250 packets of gunpowder.) It is unlikely that at this stage, the end of October 1938, he had any very clear idea how to set about his task. But he 'gathered from the daily press', though he was not a regular newspaper reader, that the next meeting at which 'the Leadership' appeared in public would take place on 8 and 9 November (the equivalent of All Saints and All Souls in the Party calendar), and he accordingly travelled to the Bürgerbräukeller in Munich, to find out on the spot 'what were the possibilities of translating my decisions into action'. Whether he also knew that security measures on this occasion were not in the hands of the police or the *Sicherheitsdienst* but of the Old Guard (*die Marschierer von '23*) whose festivity this was, it is impossible to tell. On 8 November 1938 he inspected the hall where the meeting would take place, and discovered that it and all the other public rooms of the restaurant were easily accessible at all times except during the small hours of the night. Next morning he watched Hitler's arrival in front of the restaurant, and in the afternoon took the train back to Königsbronn. Only then did it occur to him that the best place to hide an explosive charge would be a pillar with wooden panelling and a filling of brick and cement immediately behind and above the speaker's rostrum. Once the location had been decided on, it followed that for a time-bomb to go off during Hitler's speech, it would have to be detonated not by a fuse but a clockwork device.

Once Georg Elser had conceived his plan and begun to work out its details, it became evident that its execution would require his undivided attention. Accordingly, at the end of March 1939 – some days after the German occupation of Bohemia and Moravia – he gave notice at the Waldenmaier factory, and early in April went on another visit to the Bürgerbräu, this time to take measurements and photographs of the pillar. He stayed in

Munich a whole week, getting to know several of the waitresses, and tried unsuccessfully to get employment in the Bürgerbräu by offering money to the potboy who was leaving on military service. He was of course very short of money, and so he returned to his parents' house in Königsbronn where, in spite of objections from other members of the family, he could live rent free. All he had saved up was some 400 RM, which he hoped would see him through. Having a good head for figures, he was later able to account to the Gestapo for all his receipts and expenditure during those months, and there is nothing to suggest that he received money from any underground or foreign sources.

He now took a job as labourer in a quarry, which enabled him not only to increase his stock of explosives (he stole 150 cartridges there) but also to learn something about the technique of blasting. In the middle of May he hurt his foot with a stone – the injury may have been self-inflicted – and although the fracture was soon healed, he did not return to the quarry. From now on he devoted his entire time to preparing the coup. In his father's garden he conducted a few experiments to get an idea what kind of detonator would be needed and how it might be connected with a timing clock. However, as he maintained with some pride during his interrogation, the actual machine was constructed by him entirely from drawings and without further experiments. Early in August he moved to Munich. As the lodgings he rented proved too expensive, he soon moved to cheaper ones, where he could also work on his machine. His tools and spare parts, which included several clock mechanisms he had kept from the time he had worked in Constance, and the detonators together with the explosives, he kept partly in a wooden case under lock and key in his lodgings, partly in the workshop of a carpenter whom he had helped out with some joinery work. To him as well as to his landlord he explained that he was working on an invention which he hoped would be patented and bring him a lot of money.

Again, it is important to stress how readily Elser befriended people whom he met through his work, to mention his generosity in making and giving away pieces of furniture (including an inlaid wooden box for his last girl-friend), to consider the old-fashioned Swabian way in which his pride of work went hand in hand with his sociability, while at the same time he was by nature reserved, slow-spoken, often taciturn. In all but his ending he is like the half sulky, half courageous hero of one of Gottfried Keller's tales. By calling him an eccentric or solitary, German commentators insinuate that there was something cranky, perhaps slightly lunatic, about him, and thus they wish to disparage the motivation of his deed. I think the contrary is true. The fact that he trusted nobody is a discredit not to him but to the world he lived in. His great advantage was that in appearance as well as by temperament he was the most inconspicuous of men. Living in a sea of men who were at best indifferent to the injustices around them, he knew that what he had to do he had to do alone, and he prayed that it be the right thing and he should have the strength to carry it through. He was not a particularly religious man, though from childhood he 'continued to say the Lord's Prayer before going to sleep':

> I have never prayed to God in a personal way, that is freely from the heart and in my own words. And I have never made my action – I mean the wish that it should succeed – the object of my prayer. When I was a child my parents took me occasionally with them to church, later I went alone a few times, but less and less often as the years went by. Only in the course of this year [1939] I went again more often, in fact perhaps thirty times since the beginning of the year. More recently I went even on weekdays, maybe into a Catholic church if there wasn't a Protestant one close-by, to say the Lord's Prayer there. To my mind it doesn't matter whether one does this in a Protestant or a Catholic church. I admit that these frequent church-visits and prayers were connected with my deed, which preoccupied me inwardly, for I am sure I would not have prayed so much if I had not prepared and planned that deed. It's a fact that after praying I always felt a bit more composed. If I am asked whether I regard the deed I

committed as sinful within the meaning of the Protestant teaching, I wish to say, 'In a deeper sense, no!' I believe in the continued life of the soul after death, and I also believe that one day I shall go to heaven if I have had the chance to prove by my further life that I intended good. By my deed I wanted to prevent even worse bloodshed.

Those who call *this* eccentric stand self-condemned.

During the night of 5 August 1939 Georg Elser began working on the pillar that was to house his contraption, taking some thirty to thirty-five nightly sessions to complete the job. Each night he would eat his modest dinner in the restaurant, staying on at his table until closing-time, then hide in a little store-room off the dining-hall gallery until well after all the guests and personnel had left and the whole place was locked up, emerging from his hide-out for three or four hours of work and returning to it in the small hours of the morning, to leave the premises as the tradesmen and first morning guests started arriving. The task was stupendous. With tools of his own de-signing he had to remove and hinge an 8ocm square section of the panelling, chisel and gradually enlarge a hole in the cement filling, collecting the rubble and carrying it out in bagfuls. He had to build the explosive containers from scrap metal cases. To make sure it would not fail he fitted the device with two clocks, the cogs on their hour-hand axes being filed out in such a way that they slowly rolled up a steel wire at the end of which a triple detonator was set in action. He lined the panel door with tin to prevent the machine from being damaged by a chance nail driven into the pillar, and with cork in order to muffle the sound of the two clocks – and he had to rebuild the whole thing on finding that there was not enough space to house it in the cavity he had made. And since the room was being used every day, all traces of his work had to be carefully removed at the end of each nightly session. To add to his troubles, after several nights' work his knees went septic and he had to be treated by a doctor – it was the scars left by this infection which were later to confirm the Gestapo's suspicions of him.

He completed his work, installed the device and started the mechanism in the small hours of Monday 6 November 1939, setting it for 21.20 on Wednesday 8 November. So far, luck was with him; since he was not in the habit of reading the newspapers, he did not know that Hitler had originally cancelled his appearance at the celebration, but then had changed his mind at the last moment and was going to be present after all. Elser left Munich for Stuttgart, where he spent Monday night in the flat of his married sister, telling her and her husband merely that he had to leave illegally for Switzerland. He left them his clothes and a few private possessions. As he was now down to his last 10 RM, his sister gave him 30 RM for the journey. However, instead of going on to Constance, as originally planned, he allowed his perfectionism to get the better of him, and on Tuesday night he went back to the Bürgerbräu for a final inspection of the machine. It was working perfectly. He took the train to Constance.

Meanwhile his true antagonist, his moral anti-self, was also having a busy time. The Polish campaign had just been successfully concluded; in a violent interview with General von Brauchitsch, Hitler had brushed aside all criticism of the *Wehrmacht* and ordered preparations for an immediate attack against France, though eventually weather-conditions forced him to postpone the attack until the next spring. For military reasons which proved wholly wrong, the generals were opposed to continuing the war by starting a campaign in the West. They too were preparing a coup d'état, but only 'if Hitler should insist on giving the final order for the attack'. The weather, which prevented this, and Georg Elser, '*der kleine Schorsch*', absolved them from their painful duty.

At the last moment, then, Hitler decided to make his appearance in the midst of his old faithful after all, though he shortened his visit. He entered the Bürgerbräukeller at 20.00

sharp, began his speech at 20.10 and concluded after less than an hour, at 21.07, leaving the building immediately afterwards. Elser's bomb exploded at 21.20, killing one waitress and six of the Old Guard, and wounding more than 60 people of whom, one died in hospital. Hitler, who had taken the (regular) 21.3. express train to Berlin, heard of the attempt from Goebbels around midnight on the station platform in Nuremberg.

At 20.45, almost half an hour before the explosion occurred, Georg Elser was approaching the Swiss-German border in a suburb of Constance. He was stopped by a couple of customs officials, who were surveying their section of the border from a schoolhouse window while listening to a radio transmission of Hitler's speech. It was a routine examination, but as Elser's border crossing pass was out of date, they insisted on conducting a bodily search. What follows, it must be admitted, is the one part of Georg Elser's story for which there is no rational explanation: in his pockets they found some bolts, screws and springs, a picture postcard of the Bürgerbräukeller, a few notes and addresses of ammunition factories in Baden and Württemberg, and his old *RFK* badge, which he had put in his pocket 'for old time's sake'. Only when they had taken him to the police station and a radio announcement at midnight gave news of the coup and ordered full alert on all frontier stations, did the picture postcard assume significance. Before the night was out a special investigating commission (composed partly of Gestapo and partly of police officials) was set up by Himmler in Berlin, and some 120 suspects were arrested. Georg Elser, who had meanwhile been transferred to the Munich police headquarters in the Wittelsbacher Palais, was still regarded as a deserter and (in view of the notes found on him) as a possible spy. Only on 13 November, when the Gestapo head of the commission himself took over the cross-examination and, on being told by experts that the time-bomb had been mounted at floor level, asked to see Elser's knees – only then did the truth begin to emerge. Elser, who had so far denied all connexion with the coup, now broke down and asked what punishment was likely to be given to 'one who does something like that'; and at midnight, after some fourteen hours, he finally confessed.

Only the examining officials believed him. Hitler, Himmler, and the leadership of the Gestapo had their own reason for refusing to accept George Elser's confession. On the day of the coup, 9 November, two British secret agents, Captain Best and Major Stevens, were kidnapped by the SS on the Dutch border. The propaganda machinery was of course able to exploit the failure of the coup as a providential act of grace (and Hitler often referred to it as such in the years to come), but it was much more difficult to admit that the coup was perpetrated by a German worker. The Gestapo's aim, therefore, was to connect the act with the two secret agents and to build up Georg Elser as a conspirator in the pay of Otto Strasser and the British government. (The documents containing Elser's confession in the Wittelsbacher Palais were later lost, and Captain Best's became one of the versions of his story after the War.)

However, as both Hitler and Himmler had refused to believe the confession in the first place, another, much fuller cross-examination was conducted in Berlin between 19 and 23 November 1939. My source is the dossier of this second examination which the Munich court used when in 1946 it conducted an enquiry into Elser's death, and which has now been published. In the course of this second examination Elser was several times brutally beaten up, and confronted with his mother and other relations, all of whom had meanwhile been rounded up. He stuck to his story, and there is no reason to doubt that in all essentials it is the truth. It is evident that throughout his confession Elser was desperately anxious to avoid incriminating any of the people he had met in the months before the coup, and it seems that he was successful. It may be that he had in fact initiated one or another of his friends or relations into his secret. If so, then his steadfastness under torture is indeed admirable. As for the document now before us, with Elser's signature at the end of each section, its consecutively numbered pages, and its characteristic mixture of official phraseology superimposed upon his homely language, its genuineness cannot be in doubt. With its telling criticisms of the regime, its detailed account of the earlier phases of Elser's life fully verified by his surviving relations, the confession contains material which the Gestapo either could not have invented or would have been anxious to suppress.

And still they – and Hitler – hoped Elser would confess to being in the pay of the British. As 'Hitler's special prisoner' he was taken to Sachsenhausen where he met Captain Best and was kept in special detention, in the same section of the camp as Léon Blum, Kurt von Schuschnigg, Pastor Niemöller and other 'prominent prisoners'. One wonders what caused Captain Best and Pastor Niemöller to claim after the war that Elser was really in the pay of the National Socialists and that he was hired by them to kill a group of dissident party members in return for 40,000 Swiss Francs and a free pass to Switzerland; one wonders why the egregious Pastor Niemöller should add to this fabrication, gratuitously and in spite of anguished protests from the bereaved mother, that Elser was himself an SS leader.

Georg Elser did not survive to defend himself. In 1944 he was moved to Dachau and kept alive – working some of the time as a carpenter – in order to be cited as chief witness at the trial which Himmler and Hitler were proposing to stage after the War in London. When it became unlikely that such a trial would be held, Elser ceased to be of interest to the party bosses. On an order 'from the highest authority' he was murdered by the guards during an air raid on the camp on 9 April 1945, the day on which Pastor Bonhoeffer, Admiral Canaris, General Oster and Chief Army Judge Karl Sack were executed. They were of one company, after all.

The few parallels and many contrasts between the two antagonists, Hitler and Elser, are obvious enough, yet they are contemporaries. There is a point in Elser's confession when he too seems to capitulate to the ideology and make its language his own, when he too is forced to look at his own deed through the eyes of his tormentors. In the cat-and-mouse game they are playing with him during the investigation, they ask what he would do were he to be given his freedom, to which he replies, understandably enough, that he would try to find his place in the *Volksgemeinschaft*, the nation's community.

'Would you be able to do that?' he is then asked.

'I have changed my mind,' Georg Elser replies – and who will blame a man in his desperate predicament for trying to survive? It is clear that what most deeply troubles him now is not the failure of his undertaking nor his own fate but the eight people he has killed (the Gestapo have just shown him a film of their funeral), and the sixty he has injured.

'Do you say this because you have been arrested?'

'No', comes Elser's final reply. 'I firmly believe that my plan would have succeeded if my view of the matter had been correct. Since it did not succeed, I am convinced that *it was not meant to succeed*, and that my view was false.' Did he say this to save himself and because he thought this is what they would like to hear, or did he now really believe it?

At the other end of the social scale from Johann Georg Elser stands Ulrich von Hassell, German Ambassador to the Vatican and one of the conspirators of the twentieth of July 1944. Face to face with the 'People's Judge', the bestial Roland Freisler, he too falters:

> *Freisler:* Really, you know, it is very difficult to talk to you
> about what you've done. Because one can't believe a word.
> You have no feeling for the truth. You're the lie in person.
> *Hassell:* May I observe that before '44 . . .
> *Freisler:* . . . and will hang like the rest [*German proverb*].
> You know what I mean. Well then.
> *Hassell:* And secondly, my entire attitude towards foreign
> politics . . .
> *Freisler:* I don't care a damn about your attitude towards

foreign politics. Because it's not our business here to decide about attitudes towards foreign politics. That's not what we're here for, as judges. We don't presume to decide in matters which are not our business. What we have to decide here is whether the man who stands before us is a German who has remained a man of honour or not . . .

Hassell: Who in his heart of hearts did not believe in it.

Freisler: I see. Did not believe in it. And why not?

Hassell: I never believed that such an undertaking would succeed.

Freisler: Why not?

Hassell: I took it to be impossible.

Freisler: Impossible? Is that what you're saying: impossible? After all, there have been earlier attempts on the Führer's life. Attempts we know all about.

Hassell: I thought it would not come to the point.

Freisler: Ah. I thought it would not come to the point. When men like these tell you a thing like this, you don't believe it will come to the point! On what grounds?

Hassell: I don't know. With my inner feeling I did not believe that this would succeed. Of course I did not doubt what they both said . . .

Freisler: Well then!

Hassell: . . . but I was convinced that they had this view of the matter, that they had been told things of this kind, but I did not believe in its realization. I did not so to speak take the matter literally to have any substance.

'It was not meant to succeed.' 'With my inner feeling.' At this point these men, who have withdrawn from 'the people's community', enter the world of Josef K. with its insinuation that the exterminator is not wholly in the wrong, that there *is* a foothold for his authority in the victim's soul, as though his hold over the victim were more than a matter of superior might. This is the secret belief of the age of Kafka and Hitler, and of Georg Elser too. Yet his mind is not dominated by it. The freedom that Elser's deed secures for him is qualified – as all our freedom is – but untainted; the choice he made, for decency and justice, is the choice of a free man.

18 Myrmidons' Strife

Illusory expectations, a defective understanding of what the rest of Europe felt about Germany, an absence of stable political goals to which to direct their moral and religious ideals – these are the consequences of the rule through connivance-and-terror, and they are a measure of the regime's success. A major aim of its 'ideology' was the discrediting and destruction of any such goals, the negation of any alternative ideology, socialist, democratic, but also conservative, and thus the destruction of political life in any traditional form. '*Es war immer was los*' does not mean progress towards some changes or goal, whether imminent or utopian, but a determination to hang onto the *status quo*, camouflaged by a feverish display of activity, an aimless, purposeless, endless activism. This is Hitler's form of 'revolution', and this is where he disagreed with most of his advisers and party bosses. *Their* attitude is conveyed accurately enough by the protestations of one of the Old Guard in a conversation with Rauschning, then national socialist president of the Senate of Danzig:

> 'I don't intend to get pushed down again!' he screamed at me in indignation. 'Maybe you can wait. You're not sitting on a bed of hot coals! Listen, man: no job! to have no job! Rather than go through that again I'll turn to crime. I'll do anything to stay on top!'

This attitude is surely anything but 'revolutionary'. Do we not hear in such utterances simply the voice of the quintessential *petit bourgeois*? Rauschning seems right when he says that in this attitude there was not an ounce of loyalty, no faith of any kind (either in the 'Leader' or in the cause), nothing but sham and go-getting and squalid cynicism. And yet this is not the whole story. The Junker in him would not see (as Konrad Heiden, who had never been a party member, did see) that men such as this were capable of that 'absolute' loyalty – loyalty unto death – of which the members of his own (Rauschning's) class boasted. There is a contradiction here, between the desire for the security of a *petit-bourgeois* competence and the willingness, for the sake of 'staying on top', to go to any lengths including crime. Hitler created a situation in which the contradiction could be resolved. He would use the criminal heedlessness to further his own ends; thus exploited, it assumed a quality of 'fanatical idealism'. At the same time as he connived at the pocketing of the spoils, he would repudiate the desire for security as 'materialistic'. For he believed in permanent revolution: not on Gregor Strasser's terms, or Ernst Röhm's, but on his own terms of perpetual conquest and annihilation. In this warlike syndrome of a permanent revolution under his leadership, the image of personal authenticity receives its fullest embodiment.

There is some truth in the view that the original party ideology 'was the product of a declining social class, and came increasingly into conflict with the social realities created by National Socialist rule itself: the movement whose ideology had been directed towards the construction of a society of small traders, craftsmen, and smallholders brought about a tremendous acceleration in the process of concentration in industry and trade, and intensified the drift of population from countryside into towns; industry was concentrated in Central and Western Germany and drew increasingly on the population of the poorer Eastern regions as a source of labour, thus making nonsense of the policy of colonizing and settling Eastern Europe with German farmers'. But the ideology which was thus invalidated had been upheld by some of the Old Guard only (men like Anton Drexler, Gottfried Feder and Franz Xavier Schwarz, the Party treasurer). Hitler began to abandon it as soon as he saw himself on the road to national leadership. The supremacy of *his* ideas – his absolute rule – begins, not in

February 1933, but with the destruction of the SA in the summer of 1934.

The massacres of 30 June to 2 July 1934 offer a good example of Hitler's supreme ability to proceed by a series of carefully planned moves and *ad hoc* improvisations to intermediate ends, which themselves become the means that compel him to take the next steps, and so all the way to the attainment of unlimited power. In this progression he seems to be aided by good luck. On closer inspection it turns out that the only thing he is gambling on is the gullibility of his allies, the corruption and 'sense of honour' of his opponents, and the incompetence of both. The way he plays this bloody game of leap-frog at this time is a model for the tactics that will lead to the outbreak of war in September 1939. Moreover, the same tactics will be used in the persecution of the Jews.

The political problem Hitler had to face when in February 1933 he assumed supreme power in the State (power which at that point was by no means unlimited) is the main tactical problem of his rule, and it remained with him to the end. On the one hand he had to gain and retain the confidence of the conservative establishment of industrialists and bankers by assuring them that the National Socialist revolution was now completed, and that what the country needed was economic recovery and development within the framework he had created. On the other hand the impetus of the revolutionary movement must be kept going – on his own terms and under his own leadership. And both intentions must be geared to the end of warlike action, only the kind and extent of which was in question. The full complexity of this double task is reflected in Hitler's speeches throughout the next eighteen months, in which peaceable reassurances to the Conservatives alternate with reminders to the cohorts that 'the Revolution must go on'. The SA militia, four-and-a-half millions in strength by the end of 1933, was not in itself wholly unsuitable for Hitler's purpose. What rendered it unsuitable was, first, Ernst Röhm's leadership of it, for Röhm was the only man in Hitler's career who was capable of opposing him and negotiating with him on equal terms. Moreover, Röhm was prepared to risk a conflict with the *Reichswehr*, whereas Hitler was not. Less than a week after becoming Chancellor he addressed the generals and representatives of the Navy on the subject of his future policy (3 February 1933). Its exact direction must be left open, he told them, but he mentions two alternatives: 'Perhaps a fight for new possibilities of export, perhaps – and surely this would be preferable – conquest of new living space in the East and its uncompromising Germanization.' The audience responded with an instant public declaration of loyalty. There seems little doubt that Hitler's decision in favour of the Army and against the SA was made as soon as it became clear to him that he could be sure of the Army's support in the person of the weak von Blomberg and avail himself of its technical apparatus and its standing in the country, and as soon as the Army for its part showed itself ready to negotiate with Himmler (a man who, unlike Röhm, would never risk open conflict with Hitler) and the SS.

The personalities of the two leaders, Röhm and Himmler, were reflected in the character of the two paramilitary organizations they commanded. Serious discontent, of a kind unthinkable in the SS, broke out in the ranks of the SA for the first time in August 1933, when Röhm complained that his men were underpaid, discriminated against by the Party, and above all inadequately armed. It became clear that Röhm, now a minister without portfolio in Hitler's coalition government, would renew his old demands that his SA should become either a fully-fledged militia or be integrated into the *Reichswehr* (when, as he hoped, 'the brown flood would submerge the grey rock'); that Hitler would oppose these demands by insisting that the *Reichswehr* must 'remain' the sole armed force in the State (which it had not been for the last five years); and that he was coming to see the SA, and especially the condottieri round Röhm, as a liability in his negotiations with the respectable

Conservatives and with the Army itself. Towards the end of 1933 discussions about the re-introduction of national conscription were begun – this alone should have warned Röhm that his plans were in jeopardy. Moreover, in a speech on 9 November 1933, the tenth anniversary of the Munich *Putsch*, Hitler indicated quite unmistakably that he had made his choice. Interpreting the events of November 1923 in a novel way, he now presented them as 'a rift between two brothers, the Army and the Nation'. It was his 'greatest happiness' (he continued) that the hope he had cherished in those dark days 'was at last fulfilled and that we, the representatives of the Army *and* the spokesman of the Nation, now stand together, that we have again become one, and that this unity will never be broken again in Germany. *Only by this unity has that blood-sacrifice received its meaning* and has not been in vain, what we were marching for then has now become reality'. If Röhm failed to see that in this 'unity' there was no room for a third partner, he could hardly say that he had not been warned. The passage I have emphasized is of course high rhetoric, but it also represents the rationale of Hitler's actions. The débâcle of November 1923 has become a meaningful blood-sacrifice. The massacres of the SA which followed some seven months later would, in due course, be subjected to the same interpretation, the same retrospective validation. The path of his revolution lay through the 'blood-sacrifice' of *any* group of society, German or foreign, Jewish or 'Aryan', ultimately of Germany herself; what is more, some of the victims among the die-hard SA shared this interpretation – shared it to the extent of failing to oppose their own destruction.

By the early spring of 1934 a show-down with the SA seems imminent. The massacres are instigated by Field Marshals von Reichenau and von Blomberg on the understanding that, by keeping to its barracks and only occasionally supplying the SS with arms and transport, the Army will be rid of its rival, the SA, without having to fire a single shot. This much von Reichenau had agreed to in February 1933; on these terms he resumes negotiations with Himmler and the SS in May 1934. It seems likely that it had been Hitler's original plan to postpone the day of reckoning with the SA until after the President, von Hindenburg, had died. However, on 4 June, Hindenburg, now ailing and partly senile, leaves for his estate in East Prussia, and this is the signal for the beginning of the campaign. After a long and inconclusive discussion with Röhm, Hitler too leaves Berlin, for a tour of discussions with the Ruhr industrialists. Two days later there begins a barrage of speeches by Hitler, Göring (who stays in Berlin), Goebbels, Himmler, Rosenberg, Ley, Hess and Frick (Minister of the Interior in Hitler's coalition government), as well as a number of minor party officials. These speeches are aimed partly at discrediting the remaining critics of the regime (known variously as 'grousers, bleaters and spoilsports'), partly they hint at the dangers of a 'second revolution'. At the same time the Gestapo and the *Sicherheitsdienst* are fully mobilized, and a number of SS units are deployed on war-games around Munich. Röhm does not appear to suspect what is being prepared. On 7 June he goes on 'sick leave', a few days later he orders the entire SA on leave for the month of July, and on 28 June agrees to Hitler's orders for a meeting of the higher leadership of the SA for 30 June in Wiessee. Hitler is in the Ruhr, then for two days (14–15 June) as Mussolini's guest in Venice, on 21 June he flies to Neudeck in East Prussia, ostensibly to report to the President on his talks with Mussolini, in fact to reassure the worried Blomberg that the situation is under control. Meanwhile in Berlin two lists are being circulated by Göring and Himmler: one, supposedly compiled by the SA, contains the names of Army and SS officers whom the SA is said to want to liquidate when they take over power: this list is leaked to the Army. The other is simply a list drawn up by Röhm, containing the names of SA officers due for promotion to senior posts, and this list will be used by the SS in the massacres.

And now, while Hitler seems still unsure when to strike, comes his first piece of 'good luck'. Von Papen, the conservative

Vice-Chancellor, speaks at the University of Marburg on 17
June, warning Hitler against his 'false friends', warning the
country against a 'second revolution', and calling for a renewal
of national life in accordance with the principles of Catholic
conservatism. Papen's speech includes a favourable allusion to
the Hohenzollern monarchy as well as a hint to Hindenburg
who, Papen believes, will call out the Army to intervene. This
quixotic speech – courageous but out of touch with the contemporary situation – is immediately suppressed by Goebbels,
technically von Papen's ministerial subordinate. At this point
the drama turns into a farce. On the same day Hitler's propaganda compaign reaches its climax with a particularly vitu-
perative speech at Gera, in the course of which he attacks
Papen (without however naming him) as 'a tiny pigmy' and
'the little worm who thinks he can pit himself against the
gigantic re-birth of the nation'; whether the timing of Hitler's
speech was a coincidence or the result of an indiscretion is not
known. Papen, furious at Goebbels's banning of his speech,
one moment threatens immediate resignation, the next agrees
to a meeting with Hitler. Hitler talks him out of his threat to
resign 'while the nation is in danger', and solemnly promises
Papen that he will let him resign once the emergency is over.
More than that, Papen actually leaves the meeting convinced
that Hitler has taken notice of his speech and that he will
moderate his policy from now on. (Four days later Papen does
not scruple to appear in Goebbels's company at the German
Derby in Hamburg; eight days after that he is under house-
arrest and his closest collaborators, including Edgar Jung, the
actual author of that ill-fated speech, have been assassinated;
none of this prevents Papen from becoming German Minister
Extraordinary in Vienna before the year is out – where he, the
scion of the Catholic nobility, has been sent to allay the suspicion that his master was implicated in the murder of the Catholic peasant's son Dollfuss, one of the few heroic politicians of
those disastrous years.)

And now for the end-game with its characteristic pattern.

Tension in the country is mounting, Blomberg, with the President behind him, threatens (at Neudeck, 21 July) that he will declare martial law and call out the Army if peaceful conditions are not restored, and Hitler is finally compelled to act – having of course himself created the forces that push him into action. On 24–25 June Himmler and Heydrich inform the leaders of the SS that a coup of the SA is imminent, instructions for collecting arms from the supply depots of the Army are issued, the names of the supposed insurrectionists among the SA are circulated throughout the country, the watchword for the SS counter-coup is given out (there seems to be a slip-up here: it is usually the rebels who are supposed to do the attacking and therefore have to agree on a watchword, not the defenders of the state). The Army has been squared. Any doubt remaining in the minds of its officers has been dispelled by the counterfeited lists of those of its members wanted by the insurrectionists. On 25 June General von Fritsch cancels all leave and confines all troops to barracks, 28 June Captain Röhm is expelled from the German Officers' League, 29 June General von Blomberg publishes in the *Völkischer Beobachter* yet another declaration of the Army's unswerving loyalty to the National Socialist state, its President and its Leader. All is now prepared for the counter-coup, the only thing still missing is the enemy.

The second piece of 'good luck' is not long in coming, and this time again there is good reason for thinking that matters have not been left to chance. By means of forged handbills several battalions of the SA are called out on a march through Munich. And though shortly afterwards the local Gauleiter orders them off the streets, Hitler has at last got his pretext for action. The SA battalions are marching without their leaders, since most of them are assembling for the conference at Wiessee. What do the men in Munich hope to achieve? If, as Hitler will claim in his account to the Reichstag (13 July), they are really plotting to overthrow the government of the Reich, what are they doing in Munich, why are they not in Berlin (where, incidentally, the local SA commander is just setting out on his honeymoon)? There seems to be no limit to their guilelessness – or indeed to Röhm's. This is the moment for which the SS have been waiting. All over the country they take to their requisitioned butchers' trucks and Army transports; Hitler breaks off his visit to the Ruhr, and in the company of Goebbels, Dietrich (head of the press bureau) and his three adjutants he flies to Munich, where he lands at 4 a.m. on Saturday 30 June. Berating the SA officers who have come to welcome him, he strips them of their Party rank and honours, and has them arrested by the civil police. A cavalcade of black Mercedes cars now races to Wiessee; Hitler insists on being present at the kill. By 8 a.m. the homosexual Röhm and members of his circle, some with their catamites, have been chased from their hotel beds, mostly without offering any resistance, and the blood bath begins. In the course of the next three days some two hundred men are killed, a few are given the choice of committing suicide. Only in Silesia is there some resistance to the wave of arrests and executions. Hitler in his Reichstag speech of 13 July puts the number of dead at 77; he also seeks to justify his action by referring to a nation-wide plot to overthrow the government, and to an SA march through Berlin, supposedly synchronized with the Munich demonstration – no plot was ever discovered, no march in Berlin ever took place. Apart from Röhm and his SA leaders, a number of old scores were settled. Those assassinated included Gregor Strasser, General von Bredow and General Schleicher and his brave wife; Hitler's prosecutor in the 1923 trial, Gustav von Kahr; the man who corrected the grammar of *Mein Kampf*, Father Stempfle; a number of conservative civil servants; some men involved in purely private quarrels; and a number of complete outsiders, among them a music critic who suffered the fate of 'the poet Cinna' and a group of Silesian Jews, killed for the amusement of the local Gauleiter. Several senior SS officers insisted on personally shooting their SA colleagues of equal rank. Even more bizarre were the executions in the Stadelheim prison in Munich, where the prisoners believed that they,

along with Hitler, were the victims of a plot by the 'reaction-
aries', Göring and Goebbels. At the command, 'The Führer
wills it! Heil Hitler! Fire!', the SS carried out the sentences,
Their volleys were met with the same words, 'Heil Hitler!'.
on the SA men's dying lips. The Führer could do no wrong.

What is the meaning of these massacres? Do they amount to
more than the hideous strife of two rival groups of myrmidons,
both equally criminal, one rather more stupid, inflexible and
credulous than the other? Hitler's triumph was certainly complete. He had kept out the Army, allayed its fear of scandal,
and convinced it that 'its honour as an unpolitical instrument
of the State' would be preserved. To this end he now set himself up as its Supreme Commander, eventually to place the
SS – in the form of the *Waffen-SS* – in that very position which
he had denied Röhm and his SA. Professing to be scandalized
by the homosexual goings-on in the SA (which he had tolerated
for years and which were to continue in the SS), he could set
himself up as the guardian of the nation's moral health, in an
ambience in which acquiescence in political crime went hand
in hand with great moral hypocrisy in sexual matters. And he
now formally assumed the function of Supreme Judiciar,
though not without the good services of the usual toadying
academic (said to be the best constitutional lawyer of his day)
who was quick to demonstrate that 'judgeship emanates from
leadership' and that 'the Führer's act [that is, the assassinations]
is not subject to the dispensation of Justice, for it was itself the
highest form of Justice'. (Here it is again, the Nietzschean
conundrum according to which 'life' cannot be judged, or
criticized, or moralized over, by 'reason' because reason is
derivative from life and must remain subordinate to it.) On
3 July a law was passed which, in a single sentence, exempted
all acts committed between 30 June and 2 July from prosecu-
tion, and retrospectively justified the killings as lawful measures
taken in defence of the State.

Hitler's *de facto* function had now received its fullest institutional sanction: was this what persuaded the conservatives that there would be no 'second revolution'? In fact, the one thing that emerged with startling clarity was the wholly personal character of Hitler's rule, manifest in his 'will' to a permanent revolution on his own terms. Not on the Army's terms, or the industrialists', but not on the terms of his associates and henchmen either. The example made of the SA was enough. This was to be the one revolution that would not devour its children but would remain, all the way through and to the country's complete defeat, in all essentials under the control of its instigator and leader, its henchmen hardly more than creatures of his favour, its 'ideas' coextensive with *his* thinking, and null and void as soon as he was dead.

The meaning of the massacres amounts to the opposite of those fatuous hopes which the conservative establishment, civilian and military alike, had placed in them. As late as March 1934 Hitler had proclaimed, 'The revolution must go on!' and 'It will take many years, and many generations will pass, before the victorious emblems of the Reich will be engraved on all hearts – and only then will the National Socialist revolution have succeeded, only then will Germany be saved!' True, he said many things. True, the idea of a politician who wants conflict, albeit controlled conflict, for its own sake had no obvious precedent. Yet he was still the representative and leader of a generation which felt that (as Konrad Heiden put it) 'even the Devil was preferable to the emptiness of an existence that lacked larger significance'. When, with their dying breath, the men in Stadelheim prison hailed their leader, they were assenting to the 'larger significance' he had given their lives. July 1934, like November 1923, had become a meaningful blood sacrifice. 'Your god lies shattered in the dust', wrote Nietzsche fifty years earlier, 'and serpents dwell among his ruins. And now you love even the serpents for his sake.'

*

Again and again this generation had to hear how privileged it
was to have Hitler in its midst and to be placed by him (or the
Lord God, or providence, or history) in the vanguard of the
revolution. The 'blood-sacrifices' demanded of it were the
signs of its worthiness, and its reward: but were they enough?
Unlike Italy, Germany after the suppression of the socialist
uprisings of 1918–19 had never been near a state of civil war.
Unlike the Fascists, the National Socialists had never encountered the concerted opposition of the armed forces, or indeed
of any German state or municipality. The fiasco of November
1923 was a trivial affair when compared with the war-like
campaigns the Fascists had fought and won in the year preceding the march on Rome. Hitler himself said as much when
he spoke admiringly (and inaccurately) of 'the six thousand
six hundred dead' the Fascists were supposed to have lost in
their fight for Verona alone – the warlike spirit of *his* followers
had never been tested against opponents of equal strength and
determination. Strife, whether internecine or warlike, was at the
heart of his ideology. It was the element that united his idea
of personal authenticity with his conception of political life.
The discovery that belligerence could be carried from the front-
line into domestic political life he may well have owed to
Mussolini, to whom he pays tribute in *Mein Kampf*. Hitler's
original contribution to politics – the point where the disciple
turned master – came with his discovery that this belligerence
could be carried further, into international politics, and further
still, into another World War. His discovery of this continuity
was at first far from being an act of heedlessness. Its prudential
aspect lay in choosing conflicts of manageable dimensions.
This is why his first victims were the Jews. But the dynamics
of this process, which was confronted by no countervailing
principle, make it seem inevitable that in the search for further
conflict all restraint would be discarded.

It is difficult to discuss evil on such a scale as this. It is
above all difficult to follow a career whose every aspect proclaims its senselessness, in order to make sense of it. If (as it

were in spite of his saying so) this notion of conflict and strife as the only value in life really does lie at the heart of Hitler's ideological thinking, then it is clear that much of his political practice will consist in seeking out and creating emergency situations likely to keep the spirit of conflict alive. Here, it seems to me, lies the meaning of the massacres of June 1934. Once dead, Röhm and his SA bravos enter the hagiography of 'the party comrades who went wrong', and serve the renewal of its 'revolutionary spirit' in the same way as did the 'blood-sacrifices' of November 1923.

19 A Social Revolution?

The party whose propagandist Hitler became early in 1920 and whose leadership he wrested from its founder, Anton Drexler, in the summer of 1921 was neither exclusively lower-middle class, nor can it be described as 'the refuse of all the classes'. It contained a number of extreme nationalists, both from the working-class and the middle-class intelligentsia, and a number of 'political virgins', that is young soldiers, officers and students who had never used their vote and had no party connexion of any kind. The party's membership list of 1920 represents almost the entire spectrum of contemporary German society; in that sense at all events Hitler was right when he claimed that from its beginnings it was 'a classless popular party'. The character of what Martin Broszat has accurately called 'Hitler's State' cannot be explained in terms of class. The basic condition of its cohesion is Hitler's political talent, his ability to use every institution and power-group for his own purpose and to rid himself of every individual and group that showed signs of seriously interfering with it. When in January 1933 he became Chancellor of the Reich and in August 1934, after Hindenburg's death, assumed the function of President (a title he never used), he succeeded in convincing the higher echelons of industry and the civil service that he had ceased to be a party man and would subordinate all party interests to those of the Reich. Since he saw himself as the embodiment of the Reich, these claims were not only true, they were tautologous.

He promised that there would be no civil war; and with that promise, which he kept, he put to rest their worst fear. This fear had dominated the thinking of every elite and power group in Northern Germany not only since 1919 but since the days of Napoleon's defeat of Prussia a hundred years before. To allay the spectre of civil war no injustice and no oppression was too high a price to pay, especially if others – the Communists, the Jews, the Slavs, eventually the rest of Europe – could be made to pay it. No other European nation has achieved its sovereign unity for so brief a time and at such cost.

The more lasting significance of this 'achievement', hedged in by a sinister ambiguity, lies in the social sphere.

Hitler's plans involved Germany in what Ernst Jünger in an essay of 1932 called 'total mobilization', a mustering of national resources on a scale normally associated with war-like action. It is true that this mobilization, duly tempered by corruption, departmental rivalries, and the heedless pursuit of personal privilege, turned out to be a good deal less than 'total'. It has been shown in considerable detail that once Great Britain and America took their emergency measures, their mobilization of the labour force, which proceeded without lawlessness and with no permanent encroachments on the liberal-democratic way of life, turned out to be rather more effective than the strong-arm methods of the totalitarian regimes. But such comparisons are only partly relevant, for the German mobilization was of a fundamentally different kind. It began in 1933, when national expenditure on the armed forces rose from 23% to 49% in 1934 and to 74% in 1938, and it was not just a war-like process. It is characterized by Ernst Jünger in his book *Der Arbeiter* (1932) as a mobilization for 'work', and 'work' is defined as the unifying factor of war and peace. 'The clatter of the weaving looms of Manchester and the rattling of the machine-guns at Langemark' are seen as aspects of one and the same process at work in the modern world. This process, which is self-justifying, is characterized by 'lethal effort' and by 'total engagement in the area of command': the modern world *is* that undifferentiated process; 'the Worker', who is identical with 'the Soldier-Technician', is its only significant agent.

Jünger's book is a symptom rather than a cause, a Spenglerian fiction rather than a socio-political analysis. While it speculates a good deal about the metaphysical ends of this new technological society, it says next to nothing about the concrete means whereby the 'total mobilization of the soldier-worker' is to come about. Needless to say, Hitler's Germany did no more to produce a race of such 'Workers' than did any other regime. The book's affinities with the ethos of the new regime are to be sought in the concept of mobilization for war and peace. 'Every worker must regard himself as a soldier of the economy', and 'We are all soldiers of work' sound like typical slogans from Ernst Jünger's book; in fact they are pronouncements of party officials on the factory floor.

Hitler, unlike Ernst Jünger, was fully aware that his mobilization – in the course of which a peace-time economy was put on a war-time footing under the leadership not of the military but of a politician – could only be achieved through changes in the structure of German society. And these changes turned out to be so fundamental that an impeccably liberal sociologist like Ralf Dahrendorf sees in them that 'social revolution' which had been delayed by the authoritarian ethos and taboos of the Second Reich and by the dire confusions of Weimar.

Under the aegis of the least mobile power elite Germany had known in this century, a revolutionary process was set in train which neither corresponded to the intentions of that elite nor was clearly independent of them. In the armed forces and in the civil service, throughout the branches of the teaching profession and in the two Churches, in industry and in commerce, the regime created conditions for social mobility unparalleled in German history and very much greater than Weimar had been able to offer. (Thus the number of officers commissioned from the ranks during the Second World War amounted to more than twice the number raised from the ranks in the German armies since 1800). The regime was of course incapable of implementing any of its fantastic schemes for a 'Germanic' utopian community of the 'Master Race', if only because its agricultural policy (on which such a mystic community was to be based) turned out to be the least effective of its measures of reform. Moreover, the setting up of this community was to follow in the wake of extensive permanent territorial conquests in the East, and we have only Hitler's, Himmler's and Rosenberg's war-time memoranda and speeches to tell us what that would have been like.

The social revolution that did take place had little enough in common with any *völkisch* or 'Aryan' ideas. At the same time as it destroyed the basis for all due processes of law, all notions of equity and all democratic forms of government, the regime also destroyed the basis of the traditional opposition to the liberal-democratic ideology. The executions following the July 1944 coup sealed the fate of organized opposition to Hitler, but at the same time they also sealed the fate of traditional German conservatism, and of Prussia.

The regime proclaimed a classless society, and to tens and hundreds of thousands this claim must have seemed to come true. Here lay its concrete appeal. To these men – half private entrepreneurs, half party functionaries – it gave positions of prestige, affluence, and power, regardless of their formal educational and social background, guaranteeing them equality of rank with the established upper classes. As each professional and commercial association and each branch of the civil service had its parallel organization inside the party structure, there were plenty of jobs for anyone with an Aryan family tree – and only the 'old boys' with low party membership numbers and low IQs were fussy about opportunistic newcomers. The regime neither nationalized industry nor left it in private hands, but it created even in peacetime a number of semi-private state-directed consortia (along the lines of the present management of the Volkswagen works) whose interests were closely tied to the state and party while leaving the individual profit motive unimpaired. Economic security in peace-time and guarantees of increased production and consumption in war-time, as well as a regimented domestic labour force augmented by several millions of slave workers – these were the rewards offered to the industrialists. On these conditions alone state intervention was acceptable, for to the end of 1944 they, unlike the armed forces, retained a strong bargaining position. While party propaganda proclaimed its 'either-or' solutions and reiterated its 'sacred' demands of 'absolute' allegiance, the actual system which the regime had created and which kept it in power functioned through an interlocking structure of compromises. While the party's cultural programmes exalted the clod-hopping peasantry, the rights of individual provinces and the last vestiges of their independence were abolished. While the propaganda machine insisted on the primacy of inherited characteristics and on the 'natural' origin of the gift of leadership, the regime enforced its 'biological' tenets only in respect of one's admission to nationhood and to the 'national community', using allegations of doubtful ancestry (e.g. General Milch's or Reinhard Heydrich's) for the purpose of blackmail. Inside this society, 'acquired' status was dominant over 'ascribed', and life proceeded largely according to the old maxim of '*la carrière ouverte aux talents*'.

Yet there is a consistent rationale to Hitler's social policies. It is to be found in the acceleration of this social momentum towards change – an acceleration which entails attacks on every individual person or group that stands in its way by attempting to fix or institutionalize its 'acquired' status; which entails even the creation of supposedly antagonistic groups, to be attacked in order to keep up the momentum of this social process. Intention and ultimate achievement splay apart. The *intended* goal of these domestic policies, as of Hitler's conduct of foreign affairs, was disconnected from anything that might be called a social purpose.

Again and again we seem to run into flat contradictions between the claims of the regime's propaganda and its actual social practice. In his first address as Chancellor and head of government (1 February 1933) Hitler announced that he had assumed power 'in order to put an end to the destruction of family, honour, loyalty, nationhood, culture, and economy . . . wrought by fourteen years of Marxism'. Yet the purpose in founding the *Hitler Jugend* (compulsory between the ages of ten and eighteen from 1 December 1936), the *Bund Deutscher Mädchen*, and the *Reichsarbeitsdienst*, was precisely the dissolution of the traditional authoritarian structure of the German family and the neutralizing of the equally authoritarian influence of the Churches. ('The worker', Georg Elser had complained, '. . . is not master of his children.') Contradictions such as these are not, however, signs of Hitler's 'irrational' or heedless mendacity or of his pathological inability to remember in one situation what he had found it convenient to proclaim in another. (His excellent memory remained largely unimpaired to the end.) On the contrary; these are simply rhetorical ploys for pacifying the conservative element in all strata of society while he cannot afford to alienate them, to be dropped even from his public speeches when war breaks out – when, that is, the conservatives cannot turn against him without incurring the opprobrium of turning against their own nation at war. Hitler's private expatiations on the 'sclerotic old order' may be lacking in sociological finesse, but they leave no doubt that he knew what he wanted clearly enough. He needed a modern social structure, and he was prepared to do anything, to promise anything, in order to get it, even though (as Dahrendorf says) he would have thoroughly disliked certain implications of it, of which he was unaware. Only a new social order, he said *and* believed, would enable him to achieve the degree of coercive control and production necessary for the realization of his national and global plans. The old authoritarian system, whose inadequacies he saw as the cause of the defeat and 'treason' of 1918, enabled him to achieve his 'legal' consolidation of power; the conservative establishment's 'lack of political instinct' in helping him unwittingly to the top he regarded as adequate proof of their decadence. For the Papens and Neuraths and upper-echelon civil servants he reserved his deepest contempt. His favourites were the new Burnhamites – men like Todt and Speer (whom he even forgave his patrician family background). Organizer, technological expert and manager of industrial enterprises on a gigantic scale, Speer was a characteristic product of the Hitler State. It is significant that Speer found his fulfilment not only in working for that state and its master, but also in the attempt to salvage something of its material substance in defiance of Hitler's orders. But while men like Speer provided the continuity across the defeat and the early years of the Federal Republic, their attitude of 'non-political' expertise has become something of an irrelevance in present-day Germany and, what is more, seems to be felt as such.

A sinister ambiguity besets the evaluation of Hitler's revolution. What he did not know was that it would survive him, that its fullest consequences would become manifest after the war for which he instigated it was lost, in the Federal Republic that came into being in 1948. For among the few advantages which the new state had, compared with the position in 1918, was its relative freedom from the restraints of social anachronism, and its openness towards the hazards and liberties of a modern society. National Socialism was wholly incapable of creating any kind of acceptable social form. What it did create were the conditions of social mobility and equality in which such forms could come into being. Perhaps what is at work here is that dreadful 'ruse of reason' of which Hegel speaks. In such an interpretation the claims of Hitler's propaganda would at last be seen to coincide with the results achieved. Again we notice the three steps – truth, lie, truth. Major social changes, undertaken ostensibly on behalf of a national community, but actually on behalf of a single man of overweening ambitions who succeeds in uniting that community behind him, turn out in the long run to benefit that community in its progress toward enlightenment and political consciousness. This is an interpretation which a contemporary of Hitler's rule must put forward tentatively and in a spirit of sadness. It implies no revaluation of the past. Even if this view of the consequences of National Socialism is not too far from the truth, it goes without saying that these consequences correspond in no way to Hitler's intentions as far as we can make them out. To any positive issue of the process he set in train Hitler contributed nothing. The evil and the terror and the sufferings of millions of victims remain unchanged, unredeemed. The purchase, on any reckoning, was too dear.

20 The Front-line Soldier

The state of permanent though controlled institutional chaos, the fluidity of social status, the mobility of power and the controlled arbitrariness of its exercise – all these were not part of an abstract ideology but the conditions which best suited Hitler's personal rule and 'artistic' temperament. Once in power, he quickly became bored and exasperated by the daily routine of government, confining his personal interventions to speech-making and to apparently sudden, sensational decisions (which were in fact preceded by lengthy periods of vacillation and doubt), leaving the administration in the hands of an ever-diminishing group of ministers and party henchmen. But even then his delegation of powers was never definitive, no area of the life of the nation ever safe from his interference. Any decision in matters of personnel or law or administrative detail which impinged on 'ideology', or rather on his will, could be reversed at any time and without explanation. This form of rule by spheres of indefinite competence enabled him to disown decisions which led to temporary failures, such as the Austrian coup that ended in the murder of Dollfuss (25 July 1934) or the mobilization against Czechoslovakia in May 1938. More important, it helped to create and keep alive the image of a Leader who was on the side of the people and against the bureaucracy – and at this point one realizes that propaganda and ideology have caught up with arbitrary practice.

When in September 1939 he 'donned the old grey tunic' of the *Wehrmacht*, proclaiming that he would 'only take it off in victory or death', he moved the seat of government to his secret headquarters, and now his energies were concentrated on the conduct of the war with a single-mindedness which few could have expected, and which belied the desultoriness of his days at the Chancellery. Now details connected with the security of the regime and personnel questions tended to be intercepted by the increasingly powerful Bormann, whereas Hitler's attention was devoted to strategy and armaments. His technical expertise surprised the more conventional and conservative among his generals, some of whom continued to think of him as 'that Bohemian corporal' (as Hindenburg, whose judgement of men was deplorable, had called him).

Certainly Hitler's knowledge of the technology of war remained as superficial as the rest of his intellectual equipment. Just as his knowledge of history consisted in 'retaining the essential and discarding the inessential' and was designed to overwhelm his audience with obvious but often telling parallels and analogies, so his technology tended to be confined to reeling off facts and figures and impressive records, and no expert from the armed forces or the armament industry was ever allowed to call his bluff. Yet here again, he gave the impression, and not only to the man in the street, that it was possible to cut through the sinister complexities of modern science and make it subservient to concrete, visible ends. More than that: in his ready talk about the cubic capacities of engines and muzzle velocities and the relative merits of different types of bombs he is using the 'authentic' smalltalk of our civilization, of the hobby enthusiast who on a Sunday afternoon potters about with the bits-and-pieces of his car, without really knowing what makes it go.

Had war always been his ultimate purpose? Just as it was patently the purpose to which the regime's economic policy was geared, just as it was the not so distant prospect which secured him first the tacit approval and then the active co-operation of the *Wehrmacht* command, so it was the solution to the many internal contradictions and administrative half-measures in which the regime had become enmeshed in the six years of 'peace-time' administration. He knew his German history. On at least three previous occasions – 1813, 1870, 1914 – war had been used to establish and strengthen the bonds of German nationhood. This time it would be used to strengthen the bond of complicity.

War, in the mythology of National Socialism, represents the consummation of all the manly virtues, it is the area of 'authentic experience', in which the *Yes or No* mentality is given free rein, the true proving ground of men and nations. It sometimes looks as though, in evaluating it in these terms, Hitler is thinking of war as the end-purpose of his policies. Before considering that question, however, it may be relevant to ask what his own experience of it, his *Fronterlebnis* was really like.

In describing his war service, Hitler's biographers have had to rely on his own account in *Mein Kampf*, on his speeches, and on one or two regimental reports. Bullock presents him as a soldier who 'regarded the comradeship, discipline and excitement of life at the Front as vastly more attractive than the obscurity, aimlessness and dull placidity of peace'. For the rest, Bullock accepts Rudolf Olden's and Konrad Heiden's accounts, adding that Hitler 'took the war seriously, feeling personally responsible for what happened and identifying himself with the failure or success of German arms. These were not endearing qualities, but they do not detract from Hitler's good record as a soldier, at least as brave as the next man and a good deal more conscientious'. The recent publication of several long letters to his Munich landlord and acquaintances enables us to revise this portrait.

Hitler had avoided conscription into the Austro–Hungarian Army in 1908. In January 1914 he was escorted by the Bavarian criminal police to the Austrian Consul in Munich, in whose presence he wrote a lengthy apology for his failure to comply with the earlier calling-up orders. On 5 February 1914 he presented himself in Salzburg for a medical examination, in the course of which he was declared to be 'unfit for military

service' and 'too weak to bear arms', yet six months later, on
16 August 1914, in Munich, he was pronounced fit and joined
the 16th Bavarian Volunteer Regiment (*Regiment List*). Two
months later, on 20 October, he moved into the front-line in
Flanders. Almost immediately his regiment sustained very
heavy losses. On 2 December he and a handful of surviving
NCOs were awarded the Iron Cross Second Class ('it was the
happiest day of my life' he writes in one of his letters). This
ended the only period when he served as a common soldier
in the trenches. From then on to the end of the War he acted
as a regimental runner, carrying messages between Company
and Regimental Head Quarters; there is no reason for thinking
that this solitary service was any less dangerous. The letters
now published belong mainly to that first, and for Hitler most
memorable, phase of the war.

The most striking thing about these letters is their wholly
impersonal nature. They take no issue with the personalities of
their recipients, but they also give no indication of the individual reactions of their writer. In every detail and down to the
choice of verbal forms and syntax, they read like the reports of
the enthusiastic chauvinistic journalists of the time, like the
sort of blood-thirsty, cliché-ridden reports which Karl Kraus
incorporated in the macabre scenes of his gigantic drama, *The
Last Days of Mankind* (1922). Hitler's letters contain a few
solecisms and misspellings, but there is nothing in the least
illiterate about them. They reproduce exactly the inhuman
jargon of the 'popular' as well as the 'serious' German and
Austrian press of the First World War.

The journey of the regiment through Lille, its marches
through the mud of Flanders, its advances, attacks, entrench-
ment near Messines and eventual withdrawal are all described
in the hectic yet dead language of a writer who seems to have
no private feelings but is experiencing events through the
prefabricated medium of the public convention. Use of the
first person is largely confined to accounts of heroic acts ('at last
I was proposed for the Iron Cross', repeated several times; 'I

became a Corporal'; 'I am far ahead in front'). Everywhere else the descriptions are couched in plurals and awkward passive modes ('During the day . . . the immense military apparatus which imprints its stamp on the whole of Lille was being admired [by us]'). Strings of tired onomatopoeic verbs, reproducing the noise of shells, are added for dramatic effect, and repeated almost verbatim eight years later in *Mein Kampf*. Words have stereotype value-judgements built into them: '*Kerle*' for the Germans, '*Burschen*' for the enemy, whose position is like 'an ant-heap from which the fellows come oozing out'. Worn-out metaphors and images abound (the enemy 'leads us a dance', we reply with 'an iron greeting', 'like a giant serpent our column wound its way forward', 'neither devil nor death will get us to move out of here', 'I can say that each day I have staked my life and looked death in the eye'). Individual reactions are collectivized ('a thrill goes through the veins of each of us', 'none of us has any fear'). There is 'jubila- tion' when the next attack on the English is announced, and regret when they fail to launch a counter-attack. Fatigue and exhaustion (though not fear) are acknowledged, but again only through the medium of impersonal forms ('one becomes quite numb because of this eternal fighting'). All the documents we have are couched in this language.

There is no doubt that Hitler's war service was supremely exacting. If we bear in mind that the man who in February 1914 had failed to pass his medical test endured four-and-a- half years of some of the heaviest fighting in some of the most gruelling conditions the world has ever known, including both battles of Ypres, the battles on the Somme and Marne, in the Artois and in Champagne, was twice wounded, and three times decorated for bravery, we can see that his endlessly repeated claim to have shared to the full the life of the front-line soldier, and by the same token to be the spokesman of his generation, was no idle boast. My observations on the language of his letters are not intended to belittle this achievement. Obviously, their diction is as cliché-ridden and insensitive as the style of

almost any of his later utterances. Nor is it the violence of his
formulations that makes them so repellent; Frederick the
Great, the one man whom Hitler admired unreservedly, also
wrote letters full of invective and blood-curdling metaphors,
without at the same time floundering in bathos and prefabricated images and sentiments. The remarkable thing about this
embattled, impersonal language is that it seems designed to
remove the writer from the scene of the action and place him
in the cliché world of press propaganda. It seems, as far
as the evidence of these letters goes, that war could only be
endured at the cost of such an abstracting away from its
reality.

Perhaps this defection from the living experience of war
resolves the contradiction (frequently found in Hitler's biographies) between the heroism of those years of *service*, unthinkable without a concern beyond the self, and the extreme
egotism and self-regarding concern of his later career, in which
no single act, not even the training of a dog, was ever undertaken for its own or another's sake. Shock and insensateness,
it may well be, were the price of his heroism; and if that is so,
then the war-like experience he continued to vaunt to the end
of his life turns out to be precisely that which he had not
experienced to the full. But though he misrepresented its
character, he did not exaggerate the importance of that defective experience: he is the spokesman of a shell-shocked generation. The violent nervous tremors which affected him at various
periods during his life (after the coup of 1923, after June 1934,
and during the Second World War) have clearly a traumatic
origin of this kind; though here again I doubt whether his
mental condition was ever radically different from what counted
as sanity in his time.

Something of this defective experience is intimated by the
persona of the writer of these war-time letters. They have in a
sense no language of their own. Like Hitler's historicism, they
are modelled on the official German school essay (*der Sedanauf-
satz*) with its warlike topics and its notorious tendency toward

abstraction, impersonality, and dead metaphors; and this too is the staple of contemporary journalese, which Hitler imitates and unwittingly parodies. So much so that his prose reads less like an unliterary soldier's than a newspaper addict's; or rather, like the prose of a Nobody whose experiential horizon is hedged in by walls of newsprint. The letters express the 'popular' opinions of the age in the exact manner in which the gutter press of all Western countries expresses – that is, represents *and* fashions – the opinions of its readers. They are anything but articulate. Their language is not the language of the simple people who, in Germany and everywhere in Europe, suffered the horrors of war like lambs going to the slaughter, writing down their agony in words that move us by their immediacy and helplessness. (These people, too, Karl Kraus commemorates in his drama.)

Is it possible that behind the embattled clichés were those qualities – awareness and imagination, steadiness of altruistic purpose and capacity for self-sacrifice on behalf of another – which we think necessary for heroism? That they froze in him under the impact of war? Language is not an infallible guide, a man *is* free to pit himself against the convention that determines his mode of writing; but the signs of these qualities are absent. He is as solitary in the dugout as he was on the Viennese building site. He has escaped death so often that his comrades have come to think him invulnerable, and the feeling of having a charmed life will be with him to the end. He tells us he read a lot of Schopenhauer, and that the trenches were his university. Perhaps. What we do know is that, as in the men's hostels in Vienna, as in the Munich lodgings, so in the trenches too he held forth, passionately, heedlessly, endlessly: on the German war aims and conduct of war, on the perfidy of the Allies and, after five months of sick leave and with the reserve battalion in Munich, on the degeneracy of the hinterland. Was he even then staking his life on a future career as a national politician? He earned three major decorations – for the highest, the Iron Cross First Class (August 1918), he was recommended by the

Jewish regimental adjutant – and his comrades poked fun at him for being so 'keen': was he investing experience in war in anticipation of future profits?

The war experience provides him with a pattern and legitimization of the demands he will make on his followers and, eventually, on the German nation. This is the one period of his life when he subordinates himself to a collective and contributes to its working, yet serving as a dispatch runner, he remains something of the lone wolf of the Viennese casual wards. His physical health seems to have improved greatly. Though some early war-time photographs show him with the cadaverous looks of the pre-war years, on others he appears well-fed and has a rounded face. He may not be popular, but he is accepted in his function and given the recognition of status within a social hierarchy. The complex of warlike emotions allows for and indeed encourages the exertion of the self *via* hatred and resentment, and this is the pattern he will eventually choose for his politics too. The courage that is expected of him requires improvisation rather than staying power, and quick rather than responsible decisions, and this again fits his character. But, most important of all, there is *an acceptable other*: there is the concept of a national collective, 'the Fatherland', bearer of the highest and wholly uncontested evaluation, the object of his patriotism. The patriotic emotion doesn't usually play a very important part in the outlook of private soldiers in the field (with the scarlet majors at the base it is a different story). Hitler will fully recognize this, and in his numerous affectionate references to '*das arme Frontschwein*' he will be realistic enough to appeal to the common soldier's sense of duty rather than to his patriotic fervour. In his own military service, however, he clearly goes beyond the call of duty. Germany is for him a brand-new fatherland, an escape from a hopeless past, a land that knows nothing of his humiliations, a fresh start. From being the object of his patriotism, it will eventually come to be usurped by the self and identified with it, so that the self, at the summit of its power, in turn becomes the bearer of that highest and wholly uncontested evaluation. . . .

He was never offered a commission, yet it seems he was on better terms with some of his officers than with his fellow soldiers, precisely because he was 'keen' and apt to assume their patriotic and professional point of view. In his stylization of the war experience in *Mein Kampf* Hitler assures us that while the fighting went on he deliberately refrained from all political discussions; one is more inclined to believe a comrade who knew him in the trenches and writes that 'he went on and on, philosophizing in the primitive way the little man does, on all sorts of political and *weltanschaulich* questions'. As early as February 1917, on his return from extended sick leave, he began haranguing his audiences with long monologues on those themes which, after the War, were transformed into the 'stab in the back' legend. We have more than one description of life in the German trenches to show the sort of talk that went on there (and that goes on in the sergeants' messes of the Bundeswehr today). Here the young Lieutenant Ernst Jünger, in charge of a platoon of storm troopers in some of the same areas where Hitler acted as regimental runner, describes the men under his command as they engage in 'endless discussions about the war':

> They will never find the solution, for even the way they put their questions is wrong. They take the war to be, not an expression but a cause, and in this way they are hoping to find outside what is only to be found within. However, one must understand them. They are materialists through and through, and I, who have lived among them for years, hear this in every word they say. They are really material, the material which, without their knowing it, the Idea is consuming in order to reach its great aims.

Did Hitler share Jünger's contempt (he does not openly express it until thirty years later, in the *Table Talk*), and was he even then determined to be anything rather than 'material'? Was he becoming aware of his rhetorical talent, his gift for

simplification? We don't know. All we know is that the only
political passage Hitler's war-time letters contain could have
been written or spoken by him at any time in the next thirty
years. It comes from a twelve-page letter to a Munich acquain-
tance, a young lawyer, and is dated 15 February 1915. Its
syntax is rough and its spelling occasionally uncertain, and it
ends with one of those 'Austrian' phrases which are so very
different from the 'German greeting' Hitler used in later years.
But its central image, of politics as a 'reckoning' (the title of the
first volume of *Mein Kampf*) and as an act of gory revenge,
strikes a note unmistakably his own:

> . . . I think of Munich so often, and each of us has only the
> one wish, that it should soon come to a final reckoning with
> this gang, to an attack at all cost, and that those of us who will
> possess the happiness of seeing the homeland again will find
> it purer and more purified of foreignness, that through the
> sacrifices and suffering which many hundreds of thousands of
> us are daily undergoing that through the river of blood which
> here flows day by day against an international world of enemies,
> not only Germany's external enemies will be shattered, but
> our inner internationalism too will break. This would be more
> valuable than any territorial gain. Austria's fate will be what
> I have always predicted. While expressing to you once again
> my sincere thanks, I remain, with a humble handkiss to your
> honoured mother and wife,
>   Your very devoted and grateful
>   Adolf Hitler.

21 'A new life was born'

But it was not only his own note. There is interesting independent evidence to show to what extent this was the language and mode of experience adopted by a whole generation.

In the early part of June 1934 an American sociologist called Theodore Abel arrived in Germany and announced a prize contest 'for the best personal life history of an adherent of the Hitler movement', asking 'contestants . . . to give accurate and detailed descriptions of their personal lives, particularly after the [First] World War', and of the circumstances that led to their becoming active members of 'the Movement'. The announcement was posted at all local party headquarters and published in the party press. It mentioned that the contest was held under the auspices of the sociology department of Columbia University, and that its purpose was 'the collection of material on the history of National Socialism, so that the American public may be informed about it on the basis of factual, personal documents'; the closing date was September 1934. Some 680 manuscripts were sent in, and these were used as the basis of a book, *Why Hitler Came into Power*, published some four years later, which contains extracts from about a fifth of the total number submitted, and six life histories, complete and unabridged. The Party at that time had between one and two million members, in the Reichstag election it had polled over seventeen million votes. In other words, the essays were written in the months prior to, or at any rate at the beginning of, the mass growth of membership which followed once the Party had established itself in power – a prospect, inciden-

tally, which some of the writers were viewing with distrust
and anxiety about their own future position.

The 'fictitious average type of follower' that emerges from
the information supplied by the essays is described by the
author as follows:

> He is a town resident of lower middle-class origin, without high
> school education; married and Protestant; [he] participated in
> the World War but not in the military activities during the
> revolution of 1918 or later outbreaks; had no political affilia-
> tions before joining the NSDAP and belonged to no veteran
> or semi-military organizations . . . He was strongly dissatisfied
> with the republican regime in Germany, but had no specific
> anti-Semitic bias. His economic status was secure, for not
> once did he have to change his occupation, job, or residence,
> nor was he ever unemployed.

I quote these conclusions for what they are worth. These
inferences in respect of 'average types', drawn from the statis-
tical evidence, are the least illuminating part of Abel's argument; nor is it the historical narrative they are made to support
that gives the book its unique importance, but the raw material
itself, that is, the verbatim quotations of excerpts from the
essays submitted as well as the six life histories reprinted in full.

Before looking at this material, however, it might seem
appropriate to question the reliability of these 'biograms'. This
worried the author, for he finds it necessary to defend the
contestants in various ways against possible charges of distor-
tion, omission of important facts and the like. Such charges are
likely to be more justified than the author is willing to admit.
It is, for instance, worth noting that only a single mystifying
entry, by an SS man, refers to the 'Night of the Long Knives'
of 30 June 1934, which took place while the contestants were
actually writing their essays: 'A world was extinguished in me
when on that day guns were put into my hands and those of
my comrades. And a new world came into existence; a new life
was born'; yet all the contributors were active members of the
Party, and most of them belonged to the SA itself. Nevertheless,

the question of factual reliability is not really at issue. To
gauge the full significance of these apparently authentic autobiographical accounts it is essential to treat them not as a
repository of social facts but as texts; that is, as stylizations
within a certain linguistic medium, delimited by certain social
restraints. In looking at them in this way we are at a slight dis-
advantage, for we have only the author's English versions to
go by. Even so, seeing that the main effects that emerge have
the *finesse* of a *Reichsarbeitsdienst* shovel, we can be quite
certain that enough of the original survives in the translations
The answers to the question of what caused these men to join
the Party (the forty-eight essays submitted by women are not
included) do not materially differ from those given in countless
similar discussions, both friendly and hostile to the NSDAP.
More important because not available elsewhere are the
answers to the rather different question of what the writers of
these six hundred odd essays consider to be their appropriate
response and self-understanding in their roles as active and
self-consciously representative party members: how they see
themselves and how they want to be seen. The value of these
essays, then, to one side of their factual content, lies in their
nature as informal – though, as we shall see, not very informal
– propaganda. Understanding them in this way enables us to
ignore the intractable question of sincerity and personal truth-
fulness; the avowal of these and other virtues will fall into
place as a component of the roles enacted in these essays.

This is how the writers wish to be seen – but seen by whom?
The fact that their expectation is directed towards a foreign,
American, public is of course likely to influence their texts,
but in what direction? Our author remarks more than once
on the fact that relatively few writers – 60% – mention anti-
Semitism among their reasons for joining, and that several of
them – 4% – are even critical of it. These figures might be
thought to challenge the accepted view that anti-Semitism in
the early 'twenties at all events constituted a major part of the
Movement's appeal. What they certainly indicate is the desire

of at least a sizeable minority of writers to concentrate on a set of 'positive' motives, motives which they hope will be acceptable to a non-German audience; and again, what is significant are the 'positive' affirmations of the total personality picture they wish to convey. To speak, as Abel does, of 'the willingness of most people I encountered to discuss their political experiences' is something of an understatement. The prevalence of self-absorption and articulated introspection has been one of the characteristic traits of German society at all levels throughout the last two centuries. This, together with the peculiarly exasperating (as some may feel it) insistence on 'frankness' and 'sincerity' implies a relatively undeveloped capacity for *conscious* role-acting and dissimulation. (We recall Nietzsche's discovery that the great deceiver is himself the first to be deceived.) And this in turn means that, although these 'confessions' undoubtedly contain factual lies and omissions, they are unlikely to be deliberately stylized for the sake of a foreign audience. Looking over the writer's shoulder is the local party boss, who may wish to vet the essay before it is sent off; but apart from that the implicit audience envisaged is likely to be the placable self.

The untruthful apologias of ex-Nazis published in recent years must not obscure the fact that most of these men joined the Party when it was no more violent and no more lawless than its opponents the Communists; when to wear a swastika could endanger a man's life. (The fact that violence was not central to the Communist programme, as it was to National Socialism, is not likely to have made much difference to its victims.) These essays, then, are written by victors, men who are conscious of having won a fight, often in the literal sense of the word, and who do not think it odd that political 'battles' should be fought with truncheons, teargas and paper-bombs, and pistols. What they will want to keep dark is only their worst crimes, not their habitual lawlessness.

Victors they may be, yet they are anything but free men.

Although they come from all social strata and their occupations cover the whole spectrum of German society, the experiences they convey follow a simple pattern. Bewilderment and despair follow the defeat of 1918,

> Heroism had become cowardice, truth a lie, loyalty was rewarded by dastardliness. Shame reddened our cheeks and anger constricted our throats.

and the authentic experience of trench warfare is endlessly recalled:

> [The war] had taught us one lesson, the great community of the front. All class differences, staunchly entrenched before the war, disappeared under its spell. Out there it was what a person *was*, not what he seemed, that counted.

Now the questions about 'the meaning of life' demand answers with great urgency:

> 'I was a broken man, on the point of losing himself, who could no longer find God.' 'I tried various ways of finding manliness and manly action. Many circles were open to me, but I found nothing but disappointment everywhere.' '. . . though I had fallen under the spell of communistic-democratic ideas, some inner conflict, as well as certain practical considerations, prevented me from engaging in active work on behalf of Bolshevism.'

Economic circumstances are mentioned, but mostly in broad outlines rather than in their personal effects,

> 'Hunger was the daily companion of the German workingman. Added to this was the artificial whip of scarcity, wielded by the Jews.' '. . . the middle class, which still had some funds, and which had steadily opposed Marxism, without actually combating it, was completely wiped out.'

though in this context occur the only scenes in which actual human beings, rather than stereotypes, are evoked:

> All of us – parents and children – slept in one room. I saw what

happened with wakeful eyes. Others did not see that. I saw –
in my mind's eyes still see – my father standing at the window,
breathing on the frost of the window-panes. Those were cold
winters that made one's hands freeze. Buildings were un-
touched and there were no earnings. There was no unemployment relief then. I remember how, at the birth of my youngest
brother, my mother was given salt herring and potatoes to eat
right after her confinement.

For the rest, there is not a human note, a humorous aside or an
irrelevant episode in any of these testimonies, and any experience of privation is no sooner recounted than it is converted
into an abstract political generalization:

I moved to Schoenbeck, where unemployment forced me on
the dole. On these beggarly alms my wife and I managed to
subsist until 1927. From that time until 1929 I made a living
as a pedlar. When we consider that on the one hand the policies
of the Red government, particularly the inflation and taxes,
deprived me of all means of livelihood, while on the other
hand we soldiers of the front line were being ruled by a gang
of exploiters ready to stoop to any means to seize the starvation
wages of our suffering, duped comrades, it will become clear
why a number of us welcomed the activities of patriotic groups,
particularly those of the Hitler movement.

The unholy alliance of Marxism, Jews and 'the Government' is
blamed for the economic and spiritual ruin of thè country. In
this wholesale attack, 'the Government' becomes a hyposta-
tized entity like Fate or the gods, and it is charged with responsibility for the fate of men who have abdicated from rational
choices and who pride themselves on having 'no idea of politics
and forms of government':

We did not bother with politics; the subject was completely
strange to us. I saw only the flaming enthusiasm . . . [My
mother] never evaluated the Fatherland according to its social,
political or civil institutions; to her the Germany she knew
was the highest as it stood. Thus naturally a seed was sown in
our childish hearts that was to grow into a pure love for our
native land.

All the same, a number of writers seem to know enough about 'politics' to inveigh against the 'un-German class system' and to regard it as a Marxist invention; whereas what draws them to the NSDAP is its promise to heal the divisions within the nation:

The middle class had the fate of the people on its conscience. Members of this class made possible the November revolution with its devastating consequences . . . I, as a nationalist, had dared to reproach others with class arrogance. It is through this experience that I know how deeply rooted class arrogance is in the German people. . . . Now things would come right, I thought and felt, for now the mason and the scholar marched side by side and there were no more distinctions.

They may be 'non-political', but like Hitler himself they know how to exploit the main characteristic of German political life: the dominance of national fears over all social considerations, where 'the Nation', now called *Volksgemeinschaft*, is propagated and experienced as the shrine of 'private' values.

Soon hopelessness changes to hope as father, brother, or friend brings glad tidings of the Party and its leader,

'How different from this was the daring proposition that sprang from Hitler's warm, sympathetic heart!' 'The desire for a leader was evident in every political manifestation of East Prussians.' 'Around 1923 I reached the conclusion that no party, but a single man alone could save Germany: "We eagerly await the coming of the man whose strong hands may restore order".' 'These ideas were for me the fulfilment of an inner longing for clarity, and I realized for the first time how easy it was to act according to National Socialist ideas.'

though the message may still be rejected, the Old Adam may still be struggling,

'It was almost impossible to find one's way in the Hell's Kitchen of Contradictory Opinions.' 'Little by little the teachings of National Socialism were taking root in the people. But experience had made me sceptical, and I would not be immediately convinced.' 'I asked myself the question, "What is the meaning of life, anyhow? Was it the will of a higher order to leave to the Jews the domination of the world?" . . . I was struck by the thought, had not the Jewish people purposely been put into the world by our maker in order to force the other nations to battle so that they should be ennobled and perfected by this battle?'

until something 'dramatic' happens, usually a meeting addressed by Hitler himself:

> 'His never-to-be-forgotten words affected me as the words of a prophet.' 'The experience was a revelation to us, and we should have rushed blindly anywhere Hitler commanded us to go. The sun shone all the time he was there, in proverbial "Hitler weather". Before his arrival and after he left, it rained so hard we were drenched.' 'When the Führer administered our oath . . . we felt that all our sacrifices had been amply rewarded by this experience.'

It is the experience of the bewildered self, as it is taken up and reassured and given a voice in the embattled, assertive representation of one who 'speaks for us all':

> The fact is, Hitler looks every man in the eye. His looks wander from one trooper to the other as the S.A. marches by. We, oldtime National Socialists, did not join the S.A. for reasons of self-interest. Our feelings led us to Hitler. There was a tremendous surge in our hearts, a something that said: 'Hitler, you are our man. You speak as a soldier of the front and as a man; you know the grind, you have yourself been a working man. You have lain in the mud, even as we – no big shot, but an unknown soldier. You have given your whole being, all your warm heart, to German manhood, for the wellbeing of Germany rather than your personal advancement or self-seeking. For your innermost being will not let you do otherwise.'

Deep and sustained study precedes this moment of illumination:

'Through enlightening books I found confirmation of the fact that in Germany everything in politics and economics at that time depended on the Jews.' 'And then I studied the history of our people. . . . As a result of the lessons of history and my experiences both during and after the war, I became a nationalist.' After the assassination of Walther Rathenau: 'I read a great deal, and it became increasingly clear to me that international Marxism and the Jewish problem are closely bound together.' 'On our discussion evenings we occupied ourselves almost exclusively with the Old Testament, the Talmud, and the *Shulchan Aruch* . . . we were going to the root of the matter. We studied it more and more, and came to see what was necessary.'

and is eventually rewarded by the discovery of a durable, indestructible 'philosophy of life':

'One of my employers . . put his extensive library at my disposal. After two years I had with its aid formed my own opinion of life.' 'On my own initiative I was able to supplement . . . the philosophy of life with which my father had sent me on my way.' 'The philosophy of the movement endowed my hitherto aimless life with a meaning and a purpose.' 'In Nietzsche I discovered a bit of my primal self.'

At the same time, supreme value is ascribed to 'natural' and 'instinctive' motives of action, for the image delineated here is that of a man who, having read 'deeply' and pondered all alternatives 'deeply', leaves it all behind and, guided only by his instinct, makes his leap into the Führer's arms:

'In every instance [our] standpoint was based on feelings conditioned by blood and race. . . . I only want to assert that National Socialism was not *learned* by us old party members, but merely sprang from our instincts. Thus it was a matter of course that the opinion of the Leader was always inherently our own before the leader made it public. . . .'
'These first members grasped National Socialism not with their mind but their emotions. They had not learned National Socialism from books. Their blood, their natural instincts, drove them to the movement.'

Now at last all is light –

> 'My belief is that our Leader, Adolf Hitler, was given by fate
> to the German nation as our saviour, bringing light into dark-
> ness.'

though not sweetness, for the struggle 'for the soul of Germany'
is only just beginning.

The pseudo-religious character of this entire pattern is self-
evident. While its stages correspond, often down to verbal
details, to autobiographical and doctrinal passages in *Mein
Kampf* (the book which, numerous German writers have
argued, nobody had ever read . . .), the overall scheme of these
life stories is an *imitatio* of the Führer's life.

But, it may be objected, given the initial question of the
contest, how could the pattern of these pleas and apologias and
assertions be anything other than predictable? It is the paucity
of variations within the pattern and its all-encompassing
character which are so astonishing, which show up the efficacy
of indoctrination and give concrete meaning to the notion of
Gleichschaltung. The whole world is seen, or at least presented,
through this stereotype:

> 'My mother was a worthy, honest German housewife. She
> met all experiences of life with unfailing piety and faith in
> God.' 'My mother's eyes could see through all the false phrases
> and always looked straight into my heart. And those eyes could
> not be confused by Marxist theories.' 'The German mother
> and wife fought side by side with her husband in this struggle
> against an overwhelming fate.' 'Then the longing for a wife
> began, with the thought of carrying a boy in my arms.'

The set of anti-Jewish attitudes that belongs to this 'philosophy
of life' need not be illustrated, though in view of subsequent
attempts to give German anti-Semitism a 'religious' explanation it should be noted that only one writer bases his argument
on traditional Christian grounds:

'My inward aversion to these men of a foreign race which had crucified the Saviour and which now was betraying our people increased until one day it grew into hatred. The Jew was at fault for all the misery.'

It should be obvious by now that each element in the pattern of these life-stories is identical with its counterpart in the structure of National Socialist mythology as I have attempted to present it in the course of this book. And this is true above all in respect of that pseudo-religious appeal I have mentioned, and of the way *that* is reinforced, in every single case, by the idea of 'sacrifice': each writer 'sacrificing' himself for the common good of the Party, or of the Nation, for the Führer who in turn sacrifices himself for his *Volksgenossen*; everybody is ready to die for everybody else; the party and its programme are authenticated by promises not of benefits (in the shape of bigger and better Jewish properties) but of more and more sacrifices; all of Germany's history is nothing but continuous '*Opfer*', her future is assured as long as enough people are ready to carry on this 'sacrificial' tradition, and so on. . . . Perhaps this monotonous invocation is not really surprising. The idea of 'sacrifice' may be primitive enough (the point doesn't need arguing that there is nothing wrong with sacrifice and almost everything wrong with vaunting it); but as an all-purpose instrument of emotional blackmail, material extortion, and spiritual-religiose validation it cannot be improved on.

Reading these life-stories a generation after they were written, one is overwhelmed by their lifelessness. The authors themselves, the persons they describe, all move in a strange, jerky manner: from attitude to attitude, from doubt to conversion to commitment, from suspicion and hostility to enthusiasm and adoration, or again from dislike to loathing to rejection – like clockwork figures in brown or black shirts and peaked caps, or like marionettes, their strings pulled by some 'higher' power. We have observed this jerkiness in Hitler's wartime letters; we find it in those few 'personal' passages in

Mein Kampf which are not given over to direct political propaganda, and it is there again, recorded for a last time, in the
Table Talk of the 1940s. 'All my life was nothing but endless
cajolings': the heedless, incontinent flow of talk on everything
under the sun is only one aspect of those remarkable monologues in the *Wolfsschanze* that went on and on, into the small
hours of the morning, in the company of half-awake secretaries
and cooks, terrified adjutants yearning for a smoke, and snoring
party officials. But there is also another, very different aspect
to these monologues. Every now and then Hitler sets out to
represent, not a thing or a political ruse or a technical detail
or some object of contempt, but another human being on a
level of equality, and every time the attempt is made it defeats
him. A meeting with Frau Winifred Wagner late at night in
Bayreuth; the story a waitress told him in the Café Osteria in
Munich; the clever trick he played on the divinity master at
school in Linz; how a fool of a *Gauleiter* failed to introduce him
to a pretty woman who was so much more interesting than yet
another roomful of Old Party Comrades . . .: as against his
rhetorical fluency on the political platform, the effort to convey
the simplest human episode shows up the defects of his verbal
imagination. Every attempt to evoke the scene and give the
verbal picture some colour and semblance of life collapses into
a Beckmesserish incoherence. One believes his biographers
when they say he never read a novel, let alone (like Mussolini)
wrote one. Side by side with the politician there is a ghostly
Nobody, one for whom no other person exists in his own right.

But, to return for a last time to the life-stories of his followers
and imitators, are not those clichés, cumbrous formulations and
jerky sequences merely the sort of writing one would expect
from such 'ordinary men', from men who are simply unaccustomed to putting down their thoughts on paper? One notices
that the aridness of this prose increases as one goes up the social
scale: the higher the education, the more complete the verbal
surrender, the more severe the ideological restraints on the
descriptive means. These 'stories' are quite unlike the testi-

monies of unliterary people of any other age for which similar documents are available, from the confessionary autobiographies of the seventeenth century to the workingmen's journals of the late nineteenth; present-day readers' letters in German newspapers, too, read quite differently, in Federal Germany at all events. The poverty and the clichés, the jerkiness and the lifelessness, are the hallmarks of the writing of another age.

22 Conquest and Annihilation

How is the complex of 'the Führer and the People' to be related
to the War and the practice of annihilation? In attempting to
answer this question, our enquiry must now turn to the victims.
What was the situation of the German Jews? How much of
their and their fellow victims' plight was known in the Reich?
What role did war and destruction play in Hitler's mind and
in the minds of his followers? These are our last questions, and
they are the most difficult.

Hitler's discovery of anti-Semitism as the substance of his
existential project and of his political programme is likely to
have come to him gradually, probably over a period of years.
The fact that his extant letters from the trenches contain no
anti-Semitic remarks suggests that, although undoubtedly
he had been active in racialist circles in Vienna before leaving
for Munich and had belonged to a lending library specializing
in anti-Semitic writings, the full value of 'the discovery of the
Jew' may have come to him after the War. As is to be expected,
in *Mein Kampf* it is presented as a sudden, dramatic *Erlebnis*.
At the same time Hitler discovered that *he* was *not* a Jew. The
argument that follows is much the same as that following on
his discovery of the value of his war experience. Not being a
Jew meant that he was not, after all, nothing, a Nobody, and
that his 'race' was, or could become, everything: an inward
grace and a mystical attribute, yet also a thing scientifically
grounded and a political asset – in sum, a repository of all
positive attributes, as 'the Jew' was the repository of everything
negative.

Of course, there was nothing original about the introduction of the personal phobia into politics, especially not in Vienna. Two parties – Lueger's Christian Social Party and von Schönerer's *Alldeutsche Partei* – had included anti-Semitism in their programmes, though Hitler was to criticize them both: Lueger for not being rigorous – 'scientific' – enough in applying anti-Semitic criteria to his social policy, Schönerer for using the correct criteria to inadequate ends. Hitler's originality – a kind of squaring of the circle – comes at the point where the contradiction arising from the absoluteness of the doctrine has to be faced. 'The Jew', we are told, is ubiquitous. But if we find him at his destructive, parasitic work both in high finance (in the banks and on the stock exchange) *and* in working-class organizations including the trades unions, how can he be identified as the single, unitary enemy? (Not even the Jews, one might have thought, could be both the scum and the dregs of the world.) Any reasonable argument which took into consideration the actual conflict of interests on the political scene could hardly fail to come to the obvious and far from dramatic conclusion that 'the Jew' was a myth, and that the truth about the Jews was too banal to be made much of in political terms. For the truth was that they were indeed ubiquitous, a part of every social sphere and class; that their assimilation had gone farther in Vienna and, along somewhat different lines, in Germany than in any other European country; and that, to be available as a target at all, they had to be prized away from their various social contexts by an act of re-definition and myth-making. (It was this situation that caused Karl Kraus to describe the Viennese as a cross between a Jew and a Viennese.) They were still discernible and distinct in every profession as it opened up to receive them. Yet to many intellectuals it looked as though in another generation or two 'the Jewish problem' would be superseded by complete assimilation. What was needed – for a man like Hitler on one side of the argument, for Theodor Herzl, the founder of modern Zionism, on the other – was the *creation* of a distinct Jewish image – an image

which would have to be very largely the opposite of the reality
the one wished to destroy and the other to save. It must have
the attributes of a single, unified nation where the reality was
that of an ever more dispersed group held together by no
single tie; it must be distinctly alien – hence the postulate of a
biological race – where the reality covered the entire spectrum
of possible accommodations, from the pedlars in their kaftans
to the Pringsheims and Rathenaus in their cutaways; and its
vitality must be such as to warrant the harshest 'defensive'
measures. In this image, Jewish capitalism and Jewish Marxism
cease to be contradictories, as they had been in all previous
anti-Semitic doctrines, for both are seen to possess 'a fundamental unity of attitude, means, and goal'. The attitude is the
secretiveness of a world conspiracy; the means are the liberal-
Marxist press, the entertainment industry, the legal profession,
and so forth; the goal is world domination. Now a good deal of
all this is derivative – from the *Protocols of the Elders of Zion*
(which are of course regarded as genuine), but also, indirectly,
from the young Disraeli's romantic fiction of a Jewish master-
race in charge of world politics. The unbelievably naïve product
of a powerful mythopoeic imagination is turned into a political
reality by an imagination which is interested in fictions only to
the extent that they can be grafted on to a given social situation.

'The Jew', a part of this social *donnée*, was and was not
clearly visible. You could single him out by certain well-known
physical features. But if you sometimes failed to identify him,
that didn't mean that either your 'instinct' or your 'scientific'
criteria were unreliable, only that his mimicry was getting
more perfect and his cunning was increasing day by day. From
Mein Kampf to the *Table Talk* Hitler speaks of the difficulty of
telling the Jews from the rest, and stresses the need for strict
scientific and legal criteria; the seriousness with which this
'problem' was discussed in university circles is indicative of the
level of intellectual argument in the Germany of the 'thirties.
And it is precisely this utterly humourless, deadly seriousness
of German anti-Semitism, as it develops under the impact of

the intellectual fellow travellers, which makes it unprecedented and without parallel. For it is neither the channelling of mere irrational mob feelings (as in the Russian and Polish pogroms), nor a widely-held set of convictions brought to a head and discredited by a catastrophic scandal (as in France), nor again a mere personal phobia, but a *considered* ideology with full scientific and philosophical pretensions, which serves as a basis for a political *praxis* and thus proves its appropriateness to the social and psychological situation for which it has been designed. It is formulated in *Mein Kampf* – a book, it should be remembered, written by a Nobody about a political movement which is as good as dead; yet it is presented there with all the authority and appeal of a unitary and universal explanation, of a veritable *system* of thought in an age which hankered after systems and unitary explanations. (Thus for Freud, 'scientific work' was identical with the systematic elaboration of, once again, a single insight; and the same is true of men like Weininger, Spengler, Klages and many others.)

How were they to be distinguished? The horrors of the anti-Semitic campaign in its full destructiveness make it difficult to recall the extent to which the Jews of Austria and Germany had become an apparently inseparable part of the social and cultural scene, to recall that they participated in every aspect of the life of the two nations throughout the first three decades of the century. When Karl Kraus wrote *The Last Days of Mankind* (1922), the most massive indictment of modern war ever composed, he could no more leave Jewish war-profiteers and jobbers out of his scenario than their Gentile counterparts. Kraus's relentless satire takes for its objects Jewish journalism and commercial interests in the same way as it attacks '*gemütlich*' Viennese innkeepers helping out with the executions of Serbian rebels, Prussian militarism and its alliance with big business, the troglodyte mentality of the Austrian provinces, chauvinistic priests, belligerent poets writing gory propaganda behind well-fortified desks in the Austrian War Office, spineless socialists, and debauched aristocrats – all of them aspects of the process of Imperial decomposition. This would be too obvious to need mentioning, were it not that some recent cultural fantasists have accused Kraus of preparing the way for Hitler, which is very nearly the opposite of the truth. Far from wishing to isolate 'the Jews' from his giant cast – which was Hitler's first and foremost tactical aim – Kraus on the contrary showed them to be a part of it. For were they not, *in the war Kraus portrayed*, capable of every piece of infamy, corruption and betrayal (though not of physical cruelty) that was practised by their Gentile neighbours, without having any other reasons for their conduct than those which they shared with their neighbours? It was not 'Jewish self-hate' which inspired him, but an apprehension that cast its shadow before it. But the horrors to come were such that almost any criticism of its victims must seem offensive.

How complete was that assimilation which Hitler's racial doctrine set out to undo? Were the German Jews right when, in their most euphoric moments, they claimed that they were as little different from their neighbours as is a Lutheran community from its surrounding Catholic province? Or were they like the Kashubians in Danzig, the French colony in Wilhelminian Berlin? Or were they like the Czechs in Vienna, the Slovenes in Carinthia, or again the Sudeten Germans in Prague or in Moravia?

The relationship between Germans and Jews overlapped each of these relationships yet was unlike any of them. Various views have been put forward to explain that difference. Hannah Arendt holds that what distinguished the Jews of the Western Diaspora throughout the nineteenth and twentieth centuries was their accumulation of wealth without corresponding political power and social responsibility, and she sees twentieth-century Jewry as heir to this apparently enviable but in reality defenceless situation. Yet clearly something other than conspicuous wealth and political apathy – which anyway were shared by many German bankers and industrialists – must have caused the first virulent outbursts of German anti-Semitism, which began with the murder of Rosa Luxemburg and Kurt Eisner and reached their climax in the murder of Walther Rathenau. The lunatic fringe of the German New Left on the other hand accuses the Jews of responsibility for the Hitler regime because they were in cahoots with the Ruhr industrialists and big capital. Then there are the various religious explanations. The motive of Jewish guilt for the crucifixion of Christ may have been effective in the Catholic South, but significantly it doesn't seem to have been exploited by the party propagandists; and it is not even mentioned in one of the most thoughtful examinations of the whole problem, Sartre's *Portrait of the Anti-Semite* (1948). Yet this ancient accusation obviously plays some part in the pseudo-religious propaganda to which I referred at length, for as the belief in Christ dies, so the anti-Semitism that had once its roots in that belief burgeons into a new 'religion' of hate. Finally, the anomalous situation of the Jews is explained by reference to their being a people with a national God: they are unique because their national and religious identities are inseparable, and this – the old Covenant – is the reason for Gentile hatred and envy. Leaving to one side the objection that in recent times this form of divine election has not often been ascribed to them, it is not clear why the possession of a national religion should not on the contrary be a source of admiration and a special kind of sympathy. And when we recall that this is precisely what many Calvinist communities have felt toward the Jews, we must conclude that the reason for their odd place among the nations must lie elsewhere. What makes all these views unsatisfactory, or only partly satisfactory, is that they offer to explain the position of 'the Jews' as though their history, and therefore the causes of their anomalous situation, were the same, or 'essentially' the same, throughout the Western Diaspora. They are not. In one way or another, in Israel and in the Diaspora, their common fate in the modern world recedes behind the fate of each group as it develops or is stunted in its growth within the protective or hostile penumbra of its 'host nation'. And what the members of these various groups have in common first and foremost is that other men look on them as Jews and ascribe to them the qualities of Jews.

What then gives the German–Jewish relationship its distinct quality? Why are they traditionally regarded as Germanizers by both the French and the Poles or Czechs alike? What do we mean by saying that the relationship is uniquely close? Why, to give one example from among tens of thousands, does Rosa Luxemburg – born Polish speaking, at home in Russia, educated at a Swiss university - identify herself with the German language and German culture? Why does she *choose* to become a German intellectual?

Each of the minorities I mentioned has behind it something it can fall back on, a distinct culture or language or ritual which will continue in existence even after individual members of the minority group have chosen to opt out. The situation into which the Jews eagerly entered was altogether different. They were made welcome in German culture and society by some of its most articulate spokesmen. They accepted its language, and came to venerate it with great fervour and explicitness. But in so doing they had to comply with the most exacting conditions their well-meaning hosts could impose. They renounced, often within the time-span of a single generation, all that had previously characterized them: a ritual and a community, a language and a culture. But as they did so, these things ceased to exist, or at least ceased to be available to them. The relationship became uniquely close because it left them with no alternative – both individually and collectively theirs was a journey without return. The 'emancipation' of the German Jews was a child of the Enlightenment, of the German Enlightenment. On its altar their ancient faith was sacrificed, and their traditional ways became a matter of embarrassment to them and to their friends. It was the secularizing spirit of enlightened tolerance which opened German society and culture to them;

and it was the intolerance of tolerance which caused them to abandon all religious and national cohesion, and thus rendered them defenceless in their hour of need. The history of Western thought knows no crueller irony.

'The love-affair of the Jews with the Germans has on the whole remained one-sided and unrequited', Gershom Scholem has observed mildly. There has been some gratitude (he continues), but no love. And it is certainly true that no German author has written such a generously perceptive portrait of a Jew as did Charles Péguy in his obituary of the socialist-anarchist Bernard Lazares. No German work of art celebrates Jewish spiritual ardour as does Rembrandt's 'The Jewish Bride', the supreme humanity of which derives from the fact that one cannot tell whether or not the bridegroom too is Jewish. The characteristically German tributes come in the idealizations of Lessing, the idylls of Johann Peter Hebel, or again in the writings of historians like Ignaz von Döllinger and Theodor Mommsen, who spoke up against oppression and injustice and in appreciation of Jewish learning and thought. It is no accident that the least one-sided contacts between Germans and Jews took place in the world of the mind. What made it so easy for the Jews to burn their bridges was the familiar look of the road ahead.

When they left the narrow but relatively secure confines of the ghetto, the German Jews entered a world which was in many ways different from that to which their French and English fellow Jews had been or were being admitted; paradoxically, it had a good deal in common with the world they were leaving. For the culture that received them was as deeply concerned with the things of the mind – it was just as literary and speculative, reflective and unworldly – as that which they had built for themselves in their centuries of isolation. When Gershom Scholem writes that 'the intellectual encounter with Friedrich Schiller was for many Jews more real than their encounter with empirical Germans', and that '*Schiller* was the programme which to the Jew lacking in self-confidence bore the promise of all that he was looking for', he is telling only one half of the story. For it was precisely as *German* Jews that the Jewish literati of the Wilhelminian era were putting all their new 'faith' in German culture and *Geist*; it was because they were so deeply commited to certain very German intellectual preoccupations that they so often saw fit to interpret them for the benefit of less 'cultured' Germans, earning a good deal of ridicule in the process.

From its very beginnings (on that day in 1743 when the hunchbacked Moses Mendelssohn entered Berlin at the Jews' Gate and the guard's log book recorded that 'Today there passed through the Rosenthal Gate six oxen, seven pigs, one Jew'), the Jewish contribution to German literature and philosophy, music and science and every kind of scholarship was more readily given than received. Perhaps the German acknowledgement of the relationship was never more positive than in Goethe's charming words to Moses's grandson, the boy Felix Mendelssohn-Bartholdy: 'You are my David. Play to me when I am sad. Truly, I will not throw my spear at you.' Yet even so, the sheer size and importance of the Jewish contribution remains without parallel in any other country. Its dominant attributes were intellectual complexity and modernity – to call its source 'a second order of experience' is to place all important modern art under the same indictment. In philosophy and the humanities, Jewish authors closely followed prevailing modes of German thought; in music and the visual arts, they frequently anticipated them; and even in their literary treatment of Jewish themes – one thinks of Heine's late poems, of Else Lasker-Schüler, of Paul Celan – German Jewish poets followed and enriched an unmistakably German tradition. Thomas Mann, whose *Joseph and his Brothers* offers moving homage to the Jews in their darkest hour, remarks elsewhere that they alone kept the German artists alive to what was happening on the European scene. If in the arts, and even more in scholarship and the sciences, they were thus Germany's European conscience, this was to some extent made possible by their international connexions; but equally it was the heritage of the first German philosophical and literary movement to impinge on the European consciousness – the heritage of the German Enlightenment.

Of course this high intellectuality cannot have meant much to the petty tradesmen and sweatshop workers who continued to practise the ritual they had brought with them from the Polish ghetto, or to the astute businessman who (like his Gentile colleague) merely paid lip-service to it. But to their sons or grandsons it was the true hallmark of assimilation: to be a German citizen was to them not a matter of 'blood' but of the mind. What they strove after was knowledge and refinement of manner and mind. They wished to be judged by what each had made of himself, not by what others made of them. They feared the ascription of status just as they feared designation by 'natural' qualities, because they could never hope to possess the power held by those who decided that straight noses were good and bent ones evil, and who was, and who was not, an Aryan; yet as time went by, their Jewishness was sustained less and less by what they really had in common with each other, and increasingly by the names others gave them. They were democratic – at least in the sense that they knew they had everything to gain from a society that was capable of regulating fairly the acquisition of new social roles and status, and of protecting *all* its individual members against the tyranny of natural differences – but in this they followed once more the spirit of the German Enlightenment and of 1848. It seems inconceivable that they could ever have become active members of a totalitarian regime, just as it is inconceivable that Hitler could have done without them. None of the opinions they held was conducive to power. Their weakness, from which Hitler drew his strength, was endemic to their situation. In the dire circumstances of servitude and anguish each had only his personal qualities to fall back on, but no positive collective ethos – none that was distinct from the ethos of those who had abandoned them to their perdition.

Were they not all members of one culture, one Germany of
the mind, and had they not all been made equal before the
law? ('But I am innocent', Kafka's Josef K. protests, 'it is a
mistake. . . . Surely we're all human beings here, one like the
other.' 'That's right', replies the priest, 'but that is what the
guilty usually say.') They *were* treated as equals, but there was
one great difference: the Jews were without power. This did
not matter much as long as there was a law and as long as they
were allowed to devote themselves to it; and was not interpreting the law *like* having power? The position of the Jews was not,
after all, very different from that of the middle classes generally; and if the Jews were largely unaccustomed to *fighting* for
justice and liberty, so (as we have seen) were their Gentile
neighbours. It was only when, through the malevolence of their
enemies and the spinelessness of their friends, they were isolated from the community to which they had committed their
all – when they saw it become a community, a *Volksgemeinschaft*, through the act of banishing them and sending them to
their death – that their desolate position became clear to them.
'However much malicious people may warn against Jewish
solidarity, the fact remains that it does not exist and must not
be allowed to exist', Walther Rathenau had written in 1917, in
a vein of tragically mistaken satisfaction. Rathenau certainly
exaggerated. But the solidarity that did exist, like the solidarity
of the *Bürgertum*, was non-political, charitable and philan-
thropic – a purely private matter.

Everywhere in this enquiry into what started out as a high-
minded and noble experiment we come to the same simple
conclusion: that at the end of their life among the Germans no
other values and no other patterns of behaviour were available
to the German Jews than those of their erstwhile fellow-
citizens, later their enemies; by which I mean the values and
behaviour not indeed of the National Socialist thugs but of the
bürgerlich middle classes who acquiesced in what was done in
their name. The horrifyingly smooth machinery of annihilation, which included the rounding up of the Jews in their places

of domicile and the activities of the *Judenräte* in the camps and ghettos to which they were taken, cannot be understood without some reference to this spiritual predicament.

The Jews were not the only group to be annihilated, the lives of most European nations suffered irreversible and often equally grave disruption. If I have singled them out at the conclusion of this study, it is because their destruction reveals with particular clarity the true nature of National Socialism. Hidden under the verbiage of heroic propaganda yet at the same time looming through it was the spirit of its leader, the spirit of self-destruction.

However successful the party propaganda machine may have been in prizing away the German Jews from their fellow-citizens and in endowing them with subhuman attributes, one would expect their annihilation to offer an altogether different set of problems. And again it is the continuity between propaganda, intimidation, the threat of violence, individual violence, and wholesale destruction, and the growing indifference and gradual hardening of the mind of the populace to this continuity, which are the most remarkable features of the situation. The annihilation of 'inferior races' represents undoubtedly the most critical area in the relationship between Hitler and the Party on the one hand, and the people on the other.

What did the Germans know of the atrocities perpetrated in their name by their fellow-countrymen and by the scum of half-a-dozen countries of occupied Europe? The question has been asked a good many times, yet as far as I can see the answers to it have not got beyond the stage of wholesale accusation and emotional denials. What did they think when they read in *Der Stürmer* of May 1939:

There must be a punitive expedition against the Jews in Russia. A punitive expedition which will finish them off, as any murderer and criminal must expect. Sentence of death, execution!

The Jews in Russia must be killed. They must be exterminated, root and branch!

It is very unlikely that those who read this and countless similar passages either agreed or disagreed with them. It is more likely that to the majority such messages simply spelled danger and the need to take as little notice of them as possible.

How much was known in the Reich? Even if we confine ourselves to the war period, it is hard to see how, in the nature of things, there can ever be a complete answer. There is certainly enough evidence to indicate that detailed knowledge of the means of annihilation was successfully hidden from the German population, as it was hidden for as long as possible from the victims themselves. (Thus prisoners working on the railway in Lódź did not know what was happening at Auschwitz, some two hundred kilometres along the same line.) But equally there is abundant evidence – and again it is in the nature of things that it cannot be other than piecemeal – to indicate that knowledge of the bare facts of mass arrests, mass deportations and mass killings *was available* to every member of the population of the Reich. Three million German soldiers served in the East. There can be no doubt that every one of them, and every civilian travelling in the occupied territories, witnessed the rounding up and maltreatment and anguish – though not necessarily the killing – of men, women and children; and that every one of them *could* have written in his letter to his wife at home: '. . . every other day a train full of Jews from the Reich [goes] to Minsk, where they are abandoned to their fate.' At a rough guess half the photographs of life in the ghettos and extermination camps show the prisoners surrounded not by the SS or party officials (the 'gold-plumed pheasants') but by ordinary German soldiers. As the following four random samples of evidence show, these soldiers and civilians either knew or were convinced that the men, women and children they saw were going to their deaths.

The Commander of the Army of Occupation in Poland,

Colonel-General Johannes Blaskowitz, prepared two memoranda, addressed to the Commander-in-Chief, Field Marshal Walther von Brauchitsch, in protest against the conduct and depredations of the police and the SS. The second of these memoranda covers the period 23 November 1939 to 18 February 1940. Blaskowitz either witnessed or had reported to him the raping of Jewish girls, the looting of Jewish and Polish shops, and the killing of a number of men who had been herded together with horsewhips outside a synagogue. On hearing of these memoranda, extracts from which had been circulated to the chiefs of staff, Hitler spoke of the 'childish attitude' of Blaskowitz and other army commanders, and Himmler lectured them (17 March 1940) on the need to take a hard line with Poles and Jews. Blaskowitz was dismissed from several army commands, and committed suicide in the Nuremberg gaol on 5 February 1948, shortly before his trial as a minor war criminal was due to begin.

A company commander in the infantry, First Lieutenant Erwin Bingel, describes in a post-war statement how he and his men arrived on 15 September 1942 in the town of Uman, between Kiev and Odessa. There they witnessed the execution of the entire Jewish population of the town, who had been assembled in the main square under the pretext of a census. The preparations for the massacres, which included the digging of mass graves and the depositing of bags of quicklime, were in the hands of the *Feldgendarmerie*, the killings were done by Ukrainian militia under the command of SS officers. Erwin Bingel's statement ends: 'The entire operation lasted from 8 a.m. until 4.30 p.m. At 17.00 hours the square was entirely empty, only a few dogs scurried around, attracted by the smell of blood that hung heavily in the air. The sound of the shooting was still ringing in our ears.'

I have already mentioned the clandestine leaflets written and distributed by a group of Munich medical students who called themselves 'The White Rose'. The leaders of this group were Hans Scholl and Alexander Schmorell. Both served on the

Russian front as medical orderlies. Returning to Munich on study leave for the summer term 1942, they composed their first four leaflets. In the second of these they write:

We do not intend to say anything about the Jewish question, nor to enter a plea for the defence [of the Jews]; we only want to cite as an example the fact that since the conquest of Poland 300,000 Jews have been murdered in that country in the most bestial manner. In this we see the most terrible crime against human dignity, a crime not to be compared to any similar one in the history of mankind. The Jews are human too, whatever one's attitude to the Jewish question . . .

Having mentioned the killing, imprisonment and deportation of the entire Polish aristocracy, the two authors continue:

Why do we tell you all this, *since you yourselves know of these or other, similarly grave crimes* committed by these terrible subhuman people? Because a question is at issue here which concerns us all very deeply and which *must* give us all to think. Why does the German people behave so apathetically in the face of all these most dreadful and unworthy crimes?

Hans Scholl and Alexander Schmorell served as sergeants in the medical corps, and had no access to any special source of information.

Evidence of this kind is most convincing when it comes to us in a casual way – as it does in the reminiscences of Kunrat Hammerstein, son of General Kurt von Hammerstein-Equord, who was dismissed in 1933 as Chief of Army Command. On his way to his father's funeral on Easter Sunday 1943, young Hammerstein was 'overtaken by our much beloved cousin Adelaide, who told us on 6 December 1942 on her return from Lemberg [Łwów] that Jews were being killed by gas. Even before the summer of 1942 my father had spoken of "organized mass murder"; incidentally, he left the Club of the Nobility when in 1934 or 1935 they threw out their non-Aryan members.' The rambling yet caustic style of these reminiscences conveys Hammerstein's embarrassment at seeing how the members of his own class are siding with the *canaille*: 'On 25 January 1944 two hundred and fifty army generals and admirals from all fronts were assembled in the town theatre of Posen. Göring and Himmler spoke. Himmler said that all Jews, including women and children, would be eradicated: the "final solution" was being revealed to the largest war-time gathering of German generals ever held. A number of them had known since 1942 that Jewish population groups were being exterminated by mass shootings ... General Reinecke, who in August 1944 had sat with Freisler [on the bench of the 'People's Court'], stepped on to the speaker's platform in Posen after Himmler had finished, and thanked him obsequiously. In one of the side tiers sat General von Saucken, a veteran who had been wounded fourteen times; he did not clap, and was asleep only during the early part of Himmler's speech. A few rows in front of him sat the Admiral of the Aegean[?]. At the back of the house a general was trying, from a vantage point, to take a count: *five* were not clapping. The clapping generals had never heard of Eichmann. But indirectly they were applauding him.'

The picture that emerges from our evidence so far suggests that knowledge of the killing of 'inferior races', including Jews, Gypsies and Slavs, was available in very broad outlines, if only because every adult in the Reich must have witnessed the arrest and deportation of neighbours whom he knew would not return. (Moreover, the conversational habits of soldiers – German soldiers at that – make it less than likely that three millions of them can be made to keep a vow of silence concerning events of everyday occurrence.) But this picture must be complemented by what we know of a similar undertaking which produced very different reactions – the euthanasia project of 1939–41. It turned out to be a kind of trial run for the 'final solution'. Between the outbreak of war and 24 August 1941 some 100,000 German men, women and children were killed by a group of doctors, many of them members of the SS, under the direction of Dr Werner Heyde, professor of neurology and psychiatry at the University of Würzburg. A variety of means were used, including lethal injections, starvation, carbon monoxide and 'cyclon B' gas. The selection was based on the law of 14 July 1933, designed to 'prevent the propagation of congenitally diseased progeny' and on the law of 15 September 1935, 'for the protection of German blood and German honour'; incidentally, when invoked as legal authority for the taking of lives, these laws conflicted with ordinary pre-1933 legislation, which was never repealed and according to which 'premeditated killing' was the equivalent of murder and as such liable to capital punishment. The victims included certified alcoholics, 'congenital criminals', inmates of lunatic asylums, and the incurable of all ages. Some of the doctors who selected and killed the patients, wrote out false death-certificates and co-operated with the authorities in trying to keep the action secret were ordinary general practitioners and house surgeons; when in 1960 they were tried before a Hamburg court and acquitted on the grounds that 'they had not been aware of the illegal nature of their actions', one of their elder colleagues characterized them, inelegantly but accurately enough: 'It is true they have a head but it's too close to their arse, because they have no backbone.'

What is remarkable about this '*Aktion T-4*' is that it was stopped as soon as protests were raised against it. Early in 1940 the Protestant Bishop of Württemberg, Dr Theophil Wurm, wrote a letter to Himmler in which he tried to steer an uneasy course between outright rejection of the project on Christian grounds and hints to the effect that further killings are bound to bring the party into disrepute with the local population: 'Especially here in Württemberg this sort of thing is taken much to heart', writes the good bishop, because 'even among the intellectually and morally distinguished families of our small province signs of degeneration are not uncommon.' And he closes his letter echoing that astonishing belief to which I drew attention earlier, that 'it is certain the Führer does not know' what is being done in his name, because 'to this day he and the party base themselves on the tenets of Positive

Christianity, which regards charity towards our suffering *Volksgenossen* and their humane treatment as a matter of course.' This mealy-mouthed letter (which makes one wonder whether Hitler was entirely unjust in his comments about some of the Protestant clergy) was followed by wholly uncompromising condemnations from the Catholic hierarchy. The Archbishop of Breslau, Cardinal Bertram, wrote a sharp letter to Dr Lammers, head of the Reich Chancellery. The Archbishop of Munich, Cardinal Faulhaber (wearer of the Iron Cross First Class) denounced the practice in a letter to Dr Franz Gürtner, Hitler's Minister of Justice, whereas the Bishop of Münster, Graf von Galen, insisting on his rights under the ordinary criminal code, informed the police of the unlawful killings and then, on 3 August 1941, preached a blistering sermon in which he called the action by the same name as was used in the legal code, to wit, 'plain murder'. Three weeks later it was all over. The protests on behalf of Aryan Germans had proved to be effective enough. Whether similar protests on behalf of their Jewish fellow citizens would have been equally effective we shall never know. The hypothesis was not tested.

What, then, is our answer to the questions with which we began? It is certain that the authorities allowed and even encouraged some knowledge of the atrocities to act as a deterrent, and that the population at large connived at this policy. Beyond that we are confined to inferences. The people of the Reich, it seems, knew as much (for example about the killing of their German fellow citizens) or as little (for example about the killing of their Jewish fellow citizens) as they wanted to know. What they did not know, they did not want to know, for obvious reasons. But not wanting to know always means knowing enough to know that one doesn't want to know more.

The war that Hitler began in September 1939 had many aspects. The Polish campaign, which lasted four weeks, was at least partly a traditional war of territorial conquest. The *Blitz-*

krieg against France, lasting six weeks, was a no less traditional
war of revenge. Against Norway and Denmark (two months),
Holland (five days), and Belgium (seventeen days) it was a
war on the old German pattern, established by Frederick the
Great and repeated in the Belgian campaign of 1914, its intention being to anticipate encirclement and to secure bases for
further attacks. The campaign against Yugoslavia (eleven days)
and Greece (three weeks) and the North African campaigns
were largely forced on Hitler by Mussolini's miscalculations.
The declaration of war against the United States amounted to
a gratuitous act accountable in terms of a desperate gamble.
Wars such as these all have their antecedents in the history of
other states. The war against Russia, however, is unprecedented. 'Of all Hitler's decisions', Bullock concludes his examination of the origins of the war, the decision to wage war on
Russia 'is the one which most clearly bears his own personal
stamp, the culmination (as he saw it) of his whole career.'

At various points in this study I have stressed the singleness
of purpose and consistency of aim of Hitler's policies and
beliefs. One example of this was the continuity he established
between persuasion, propaganda, threats of terror and terror
itself. Another is the continuity, so utterly bewildering to his
French and English negotiating partners, between 'peace' and
'war' on which his foreign policy was based, where subversion,
propaganda, diplomatic and economic pressure, war of nerves,
threat of war, localized war and general war itself all merged
into a single spectrum, and he alone knew the stage that had
been reached at any one time. And again, there is Hitler's
innermost conviction, the 'sincerity' of which is explained in
Nietzsche's observation about the deceiver deceived, that
throughout his career he was faithfully following the *weltanschaulich* principles with which he began in 1919; his conviction that there was an alliance amounting to an identity
between his internal enemies and his enemies abroad, and
consequently that this war against foreign states was nothing
but a continuation of his early party political struggle: 'I am

firmly convinced', he proclaims in 1940, 'that this fight will be concluded in exactly the same way as the fight which I waged inside Germany.' And in the fifth year of the war he restates this continuity of ideology and *praxis*, of war and peace, of private mania and public policy, in one of his last radio speeches:

> One day the World War of 1939 will enter history as a gigantic repetition of the 1924 [Munich] trial against the Party. Just as that attack, which was intended to destroy the Movement, helped in fact to disseminate its ideas over the rest of Germany with the force of an explosion, so will this fight open the eyes of the [other] nations with regard to the Jewish question, and will show them that the National Socialist answer to this question and the measures taken to dispose of it are obvious and worthy of imitation.

Hitler reached the summit of his life not in the years of his chancellorship (the duties of which soon bored him), nor even in the first two years of war (the period of his greatest military successes), but in the first years of the Eastern campaign, for now at last he was able to indulge to the fullest extent his destructive passion without as yet having to bear the ultimate consequences of it. This destructiveness had always been near the centre of his picture of the world, and at this time, during those years in the shadow of catastrophe, when his means of gratifying that passion had increased immeasurably, it came to displace all other motives, considerations and ambitions. This destructiveness engenders a community spirit of connivance on the national scale (as the massacres of 1934 had done on a party-political scale), when in the face of other men's death and the threat of one's own all retreat is cut off; and this is the only kind of community he does not seem to despise. However, it would be wrong to think that the holocaust is unleashed as a revenge for military setbacks; it simply begins at a time when a larger number of victims than ever before is in German hands. Thus the decisions affecting the fate of European Jews are taken simultaneously with the final preparations for the war against Russia: Himmler's 'special tasks' are marked out in a speech of

31 March 1941, the military campaign begins with an entirely unprovoked attack on Russia on 22 June, and on 31 July Heydrich is given the task of 'implementing the desired Final Solution'. In other words: to understand the special and unprecedented nature of the war in the East it must be seen as being of a piece with Hitler's anti-Jewish policy; to understand the full force of his anti-Jewish measures they must be seen as part of an essentially war-like action; and both are the consummation of his political and existential ambitions.

Fancy stories about Colditz do nothing to help us understand that the war against Poland and Russia was a war which had annihilation for its immediate as well as its ultimate purpose – annihilation and nothing else. The pretence that this was a war of conquest was still kept up. There was still talk, as there had been in *Mein Kampf* and before, of 'the Ukrainian corn-stores of Europe'. There were grandiose plans for model farms on a 'Germanic' pattern, connected by thousands of kilometres of *autobahnen*, and designs for huge mausoleums (*'Totenburgen'*) to house the dead of the Master Race. There was even an attempt to start a settlement in the Warthegau (east of the old Reich frontier with Poland), but the Germans from the populous Western areas, far from feeling that they were 'a People without Space', proved unwilling to move east even when tempted by state subsidies, and the scheme was soon given up as a dismal failure.

However, as the administrative pattern for Poland (under its 'Governor General', Hans Frank) and for the Eastern territories was established in the wake of the conquering armies, and the SS and various branches of the police took over, so the true nature of the war was revealed as a thing unprecedented in European history – unprecedented in its concrete, immediate objectives and even more in its long-term aims. The notorious Army order for the 'immediate execution' of all captured Russian commissars is indicative of the treatment to which large sections of the Polish, Ukrainian, Czech and Russian intelligentsia were subjected. What is less well known is that soon after the order was promulgated, the professor of anatomy at the Reichsuniversität Straßburg, Dr August Wirth, prepared detailed plans for the acquisition of the severed heads of these 'Jewish–Bolshevist commissars' for the purpose of racial studies at the ethnological institute attached to his university.

The measures of annihilation were not to be confined to the war. German physicians, nutritional scientists and university teachers vied with each other in their eagerness to supply Hitler and Himmler with long-term schemes regulating education, sanitation, food supplies, medical services and birth control in the conquered Eastern territories, designed to reduce their populations, keep the survivors at subsistence level, and turn them into ignorant and abject slaves. There was nothing very remote about these plans. Experiments for mass sterilization (by drugs, X-rays, and surgical means), conducted on several hundreds of Jewish concentration-camp prisoners and on Eastern civilians and prisoners of war, were so successful that one professor of medicine, Clauberg, claimed in a letter to Himmler (7 June 1943) that the use of his method made it possible to sterilize one thousand women a day. As the motive of these genocidal measures could hardly be said to be revenge, so the aim was no longer any form of national gain (though of course private looting, for instance by the railwaymen in Auschwitz, appears to have been common enough). In fact, the schemes of annihilation went ahead at considerable cost to the German war effort. In the autumn of 1942 several hundred Polish Jewish steel workers were killed, and the death transports continued at a time when labour and rolling stock were badly needed for armaments and troop reinforcements along a series of disintegrating fronts reaching from the Karelian Isthmus to the Mediterranean.

To be in command. To be responsible for the conduct of such a war of annihilation, to be its leader not its victim, to commit all his nervous energies and mental powers to its manifold tasks and offer himself as a 'sacrifice' in its cause – this is the fulfilment of Hitler's ambitions at the same time as it is his 'revenge', that is, his compensation for the *Fronterlebnis* of thirty years before. Now at last everything around him proclaims that he is no longer the 'poor bloody infantryman' of the Flanders trenches. He can make and unmake Field Marshals, garrotte Generals, send a third of a million soldiers to their doom in a single protracted battle – and yet, it is the experience of trench warfare that continues to determine his strategy as supreme war lord.

This may seem a surprising claim to make. After all, Hitler's greatest strategic successes came to him in the 'lightning' campaigns of 1939–41. Throughout these campaigns he made all the strategic and even tactical decisions, certainly down to regimental level, single-handed, against the advice of the military and with minimal losses, achieving successes they had regarded as impossible. There is no doubt that this was the kind of war he had been preparing for, both psychologically and in the phasing of armaments, from the time of Göring's Four Year Plan of 1934 onwards. When France fell Hitler was at the height of his popularity, both in the party, which at that time attained its peak membership of eight millions plus one million in the *Waffen-SS*, and in the country as a whole. (When war was declared Hitler was at first taken aback, while the mood of the people is said to have been sombre; it does not seem to have taken either of them long to recover.)

These, then, were undoubtedly the months of Hitler's greatest glory. Yet the question arises why he made not the least attempt to consolidate his amazing territorial and economic gains in a Continental peace – a peace which, in the short run at all events, no power could have challenged. It seems clear that the conquests those swift and strategically elegant campaigns yielded were not his ultimate aims.

These aims are not detached from the rest of his life but form a terrible continuity with it. Just as Hitler's diplomatic victories of the 'thirties were a repetition of his domestic successes of the 'twenties, so the successes of the first years of the war, including the early part of the Russian campaign, repeat the pattern

of the 'thirties – a pattern, broadly speaking, of less and less
calculated risks under the growing shadow of personal and
national doom, his decisions informed by an ever-growing
certainty of the coming annihilation of the entire world in his
power. It is clear from General Alfred Jodl's and other men's
testimony that either as early as the winter of 1941–42, which
marked the disastrous repulsion of the German armies before
Moscow, or during Rommel's retreat to Tripolitania at the end
of 1942, Hitler knew that the War was lost. If then we ask why
he insisted on prolonging it for another three years; why his
strategic directives became ever more reckless, costly in man-
power, rigid, and increasingly out of touch with the realities
of the military situation; and why, in the face of defeat, he insisted on putting into practice that 'Final Solution of the Jewish question' which he had discussed with his friend Dietrich
Eckart more than twenty years before, the answer is not that he
had hope of victory to the last, but that, on the contrary, being
incapable of envisaging his own survival, he was lured by the
prospect of a universal annihilation which included his enemies,
his victims, his people and himself.

There is nothing novel about this interpretation of Hitler's
end purpose. It was suggested by Rauschning in his discussion
of Hitler's 'nihilism'; and again by Carl Burckhardt, who between 1936 and 1939 served as High Commissioner of the
League of Nations in Danzig and met Hitler a good many times.
Burckhardt argues convincingly that 'the insatiable hatred
within [Hitler] was connected, in the subconscious part of his
being, with one concealed but ever-present certainty: the
certainty that what awaited him in the end was the most appall-
ing failure and a personal fate such as did in fact overtake him
in the Reich Chancellery on 30 April 1945'. However, a more
concrete analysis of this all-encompassing spirit of destructiveness is to be found in the memoirs of Erich von Manstein, who
regularly attended the briefings at Hitler's secret headquarters
throughout his period as Chief of Command on the southern
sector of the Russian front, 1942–44.

There is no snobbery or superciliousness about any of the severe criticisms the Field Marshal levels against the self-taught strategist. He points to Hitler's lack of understanding of the part played by defensive warfare, and to his absurd overestimation of the political and propagandist value as opposed to the strategic significance of military gains and losses. He criticizes Hitler's failure to distinguish between territorial conquest and military victory, and he exposes as chimeric and disastrous in its consequences Hitler's 'excessive' belief in his own will-power. But it is von Manstein's technical observations which directly support and consolidate the interpretation I have outlined. The defeat of the German armies before Moscow marks the moment when Hitler abandons the highly mobile warfare which brought him spectacular victories during the early campaigns; it is from this point onwards that he takes over Stalin's recipe of rigidly holding on to every position gained. This invariable practice is supported by Hitler's conviction, originating in his Flanders experience, that the only way to prevent the 'poor bloody infantry' from abandoning their forward positions is to order them to dig in (a theory which would have appealed to Hitler's hero, Frederick the Great). In this way he hits on the often-repeated device of allowing a full encirclement of his troops in order to attract a maximum number of enemy forces and destroy them in a subsequent break-out operation – and here Stalin's bigger battalions are likely to carry the day. However, it is by no means only military considerations which lead Hitler to adopt this suicidal device. At least as important to him is the propaganda value of the 'miraculous' deliverance at the last moment and against impossible odds, the *Kitsch* drama intended to confirm the people's faith that the Führer is inspired and guided by Fate. Hitler meanwhile derives comfort from the belief that he is repeating in military terms a manoeuvre which served him well enough in his diplomatic dealings with the European politicians of the 'thirties. The analogy is lost on Stalin.

And this, too, is the gamble that goes wrong at Stalingrad,

for by now Hitler's every move has become the inflexible, dogmatic reaction of one who is a prisoner of his own myth – the myth of 'the man of Will':

> He was a man [writes von Manstein] who recognized nothing but brutal struggle to the uttermost. What governed his thinking was the wishful image of masses of enemy soldiers bleeding to death before our lines, rather than the image of a polished swordsman who on occasion knows how to step aside, so as to strike the decisive blow with the greater sureness. Ultimately, to the concept of the art of war he opposed that of crude force, and the full effectiveness of this force was supposed to be guaranteed by the strength of will behind it.

The point von Manstein does not make is that those masses bleeding to death were not always enemy soldiers. In an age when everything seems permitted, in a situation where everything – every evil deed at all events – is possible, the guiding imagination which von Manstein attributes to Hitler no longer distinguishes between armed conflict and the massacre of the defenceless, between the battle front and the extermination camps:

> I walked round a mound of earth and stood before the gigantic grave [an eye-witness reports]. People lay so closely pressed together that only their heads could be seen. Blood was running from almost all the heads across the shoulders. Many of those who had been shot were still moving. Some raised their arms and turned their heads to show that they were still alive. I looked round for the marksman. It was an SS-man sitting on the edge of the short side of the pit, his legs hanging down into it; on his knees lay a submachine gun, and he was smoking a cigarette. The people, entirely naked, walked down some steps which had been dug into the clay wall of the pit, and then slid across the heads of those who lay there until they reached the place which the SS-man had pointed out to them. They lay down in front of the dead or wounded, some were stroking those still alive and talking to them quietly. Then I heard a series of shots. I looked into the pit and saw bodies moving

convulsively or heads which were lying quite still on the bodies in front. Blood poured from the napes of their necks.

This scene, which Hitler himself may well have been physically incapable of witnessing, is the end-purpose of his ambitions. If in his public pronouncements he hoped for a miraculous rescue almost to the end, this unreasonable hope was no more than a mask behind which he hid his own fullest intentions, not only from the German people, but also from himself. Yet enough evidence has been offered in the course of this study to suggest that he knew the truth about himself – the truth that not con-quest but indiscriminate annihilation was his aim. This, rather than any heroic self-assertion or the prospect of material gain, emerges as the secret that bound his followers to him; and not his followers only. On this dark understanding his whole career is based.

Notes

ABBREVIATIONS

Broszat   Martin Broszat, *Der Staat Hitlers: Grundlegung und Entwicklung seiner inneren Verfassung*, München 1969
Bullock   Alan Bullock, *Hitler, A Study in Tyranny*, second edition Harmondsworth 1962
Domarus   Max Domarus, *Hitler: Reden und Proklamationen 1932–1945, kommentiert von einem deutschen Zeitgenossen*, München 1965
Frank   Hans Frank, *Im Angesicht des Galgens: Deutung Hitlers und seiner Zeit auf Grund eigener Erlebnisse und Erkenntnisse*, München 1953
Machtergreifung Karl Dietrich Bracher, Wolfgang Sauer and Gerhard Schulz, *Die nationalsozialistische Machtergreifung: Studien zur Errichtung des totalitären Herrschaftssystems in Deutschland 1933/34*, Köln 1960
Nolte   Ernst Nolte, *Der Faschismus in seiner Epoche: Die Action française. Der italienische Faschismus. Der Nationalsozialismus*, München 1963
Tischgespräche Dr Henry Picker, *Hitlers Tischgespräche im Führerhauptquartier 1941–42*, edited by Percy Ernst Schramm, Stuttgart 1963

References to Hitler's *Mein Kampf* are to the seventeenth edition, München 1943.

Preface

Page
7 'My business . . . to believe it' / Herodotus, *The Histories*, VII, 152, 3. See the Penguin edition, translated by Aubrey de Sélincourt (1963), p. 467.

1 The Representative Individual

9 A Munich historian . . . 'I shall never forget' / Professor Karl

Alexander von Müller, whose lectures Hitler attended, quoted from Konrad Heiden, *Der Fuehrer: Hitler's Rise to Power*, Boston 1944, p. 190.

'For the first time . . . an expression of blissful egotism' / Professor Max von Gruber, quoted from Heiden, loc. cit.

10 'Then Adolf Hitler steps forward . . . fit for the kindergarten' / Karl Tschuppik is writing in 1927; I quote from the introduction to *Reden des Führers*, edited by E. Klöss, München 1967, pp. 16–17. 'Bombast' here renders the German *Pathos*, which in later contexts I shall leave untranslated.

12 'Leader of the Nation . . . and Leader of the Party' / These are the titles Hitler conferred on himself by the decree of 26 April 1942, passed by the Reichstag with acclamation. See *Gesetze des NS-Staates*, edited by U. Brodersen, Bad Homburg, Berlin and Zürich 1968, p. 41.

16 the appearance of spontaneity . . . if the situation demanded it / e.g. in the parliamentary debate with Otto Wels; see below, p. 99ff. See also Bullock, p. 775.

speculations about Hitler's . . . sexual habits / For a particularly rich example of this, see W. C. Langer, *The Mind of Adolf Hitler*, London 1972, which purports to be based on a 'secret wartime report', and which dwells at length on a number of mistresses and prurient episodes not mentioned anywhere else.

'a haunted man . . . the Jewish world conspiracy' / Norman Cohen, *Warrant for Genocide* (Penguin), 1967, p. 194.

'Reared in an age of security' / The phrase is from the opening of Ernst Jünger's *In Stahlgewittern* of 1920.

17 'moral . . . cretinism' / Bullock, p. 804.

18 'I have come from the people . . . representative of his people!' / Domarus, p. 609 (20 March 1936).

With fuller evidence of his studies in Vienna and Munich / See W. Maser, *Adolf Hitler: Legende, Mythos, Wirklichkeit*, München and Esslingen 1972, especially chapter 5. Maser exaggerates. On p. 279 he offers a long list of Hitler's intellectual 'sources', which includes Malthus, Clausewitz, Schopenhauer, Darwin, Gregor Mendel, the Austrian poet Robert Hamerling (a relation of Hitler's), a eugenicist called Alfred Ploetz, the racial biologists Wilhelm Bölsche and Ernst Haeckel, the sociologists Gustave Le Bon and William McDougall, the cosmologist Hanns Hörbiger (whose glacial theory Hitler defended), the arctic explorer Sven Hedin, the historian Alexander von Müller (see above, p. 9 and below, p. 94), and Sigmund Freud. By a 'source' Maser means a mention or a reference or a recognizable allusion. In the case of Freud no evidence whatever is offered, though it is true

that in his *Table Talk* Hitler on more than one occasion mentions 'inferiority complexes' and the like.
'A man who has no sense of . . . no hearing or sight' | *Tischgespräche*, p. 72 (27 July 1941).
'Surely that has . . . leave the battlefield!' | Compare *The Eden Memoirs: Facing the Dictators*, London 1962, p. 135.
'Because of my origin . . . the imperial idea' | *Tischgespräche*, p. 174 (4 February 1941), my italics.

20 'the essential in history' | *Mein Kampf*, p. 12.
'the deepest aspirations, hopes, fears and sense of destiny' | Richard Crossman, in *The Times*, 10 January 1973.

21 In a period of prolonged drought . . . 'of goodness even' | C. M. Turnbull, *The Mountain People*, London 1973, p. 130.

2 The Authentic Experience

24 Courage and personal resoluteness . . . an ideological end | See Nolte, pp. 217f.

25 For Hitler . . . his national programme | See, e.g., *Mein Kampf*, pp. 460–1: '. . . der völkische Staat [hat] die Bildung des Charakters in jeder Weise zu fördern . . .'

26 The hardest decision . . . a political career instead | See Domarus, p. 1421 (23 November 1939).
And this decision . . . gift as a public speaker | *Mein Kampf*, p. 225: 'Ich aber beschloß, Politiker zu werden'; and p. 235: '. . . und was ich früher immer, ohne es zu wissen, aus dem reinen Gefühl einfach angenommen hatte, traf nun ein: ich konnte "reden".'
Others beside him . . . Brest–Litovsk and Versailles | See R. H. Phelps, 'Hitler als Parteiredner im Jahre 1920', in *Vierteljahrshefte für Zeitgeschichte*, 11 (1963), and 'Hitler and the *Deutsche Arbeiterpartei*', in *American Historical Review*, 68 (1963), pp. 974–86.
'*Parteierzählung*' | The term was coined by Domarus; see p. 49.

27 Trilling's discussion of Joseph Conrad's *Heart of Darkness* | See *Sincerity and Authenticity*, London 1972, pp. 109 and 133.

3 The Language of Sacrifice

28 not exactly a 'heroic phenomenon' | Hitler used the phrase 'keine heroische Erscheinung' (see Joachim C. Fest, *Hitler: eine Biographie*, Frankfurt/M 1973, p. 1034) about Gustav von Kahr,

his antagonist during the *Putsch* of 1923; von Kahr was murdered
on 30 June 1934.
While Ernst Röhm . . . Hitler in person . . . their wives and
children / See Fest, op. cit., pp. 640–1, and Konrad Heiden, op.
cit., e.g. p. 764.
The man who planned . . . she was Jewish / See Maser, op. cit.,
p. 255.
'nothing was genuine except fear . . . physically sick' / From the
diary of an anonymous general, quoted from P. E. Schramm,
*Hitler als militärischer Führer: Erkenntnisse und Erfahrungen aus
dem Kriegstagebuch des Oberkommandos der Wehrmacht*, Frank-
furt/M 1965, p. 133.

29   'all too many lovers . . . of world-political misfortunes' / Quoted
from Fest, op. cit., p. 524.
'I have come to know . . . mankind is now roasting' / Franz
Werfel, *Zwischen oben und unten*, Stockholm 1946, section 'Theolo-
gumena', para. 126: '. . . Unter dem amüsiert empörten Geläch-
ter einiger Philister waren wir die unansehnlichen Vorheizer
der Hölle, in der nun die Menschheit brät.' See also W. Muschg,
Die Zerstörung der deutschen Literatur, Bern 1956, and Joachim C.
Fest, *The Face of the Third Reich*, Harmondsworth 1972, p. 393.
For a literary counterpart to this argument, see J. P. Stern, 'The
Dear Purchase', in *German Quarterly*, 61 (1968), pp. 317–337.
'intellectual war service with weapon in hand' / Thomas Mann,
Betrachtungen eines Unpolitischen, Berlin 1919, p. ix.

30   *Frederick and the Great Coalition* / *Friedrich und die große
Koalition*, Berlin 1916; the volume contains two further pieces,
not reprinted in the *Betrachtungen eines Unpolitischen*.

31   'He was victim . . . True, he believed . . . mission should be
fulfilled' / *Friedrich und die große Koalition*, p. 118.

32   'The ox must draw . . . I must make war' / ibid., p. 112.
'It was only if success . . . had been in the right' / ibid., p. 99.
'*die es am schwersten hatten*' / From 'Gedanken im Kriege', in
Friedrich und die große Koalition, p. 30, my italics.

33   'There are individual people . . . a doctrine of sacrifice' / Domarus, p. 571 (30 January 1936).
'All in all . . . funeral pyre!' / *Hitler's Table Talk 1941–1944*,
introduced [and edited?] by H. R. Trevor-Roper, London 1953,
p. 316 (February 1942). This is not included in *Tischgespräche*.
See also H. R. Trevor-Roper, *The Last Days of Hitler*, 4th ed.,
London 1971, p. lx, and Fest, *Hitler: eine Biographie*, p. 988.

34   'to perish in King Attila's hall like ye Nibelungs of olde' / The
quotation – 'wie die weiland ollen Nibelungen in König Etzels
Saal' – comes from Bormann's last letter to his wife, dated 2

April 1945; compare *The Bormann Letters*, edited by H. R. Trevor-Roper, London 1954, p. 198.
'Under the debris . . . everything old and outworn has gone' / Goebbels's address on Radio Werwolf; quoted from Trevor-Roper, *The Last Days of Hitler*, p. 58, author's translation. Goebbels himself wrote an Expressionist novel, *Michael: ein deutsches Schicksal in Tagebuchblättern* (München 1926), which is not *much* worse than some of the more extravagant productions of that school.

4 Propaganda as Perlocutionary Act

35 'Mein ganzes Leben . . . ein ständiges Überreden' / *Tischgespräche*, p. 156 (18 January 1942).
'In all great deceivers . . . so miracle-like, to the audience' / *Menschliches, Allzumenschliches*, para. 52, Nietzsche's italics.
36 Several commentators . . . unmistakably sexual terms / See, e.g. Fest, *Hitler: eine Biographie*, p. 463, and compare *Mein Kampf*, pp. 44 and 201.
Hitler observes . . . tension and keyed-up expectation / See *Mein Kampf*, p. 531.
37 a perlocutionary act / I refer to the theory of such acts in J. L. Austin, *How to Do Things with Words*, Oxford 1971, especially 'Lecture viii'; it is sufficient for our purpose to define such acts as being of the kind '*By* prophesying x Hitler is doing y', rather than of the kind '*In* prophesying x Hitler is *saying* y will occur'.
This is the elimination of freedom . . . in mass politics / See *Mein Kampf*, p. 532.
the informational element should indeed be slight / My present argument owes much to Harold Weinrich's very stimulating *Linguistik der Lüge*, Heidelberg 1966, especially pp. 56–8.
38 a sort of Tinkerbell ploy / Domarus, on p. 607, speaks of 'der Stil der Kasperltheaterbefragung'.
'A chi l'Italia?' . . . / Quoted from Nolte, p. 241.
'I put this question . . . And I shall further ask . . . "No, we do not want that!" ' / Domarus, p. 607.
39 'I ask myself . . . succeeded in their intentions' / Domarus, p. 621.
'Do you believe with the Führer . . . imagine it today?' / Goebbels's speech of 18 February 1943, quoted from Domarus, pp. 607 and 1990; parts of the speech are recorded, see note to p. 62.
40 that he must at all times structure . . . according to his will / See *Mein Kampf*, p. 536.
a pattern established in his private relationships / August Kubizek's

Young Hitler: The Story of our Friendship, London 1954, still contains the best, and as far as we can tell the most reliable, description of those early days.

one big, overall, 'unitary' national situation / the concept of *'Gleichschaltung'* is adumbrated as early as *Mein Kampf;* see p. 203.

'the absolute, single-minded, insolent lie' / *Mein Kampf*, p. 202.

'I will reveal . . . rise to my position' / Domarus, p. 580.

41 Its intellectual and literary history . . . the security of tradition / See Erich Heller, *The Disinherited Mind*, 3rd ed., London 1971.

a longing for a 'breakthrough' / This is the burden of the polemical parts of Ronald Gray's *The German Tradition in Literature 1871–1945*, Cambridge 1965.

'The history of this age . . . there is no third way' / Oswald Spengler, *Der Untergang des Abendlandes*, vol. II, München 1918, p. 539.

like the meaning of certain other parts of his ideology / See especially below p. 173.

5   Nineteenth-century Roots

44 'Let your speculative thinking' . . . 'in the child' / *Also sprach Zarathustra*, Part II, 'Auf den glückseligen Inseln' and 'Von den Tugendhaften'.

'Only as an aesthetic phenomenon . . . justified' / *Die Geburt der Tragödie*, end of section 5.

45 'Such beings are incalculable . . . like lightning . . . justified in her child' / *Zur Genealogie der Moral*, section II, para. 17.

'When the masses are like wax . . . the vision he has conceived?' / Mussolini talking to his biographer Emil Ludwig in 1932; quoted from Denis Mack Smith, 'The Theory and Practice of Fascism', in *Fascism: an Anthology*, edited by N. Greene, New York 1968, p. 82.

'Lenin is an artist . . . marble and metal' / Mussolini quoted from Nolte, pp. 245–6.

6   The Language of Nature

51 'As soon as you cut . . . a little Jew!' / *Mein Kampf*, p. 61. There is an extraordinary parallel between this and Kafka's image of the wound in the boy's thigh in the story 'Ein Landarzt'. Hitler's image is varied to 'a leech on the Nation's body' on p. 340. The

sources I have used for the earlier parts of this paragraph are scattered throughout both volumes of *Mein Kampf*. 'Thus it is that today . . . the work of the Lord!' / *Mein Kampf*, p. 70: 'So glaube ich im Sinne des allmächtigen Schöpfers zu handeln: indem ich mich des Juden erwehre, kämpfe ich für das Werk des Herrn.'

the writings of politicians like Georg von Schönerer / See *Zwölf Reden des Reichsabgeordneten Georg Ritter von Schönerer*, Horn 1886, e.g. pp. 37f.

Otto Weininger . . . Dietrich Eckart, Hitler's friend and mentor / See *Dietrich Eckart: ein Vermächtnis*, edited by A. Rosenberg, München 1937, p. 207; see also *Tischgespräche*, p. 152 (1 December 1942), and F. Heer, *Der Glaube des Adolf Hitler*, München and Esslingen 1968, pp. 386f.

54 'Even at this time . . . devotion to their duty' / The italics in this passage are mine.

Stefan George's nostalgic solemnities / I have in mind the concluding stanzas of 'Der Krieg' of 1913.

the German 'scholar in his study' / However, I have no mind to perpetuate ethnic clichés. The bad-tempered earnestness of intellectuals seems to be largely a twentieth-century phenomenon. The German *savant* of the nineteenth century was certainly serious and often otherworldly, but he was also by no means without humour and had a good deal of charm.

7   Hitler's Ideology of the Will

56 As to their numbers . . . 'The German nation . . . loyal to him to the end' / Frank, p. 381.

57 a few catch-phrases . . . 'lives fully' / Frank, p. 315; *Tischgespräche*, p. 82.

60 'You had worked your way . . . but in their persons' / From 'Brief an den Vater' (1919), in *Hochzeitsvorbereitungen auf dem Lande*, New York 1967, p. 169.

This is the right . . . 'the personal right in success'/ *Mein Kampf*, p. 419: '. . . bis sich aus dem Wellenspiel einer freien Gedankenwelt ein eherner Fels einheitlicher glaubens- und willensmäßiger Verbundenheit erhebt.'

61 'Stalingrad must simply be held' . . . 'The Sixth Army remains at Stalingrad!' / See Albert Speer, *Erinnerungen*, Berlin 1970, pp. 262–3.

'Success failed . . . *did not want* success' / Bullock, p. 754.

62 'It has been my task . . . repair the affair somehow' / Bullock, pp. 755–6; *Tischgespräche*, p. 101.
'For five years . . . this fight cannot be won' / Bullock, p. 756; *Tischgespräche*, p. 102; my italics.
'There is one thing . . . nothing can wear me down' / Bullock, pp. 762–3; Domarus, p. 2175; my italics.
'If we form a community . . . and triumph over it' / Domarus, p. 1317. This part of the speech is recorded on side 4 of *Deutschland im zweiten Weltkrieg*, a series of excerpts from German war-time speeches, selected and commented by Horst Siebecke, Athena Company.

63 the passionate rise-and-fall of '*Not*' / In September 1916 Thomas Mann took Romain Rolland severely to task for translating 'Not' as mere *nécessité*. On the contrary (Mann insists), it is always '*heilige Not*'; it is 'the highest creative *Pathos*' of which German soldiers – and Richard Wagner! – are capable. See *Betrachtungen eines Unpolitischen*, p. 151.
And this rapport . . . the spoken word / See *Mein Kampf*, pp. 520ff.

64 'I remember for instance . . . power that had worked upon him' / A. Zoller, *Hitler privat*, Düsseldorf 1949, p. 30.

65 In the same month . . . 'a piece of his mind' / The episode is described by F/M Busch's adjutant; see Maser, *Adolf Hitler: Legende, Mythos, Wirklichkeit*, p. 385. A few weeks later, 18 April, Busch was helping Speer to preserve the bridges across the Elbe; see Speer, op. cit., pp. 591–2.

8   'There is no such thing as the Will'

66 *Mario und der Zauberer* is printed in *Ausgewählte Erzählungen*, Stockholm 1954. The English version is 'Mario and the Magician', in *Stories of three Decades* [translated by H. T. Lowe-Porter], London 1936.

67 Hans Frank slavishly echoes . . . 'hardships of those days' / Frank, p. 312: '*Er gab aber auch sein letztes an Kraft, um die ungeheuerlichen Strapazen dieser Tage zu bestehen.*' I have italicized the characteristic Hitlerian turn of phrase.

69 'As we form such a *community* . . . and by our abilities' / Domarus, p. 2198, my italics.
On 20 May 1943 . . . 'What is decisive is the Will!' / General Warlimont's report, quoted from Maser, op. cit., p. 392.
The state . . . 'several will-forming agencies' / '. . . mehrere Willensbildner'. Quoted from Broszat, p. 353; see also pp. 358 and 361.

admiration for Frederick the Great . . . 'strength of soul' / Domarus, p. 1237.

70 Even Alan Bullock . . . 'unusual consistency of purpose' / Alan Bullock, 'Hitler and the Origins of the Second World War', in *Proceedings of the British Academy*, 53 (1967), p. 286.

71 'He who wills an end . . . means that are in his power' / *Grundlegung zur Metaphysik der Sitten*, section 2; see *Kant's gesammelte Schriften*, edited by the Königlich Preussische Akademie der Wissenschaften, vol. IV, Berlin 1903, p. 417.

73 'This is a metaphor . . . clarity of direction' / *Nietzsches Werke: Kritische Gesamtausgabe*, edited by G. Colli and M. Montinari, vol. VIII/iii, Berlin 1972, p. 186.

74 It denotes a wanting . . . *'trying to get'* / G. E. M. Anscombe, *Intention*, Oxford 1957, author's italics.

76 'He is almost an image-maker's model . . . and unpredictable' / 27 April 1972.
'I do not merely imagine . . . the greatest authority' / Domarus, p. 1603.
the absolutization of his Will . . . drawing attention to that self / Compare G. E. M. Anscombe, op, cit., p. 45, and her reference to Wittgenstein's *Philosophical Investigations*, para. 659.

9 The Language of Prophecy

78 'Whatever falls – it should be kicked, too!' / *Also sprach Zarathustra*, Part III, 'Von alten und neuen Tafeln', section 20: 'O meine Brüder, bin ich denn grausam? Aber ich sage: was verfällt, das soll man auch noch stoßen! / Das Alles von heute – das fällt, das verfällt: wer wollte es halten! Aber ich – ich *will* es noch stoßen!'

79 'In the course of my life . . . the Jewish race in Europe' / Domarus, p. 1058 (30 January 1939).

81 Sir Nevile Henderson . . . 'among Jews and anti-Nazis' / This, at any rate, is the official version of Henderson's discussion with Hitler, 23 August 1939, published by the German Foreign Office and quoted by Domarus on p. 1249.
'It is part of the great leader's genius . . . the justice of their own case.' / *Mein Kampf*, pp. 128–9.

82 one readily agrees . . . that 'Cathedral built of ice' / See Albert Speer, *Erinnerungen*, pp. 71–2. The fact that Speer is literally the only one among the higher party officials with whom it might not be wholly intolerable to be personally acquainted has caused English and American reviewers of his memoirs to acclaim him as

a man of honour, a victim of Hitler's demonic powers, and so forth. Geoffrey Barraclough, in his excellent article in *New York Review of Books*, 7 January 1971, is the only reviewer I have read who refuses to accept Speer's apologia from 'the mystique of technology'.

'Hitler was the first . . . modern technology' / Speer, op. cit., caption at p. 481.

83 He was singularly accurate . . . it reached that point / This is true, e.g., of Feder's or Strasser's economics, of Hauer's religious speculations (see below, pp. 107–9) and of Alfred Rosenberg's racial theories.

The background of Speer's argument . . . 'terrorization by technology' / See Barraclough, op. cit., p. 6.

On at least two . . . as good as his word / See his speeches of 30 January 1941 (Domarus, p. 1663) and 30 January 1942 (Domarus p. 1829).

84 Hannah Arendt warns . . . 'propaganda disappears entirely' / See *The Origins of Totalitarianism*, London 1962, p. 344.

10 The Religious Expectation and its Ritual

85 The year begins on 30 January . . . / The following chronicle is taken from Frank (pp. 298–330), Domarus (pp. 329–30), Nolte (pp. 467–72) and Heer, *Der Glaube des Adolf Hitler* (pp. 226–68).

the 'immutable' party programme / See *Tischgespräche*, pp. 158–9.

86 the average number . . . 950,000 in 1938 / See H. T. Burden, *The Nuremberg Party Rallies: 1923–1938*, London 1967.

'Here all centred on the Party . . . "objectively-politically"' / Frank, p. 306; 'objective' was one of the dirty words in the Party vocabulary.

87 'No country in Europe' . . . the NewYork *Times* / See Burden, op. cit., p. 130.

'my hunchbacked ancients' / 'Uralte Höckergreise'; see Frank, p. 306.

89 'As he appeared . . . indescribably beautiful' / Quoted from Burden, op. cit., p. 128.

the spontaneous speech habits . . . / See, e.g., *Tischgespräche*, p. 129.

90 'How deeply we all feel . . . and now we are Germany!' / Domarus, p. 641; compare p. 570. See also F. Heer, *Gottes erste Liebe*, München 1968, p. 388, and *Der Glaube des Adolf Hitler*, pp. 314–15.

11   A Society Longing for 'Transcendence'

92   'Je suis athée, mais je suis catholique' / See Heer, *Gottes erste Liebe*, pp. 389 and 435, and *Der Glaube des Adolf Hitler*, p. 223.
his boyhood impressions as a server at Mass / See *Tischgespräche*, p. 49.
He professed a cynical admiration for the Catholic hierarchy / See *Mein Kampf*, p. 4.
'the soiled collars and stained frock coats' / *Tischgespräche*, p. 259 (7 April 1942).
his need of 'a visible enemy' / To H. Rauschning, in *Gespräche mit Hitler*, New York 1940, p. 222. Rauschning's two books impute to Hitler a speculative philosophical – mainly Nietzschean – outlook which is found nowhere else; I have therefore used them only where they seemed to provide an authentic account of Hitler's entourage, especially during the afternoon parties (coffee with lashings of whipped cream and crumbly cake) at the Reichskanzlei.

93   and there are his plans . . . all religious bodies / *Tischgespräche*, p. 176 (8 February 1942).
'the hard inward struggle . . . a foal in a meadow' / Domarus, p. 745.

94   More is wanted (Hitler writes) . . . 'So the circle closes' / *Mein Kampf*, pp. 416–17.
the historian Alexander von Müller . . . the spring of 1918 / See Maser, op. cit., pp. 161ff.

96   Ernst Nolte's extended description . . . its implacable enemies / See his last chapter, pp. 515–45; 'a reaching-out of thought' / p. 520; 'matter or spirit' / p. 517. A regrettable, though un-wonted, dogmatism disfigures the last section of Nolte's book, as when he speaks of his highly problematic distinction between transcendence and immanence as 'inviolable and the foundation of all truth'. Whether or not this *hauteur* is intended to hide the moral indifferentism of his idea of transcendence, this is certainly a style unbecoming in a critic of fascism.

97   the wrong, 'a-metaphysical solution' / Ernst Jünger, *Strahlungen*, Tübingen 1949, p. 343, diary entry for 22 June 1943.

12   The Indifference to Liberty

99   'the more primitive . . . an act of undue coercion' / *Tischgespräche*, p. 271 (11 April 1942).

101 It has been said . . . a real parliamentary debate / See Domarus,

p. 238; for Hitler's opening and closing speeches, and Wels's address, see pp. 229–46.

It is certainly, as Bullock says, ungenerous / See Bullock, p. 269.

'Is it morally . . . Just as in 1919 . . . the rest is bound to follow' / Letter of Karl Bachem, 25 March 1933, quoted from *Justiz im Dritten Reich: eine Dokumentation*, edited by I. Staff, Frankfurt/M 1962, pp. 52ff.

102 'We are entering the Reichstag . . . that's how we come' / Josef Goebbels in *Der Angriff*, 30 April 1928, quoted from G. Hufnagel, 'Das Scheitern der Weimarer Republik', in *Geschichte* (Tellekolleg Südwestfunk), München 1972, p. 189.

13 Three Wise Men

104 'the spiritual situation of the age' / Karl Jaspers, *Die geistige Situation der Zeit*, Berlin 1931, [5th ed., summer of] 1932. I quote from the reprint, Berlin 1965; the original appeared as volume 1000 of the *Sammlung Göschen*.

'the mechanical dialectics of Marxism' / Jaspers, op. cit., e.g. p. 11; even homosexuality / p. 54; and psycho-analysis / p. 159; 'genuine leaders' / p. 98; 'those who . . . escape from themselves' / p. 192; control through public opinion . . . the idea of the state / p. 98; Alternatively, freedom . . . 'modern technology' / p. 210.

105 Freud's *Civilization and its Discontents* / *Das Unbehagen in der Kultur*, 1930; I quote from the reprint, Frankfurt/M 1953.

106 'This danger . . . leader-individuals . . . mass-formations occur' / Freud, op. cit., p. 105.

107 C. G. Jung's notorious essay / See 'Wotan', reprinted in Jung's *Aufsätze zur Zeitgeschichte*, Zürich 1946.

Wilhelm Hauer's *Deutsche Gottschau: Grundzüge eines deutschen Glaubens* / Stuttgart 1934.

108 'the breakthrough . . . adequate faith may arise' / '. . . der Durchbruch des Menschen zu einer lebensunmittelbaren Selbständigkeit, aus der erst wieder echter, der Lage gewachsener Glaube entsprießen kann . . .' ibid., p. 195.

109 *furor teutonicus* / Jung, op. cit., p. 12.

Hauer's book . . . 'and seized by him' / ibid., p. 21.

'seized' / '. . . ergriffen': the word Jung uses is not quite the equivalent of 'possession'.

Indeed Hitler himself . . . to the people / Jung, op. cit., p. 113. Hitler is not mentioned by name, but I do not see who else can be

intended: 'Das ist aber das Eindrucksvolle am deutschen Phäno-
men, daß Einer, der offenkundig ergriffen ist, das ganze Volk
dermaßen ergreift, daß sich alles in Bewegung setzt . . .'
'There are representatives . . . a tragic experience' / ibid., p. 22,
author's italics.

14 Institutional Patterns

111 'express all their . . . sense of destiny' / see note to p. 20 above.
Gauleiter Joseph Wagner . . . Robert Ley . . . Hess . . .
Himmler . . . 'to compare with him' / Frank, p. 323.

112 'I, together with the Duce . . . the front-line crock' / Frank, p.
352: '. . . für den kleinen Frontkrüppel'.
How strong and persistent . . . 'the Führer does not know' / See,
e.g., Frank, p. 252.

113 'At no time did Hitler . . . a *fait accompli*' / Joachim von Ribbentrop, *Zwischen London und Moskau: Erinnerungen und letzte
Aufzeichnungen*, Leoni am Starnberger See 1954, p. 276.
'a state where . . . social system' / Durkheim's definition is
quoted from Talcott Parsons's 'Some Sociological Aspects of the
Fascist Movements' (1942), reprinted in *Essays in Social Theory*,
Glencoe 1954, p. 125.
that the party-programme . . . to be unalterable / See his speech
of 31 August 1928, in *Gesetze des NS-Staates*, p. 15.

114 '*Es war immer was los*' / Compare also the contemporary testimony of an underground student group which, in the spring of
1942, attributed to the regime the belief that 'the people must be
kept in a state of permanent tension, the bridle must never be
loosened'. See Christian Petry, *Studenten aufs Schafott: Die
Weiße Rose und ihr Scheitern*, München 1968, p. 161.

15 The Spirit of National Socialist Law

117 This was especially . . . more than a century / For the figures
showing this dominance, see Ralf Dahrendorf, *Gesellschaft und
Demokratie in Deutschland*, München 1965, especially chapter 16.
'For the first time . . . I am your leader!' / Domarus, p. 1628.

118 the legal spirit the Party attempted to put into practice / The main
sources of the account that follows are: Broszat, chapter 10
('Recht und Justiz'); Karl Peters, 'Die Umgestaltung des Straf-
gesetzes in den Jahren 1933–1945', in *Deutsches Geistesleben und
Nationalsozialismus*, Tübingen 1965, pp. 160–78; *Justiz im*

Dritten Reich, edited by I. Staff; and the excerpted collection of laws in *Gesetze des NS-Staates*.

'I shall not rest . . . become so in time' / *Tischgespräche*, pp. 222ff (29 March 1942); 'But alas . . . a ridiculous verdict' / p. 326; 'Besides, to spend . . . no difference between them' / p. 467 (22 July 1942): 'Im übrigen könne man es doch wirklich nicht als einen anständigen Beruf bezeichnen, ein ganzes Leben lang Bazis zu verteidigen . . .'; 'No reasonable human being . . . Germany will not perish' / p. 223. The man who meticulously recorded these and similar remarks in shorthand, and solemnly edited them with commentaries and headings, was an official of the legal administration, Landrat Dr Henry Picker.

120 'Anyone setting a motor trap . . . punished by death' / Broszat, p. 418.

the 'Law in Defence of the State' / See *Gesetze des NS-Staates*, p. 75; and see below, p. 63.

On the day following . . . convicted of the crime / See *Gesetze des NS-Staates*, pp. 70 and 91.

The complex anti-Jewish legislation / ibid., pp. 124–45. Point Four of the Party Programme reads: 'Only fellow nationals can be citizens. Only those of German blood, irrespective of their religion, can be fellow nationals. Consequently no Jew can be a fellow national.'

The immense increase . . . once war broke out / In 1938 the number of people condemned to death *by German public civil courts* was 23, in 1943 it was 4438, and in the first six months of 1944 (the last period for which official statistics are available) 2015; see Broszat, p. 420.

121 One of the speakers . . . 'the point of view . . . the German national community' / I quote from Karl Peters, op. cit., pp. 160–1; the speaker was Graf Gleispach.

122 Roland Freisler in his commentary on the Nuremberg laws / See his *Nationalsozialistisches Recht und Rechtsdenken*, Berlin 1938.

'justice must be . . . the whole Nation' / Frank, p. 170.

'It is the first time . . . a concept in law' / Frank, reported in *Völkischer Beobachter*, 30 June 1935; see *Facsimile Querschnitt durch den 'Völkischen Beobachter'*, München 1967.

'Whether the Führer . . . issue of our time' / Frank, p. 467.

the law of 26 April 1942 / See *Gesetze des NS-Staates*. p. 41; and see above, p. 12.

124 yet the fact is . . . the Federal Republic / See Peters, op. cit., p. 166.

125 'the National Socialist conception of law and order' / See Broszat, p. 412.

126 Thus it was not until 30 June 1943 . . . 'sentence of death' /
Broszat, p. 422: '. . . wenn dies "aus stimmungspolitischen
Gründen" angezeigt erscheint "und durch vorherige Fühlungs-
nahme sichergestellt ist, daß das Gericht die Todesstrafe
verhängen wird." '
'Unless otherwise instructed . . . take place forthwith' / Broszat,
p. 412.

127 Kafka's unfinished novel, *The Trial* / I shall quote from Max
Brod's edition of *Der Prozeß*, New York 1946.
'But I am innocent' . . . 'the guilty usually say' / *Der Prozeß*, p.
222; the verdict will be not 'true' but 'necessary' / p. 232; 'You
have a trial' / p. 145; many people   see him as an asshole / p.
18; and won't shake hands with him / p. 30; 'If you want . . .
give notice to!' / p. 32; 'the question . . . simplify the matter' /
p. 160; neither a stable code of law nor acquittal / p. 164; to be
involved . . . losing it / p. 107.

128 'Why, do you think . . . hasn't done anything?' / 'Glauben Sie
denn, wir laden jemand vor, der nichts verbrochen hat?' – quoted
from *Justiz und NS-Verbrechen: Sammlung deutscher Strafurteile
wegen nazionalsozialistischer Tötungsverbrechen 1945–1966*, vol.
VI, Amsterdam 1971, p. 417.
'the verdict doesn't come . . . merges into the verdict' / *Der
Prozeß*, p. 222; ' "All men are intent" ' . . . ' "I shall now go and
shut it" ' / p. 226; 'True, he couldn't . . . "like a dog" ' . . .
should survive him' / pp. 238–9.

16 The Leadership Principle

130 The basic principle of life . . . '. . . Only then can I state . . .
that is, by democracy' / Domarus, pp. 72ff.

131 the fact that the speech . . . attack on the Jews / See Golo Mann's
essay in *Deutschland und die Juden*, Frankfurt/M 1967, pp. 61–62.
Mommsen's observation on the Jews . . . of the preceding twenty-
five years / As has been frequently pointed out (e.g. by Heer,
Der Glaube des Adolf Hitler, pp. 426 and 604; and Nolte, p. 592),
T. Mommsen's description of the Jews as 'the ferment of decomposition of peoples and states' was intended as a positive evaluation of their function in static European societies. See Mommsen's reply to Treitschke, 'Auch ein Wort über das Judentum',
in *Reden und Aufsätze*, Berlin 1905, p. 416.

132 But the strongest applause / See Domarus, p. 83.
What matters . . . 'Will of the whole nation' / Domarus, p. 84;
'Wesentlich ist die politische Willensbildung der ganzen Nation.'

'*Taktik und Prinzip*' / See Frank, p. 306.

The *Autobahn* projects . . . in the late 'twenties / Most of the data here come from Broszat, chapter 5.

133 Even a major aspect . . . in September 1932 / See H. Childs, *Germany since 1918*, London 1971, p. 59.

Ford's anti-Semitic explanation . . . an added recommendation / See Nolte, p. 406.

And of course . . . the re-armament programme / In 1933, 23% of all public investments went on armaments; in 1934, 49%; in 1938, 74%. See Broszat, p. 225.

the re-introduction of the old *Arbeitsbuch* / See Broszat, p. 205.

134 'German concepts of social conscience and honour' / Broszat, p. 195.

Under these concepts . . . 'a true national community' / Speech of 29 November 1933, quoted from Broszat, p. 193.

'There is no such thing . . . being and not-being' / Hitler quoted from Frank, p. 367.

17 Conservative Opposition and the True Antagonist

135 They are more typical . . . July 1944 / See Childs, op. cit., pp. 98–99.

their numbers are in the ten thousands / H. Rothfels, in *Die deutsche Opposition gegen Hitler*, Frankfurt/M 1958, p. 106, quotes a trade union leader's estimate of an 'anti-Nazi front' of 125,000.

as some German historians still fail to understand / See Golo Mann, *Deutsche Geschichte 1919–1945*, Frankfurt/M 1962, p. 219.

136 Goerdeler's peace plans . . . protection against Russia / The document is quoted in G. Ritter, *Carl Goerdeler und die deutsche Widerstandsbewegung*, Stuttgart 1954, pp. 562, 570ff.

Goerdeler's proposals . . . these laws were based / See *Beck und Goerdeler: Gemeinschaftsdokumente für den Frieden 1941–1944*, edited by W. von Schramm, München 1965, pp. 106–7.

137 'What does our death matter . . . The students are bound to revolt!' / J. P. Stern, 'The White Rose', in *German Life and Letters*, N. S. 11, No. 2 (1958), p. 97.

The figure of 3,000 . . . may well be exaggerated / See Petry, *Studenten aufs Schafott* p. 221.

'Hundreds of students . . . with open arms' / ibid., p. 122.

'I beseech you . . . your reasonable service' / Romans 12. 1.

138 His name is Johann Georg Elser / The Gestapo material as well

as the post-war investigations were first sifted by Anton Hoch in 'Das Attentat auf Adolf Hitler im Münchner Bürgerbräukeller 1939', in *Vierteljahrshefte für Zeitgeschichte*, 17 (1969), pp. 383–413. My own account in this section follows *Autobiographie eines Attentäters: Johann Georg Elser*, edited and introduced by Lothar Gruchmann, Stuttgart 1970, see also Bundesarchiv Koblenz, File R22/3100; additional facts from Hoch's excellent article.
In Bullock's biography . . . betrayed by his masters / The source of Bullock's almost wholly misleading account (see pp. 566–7) is Captain S. Payne Best, *The Venlo Incident*, London 1950, pp. 127–36. I shall refer to it below, p. 150.
the familial pattern described in *Mein Kampf* / e.g. on pp. 28ff.

140 'I was never interested . . . a Communist orientation' / Gruchmann, op. cit., p. 78 and note on p. 160.

141 the *Völkischer Beobachter* . . . 'a satanic monster' / quoted from Gruchmann, op. cit., p. 22.

142 'It was clear to me . . . the conquest of Poland was laid' / See Domarus, p. 1422 (23 November 1939). See also Bullock, p. 569, whose translation I have slightly adapted.

143 he was stubborn and courageous enough . . . Hitler's speeches / See Hoch, op. cit., pp. 396–7.
a man is possessed . . . to interfere with them / ibid., p. 398.

146 'I have never prayed to God . . . to prevent even worse bloodshed' / Gruchmann, op. cit., pp. 74–5.

148 As he was now . . . 30 RM for the journey / See Hoch, op. cit., pp. 406–7.
a violent interview with General von Brauchitsch / See Bullock, p. 568.
They too were preparing . . . 'order for the attack' / Bullock, p. 566.

149 Hitler, who had taken . . . platform in Nuremberg / See Domarus, pp. 1414–15.
Elser's border crossing pass / Elser had an old pass *für den kleinen Grenzverkehr* from the time when he had lived in Constance and worked in Switzerland; see Gruchmann, op. cit., p. 7.

150 In the course of . . . brutally beaten up / i.e. '*verschärfte Vernehmungen*'; see Hoch, op. cit., p. 412.

151 One wonders what caused . . . free pass to Switzerland / ibid., pp. 389 and 397.

152 'I have changed my mind' . . . 'I firmly believe . . . my view was false' / Gruchmann, op. cit., p. 157, editor's emphasis: 'Ich habe meine Ansicht geändert.' 'Dadurch, daß Sie festgenommen worden sind?' 'Nein, ich glaube bestimmt, daß mein Plan gelungen wäre, wenn meine Auffassung richtig gewesen wäre. *Nachdem er*

nicht gelungen ist, bin ich überzeugt, daß es nicht gelingen sollte und daß meine Ansicht falsch war.'
'Really, you know, it is' . . . 'literally to have any substance' / From the OSS film of the July plot trial at the Imperial War Museum: 'Ich hielt das für undurchführbar' . . . 'Nach meinem inneren Gefühl habe ich nicht daran geglaubt' . . . 'Ich nahm die Sache sozusagen nicht wörtlich als substantiiert an.'

18   Myrmidons' Strife

154 'I don't intend . . . anything to stay on top!' / *Gespräche mit Hitler*, p. 96.
155 There is some truth in the view . . . 'Eastern Euope with German farmers' / T. W. Mason, 'Economics of National Socialist Germany', in *European Fascism*, edited by S. J. Woolf, London 1968, p. 194.
157 Less than a week after . . . 'Perhaps a fight . . . its uncompromising Germanization' / See General-Lieutenant Liebmann's notes about this private meeting with general army officers, in T. Vogelsang, 'Neue Dokumente zur Geschichte der Reichswehr', in *Vierteljahrshefte für Zeitgeschichte*, 2 (1954), pp. 434–6. The whole passage – 'Vielleicht Erkämpfung neuer Exportmöglichkeiten, vielleicht – und wohl besser – Eroberung neuen Lebensraums im Osten und seine rücksichtslose Germanisierung' – precedes the disputed Hossbach memoir by nearly five years, and destroys A. J. P. Taylor's thesis about the adventitiousness of Hitler's plans for war. Compare Nolte, p. 424, Domarus, pp. 197–8, and J. W. Wheeler-Bennett, *The Nemesis of Power: The German Army in Politics 1918–1945*, London 1964, p. 291. The rest of the speech contains some of Hitler's ideas on European and domestic policy, which are hardly more than repetitions of corresponding passages in *Mein Kampf*. The generals, however, achieved the singular distinction of not believing a word of what they helped him to accomplish.
     Serious discontent / See Konrad Heiden, op. cit., pp. 726–770.
158 discussions about the re-introduction of national conscription / See W. Sauer's account, in *Machtergreifung*, p. 491.
     Interpreting the events . . . his 'greatest happiness' . . . 'has now become reality' / *Machtergreifung*, p. 937.
     The massacres are instigated . . . / See Sauer's account, in *Machtergreifung*, pp. 952–60.
159 'grousers, bleaters and spoilsports' / 'Nörgler, Meckerer und Miesmacher'; see Frank, passim.

160 Papen's speech includes . . . the Army to intervene / See Bullock, p. 298.
'the little worm . . . re-birth of the nation' / Domarus, p. 390.
Hitler talks him out . . . once the emergency is over / See *Machtergreifung*, p. 955.
None of this prevents Papen . . . those disastrous years / See *Machtergreifung*, p. 256.

161 General von Blomberg . . . its President and its Leader / See Bullock, p. 301.
By means of forged handbills . . . a march through Munich / See Domarus, p. 395.

162 Several senior SS officials . . . of equal rank / See Domarus, p. 395. Rosenberg claimed after the war that Hess and Amann (manager of the *Völkischer Beobachter*) vied for permission to take part in the killings. See *Machtergreifung*, p. 961.

163 Their volleys . . . the SA men's dying lips / See Konrad Heiden, op. cit., p. 767.
its fear of scandal / Sauer speaks appropriately of 'das in Ehrenfragen sonst so mimosenhaft empfindliche Offizierkorps'; *Machtergreifung*, p. 965.
'judgeship emanates . . . highest form of Justice' / Carl Schmitt, quoted from Sauer in *Machtergreifung*, pp. 966–7.
On 3 July . . . in a single sentence / i.e. 'Die zur Niederschlagung hoch- und landesverräterischer Angriffe am 30. Juni, 1. und 2. Juli [1934] vollzogenen Maßnahmen sind als Staatsnotwehr rechtens' (*Machtergreifung*, p. 963).

164 As late as March 1934 . . . 'will Germany be saved!' / Domarus, p. 371; 'Revolutionsappell der alten Kämpfer', 19 March 1934.
'even the Devil . . . larger significance' / Heiden, op. cit., p. 774.
'Your god lies shattered . . . for his sake' / Quoted from *Die Unschuld des Werdens: der Nachlaß zweiter Teil*, edited by Alfred Bäumler, Alfred Kröner Verlag, Leipzig 1931, p. 337. The passage has not as yet appeared in the *Kritische Gesamtausgabe*.

165 Hitler himself said as much / See *Tischgespräche*, p. 260 (6 April 1942).

166 'the Party comrades who went wrong' / 'Kameraden, die sich verfehlt hatten . . .' H. Himmler in his address to the SS leaders in Posen, 4 October 1943; quoted from *Official Record of the Trial of the Major War Criminals before the International Military Tribunal*, vol. XXIX, Nuremberg 1948, p. 145.

19   A Social Revolution?

167 'the refuse of all the classes' / Hannah Arendt, *The Origins of Totalitarianism*, p. 155.
'a classless popular party' / Nolte, p. 387; for a cross-section of members' occupations, see his note 59 on pp. 596–7.
He promised . . . civil war / See Nolte, p. 415, and *Machtergreifung*, p. 953.

168 It has been shown in considerable detail . . . the totalitarian regimes / See, e.g., B. H. Klein, *Germany's Economic Preparations for War*, Cambridge (Mass.) 1959, and Nicholas Kaldor, 'The German War Economy' (1946), reprinted in *Essays on Economic Policy*, vol. II, London 1964, pp. 203–32.
It began in 1933 . . . a war-like process / See Broszat, p. 225.
'The clatter . . . at Langemark' / *Der Arbeiter*, para. 39 (in Ernst Jünger, *Werke*, vol. VI, Stuttgart [1963], p. 145).

169 'Every worker . . . We are all soldiers at work' / Quoted from Broszat, pp. 189–90; the second statement comes from Robert Ley, Reich Minister of Labour, addressing the workers in the Siemens electrical works in Berlin in October 1933.
And these changes turned out . . . dire confusions of Weimar / See Dahrendorf, *Gesellschaft und Demokratie in Deutschland*, p. 432.
the least mobile power elite / See W. Zopf, quoted from Dahrendorf, op. cit., p. 254.

170 The social revolution . . . the liberal-democratic ideology / See Broszat, p. 441.
half private entrepreneurs, half party functionaries / See Broszat, p. 229.

171 to the end of 1944 . . . a strong bargaining position / See Broszat, p. 242.

172 'in order to put an end . . . fourteen years of Marxism' / Domarus, p. 192.
'The worker . . . children' / See above, p. 142.
his pathological inability . . . to proclaim in another / This is how Carl Burckhardt, the League of Nations' commissioner in Danzig, 1936–39, saw him; see *Meine Danziger Mission*, München 1960, p. 270.
He needed a modern social structure . . . he was unaware / Dahrendorf, op. cit., p. 434: 'Hitler brauchte die Modernität, so wenig er sie mochte.' See also Geoffrey Barraclough, 'The Liberals and German History', in *New York Review of Books*, 2 November 1972, and Walter Laqueur's retort, 'Rewriting History', in *Commentary*, March 1973, especially p. 55.

173 that dreadful 'ruse of reason' of which Hegel speaks / e.g. in the introduction to his *Philosophie der Geschichte*, II, b (Reclam edition, Stuttgart 1961, p. 78).
Major social changes . . . political consciousness / See Hegel, op. cit., p. 61.

20 The Front-line Soldier

175 Once in power . . . routine of government / See Broszat, p. 352.
176 'retaining the essential and discarding the inessential / *Mein Kampf*, p. 12.
177 Bullock presents him . . . 'a good deal more conscientious' / Bullock, p. 53.
The recent publication of several long letters / See W. Maser *Hitlers Briefe und Notizen*, Düsseldorf [i.e. Dusseldorf Wien] Wien 1973.
178 The journey of the regiment . . . couched in this language / The references in this paragraph are to *Hitlers Briefe und Notizen*, pp. 63–88.
179 and repeated almost verbatim / See *Mein Kampf*, p. 180.
. . . the battles . . . in Champagne . . . / for a full list see Maser, *Adolf Hitler: Legende, Mythos, Wirklichkeit*, pp. 134–6.
181 He has escaped death . . . think himself invulnerable / See Fest, *Hitler: eine Biographie*, p. 105.
He tells us . . . his university / See *Hitler's Table Talk 1941–1944*, p. 720 (16 May 1944); this is not included in *Tischgespräche*.
182 and his comrades . . . so 'keen' / Fest, *Hitler: eine Biographie*, p. 103: 'Der Spinner will halt seine Bandel.'
The war experience . . . / The data in this section are taken from Maser, *Adolf Hitler: Legende, Mythos, Wirklichkeit*, chapter 4, and Fest, *Hitler: eine Biographie*, book 1, chapter 5.
183 Hitler assures us . . . political discussion / See *Mein Kampf*, p. 182.
'They will never find the solution . . . to reach its great aims' / Ernst Jünger, *Der Kampf als inneres Erlebnis* [1922], Berlin 1938, p. 87.
184 a twelve-page letter . . . dated 15 February 1915 / *Hitlers Briefe und Notizen* p. 100. In a single sentence at the end – 'Mit Osterreich wird die Sach kommen, wie ich es immer sagte' – Hitler uses that wholly unselfconscious and genuinely popular language I mentioned.

21 'A new life was born'

185 *Why Hitler Came into Power* / The facsimile reprint (New York
1966) is entitled *The Nazi Movement: Why Hitler Came to
Power*. The original edition (New York 1938) had a subtitle, 'An
Answer Based on the Original Life Stories of Six Hundred of his
Followers'. For the conditions of the contest quoted above, see
pp. 1–9. The quotations in the rest of this section are taken from
the various parts of this book, which will be referred to as
'Abel'.

186 'He is a town resident . . . nor was he ever unemployed' . . .
'A world was extinguished . . . a new life was born / Abel, p.
245.

189 Although they come from all social strata / In Abel's rough classi-
fication: skilled and unskilled workers, 35%; peasants (and smallholders), 7%; lower middle class (corresponding presumably to
'Mittelstand'), 51%; upper middle class and aristocracy, 7%.
'the meaning of life' / See Abel, pp. 226, and 279.
'Hunger was the daily . . . wielded by the Jews' / Written by an
unskilled labourer; Abel, p. 126.

190 'I moved to Schoenbeck . . . the Hitler movement' / The writer
is described as 'a petty tradesman'; Abel, p. 126.

191 'Around 1923 . . . "restore order" ' / A high-school teacher,
quoting from an inscription on a monument; Abel, p. 151.

193 'In every instant . . . the leader made it public' / From the story
of a clerk who, through his party connexions, rose to being
Vice-President of his bank; Abel, pp. 275 and 279.
'"These first members . . . to the movement' / By a young farmer;
Abel, p. 296.

194 'My belief is that . . . light into darkness' / Abel, p. 244; compare
the almost identical formulation on p. 54.

22 Conquest and Annihilation

198 his discovery of the value of his war experience / See above, p.
25.

200 The *Protocols of the Elders of Zion* / As Cohen's *Warrant for
Genocide* shows, not many stories of forgery manage to be as
dreadful *and* dreary as does this one.
The unbelievably naïve . . . mythopoeic imagination / Hannah
Arendt, in *The Origins of Totalitarianism*, p. 76, speaks of
Disraeli's 'unbelievable naïvete' in attributing to the Jews the

leadership of all secret societies, including Communists, Jesuits, Protestants, atheists etc.
Hitler speaks . . . telling the Jews from the rest / See *Mein Kampf*, pp. 253–4, and *Tischgespräche*, p. 152 (1 December 1941).
the seriousness with which this 'problem' was discussed / Thus Dr Ernst Forsthoff, Ordinary Professor of Law, speaks of 'the need to recognize the difference of the species especially in all those cases where, because the individual is not a member of a foreign nation, that difference is not easily visible'; and Professor Carl Schmitt (see above, p. 117) makes the same point, adding that 'the smallest mistakes in this respect are apt to be magnified, to create confusion . . . and to become harmful to young students etc.' – See *Justiz im Dritten Reich*, pp. 165–6 and 171–2.

202 Hannah Arendt holds . . . defenceless situation / See *The Origins of Totalitarianism*, chapter 3.

203 The lunatic fringe . . . German New Left / See *Frankfurter Allgemeine Zeitung*, 15 December 1972.
Finally, the anomalous situation . . . Gentile hatred and envy / See Lionel Kochan, *Pogrom in November 1938*, London 1957, p. 13.

204 other men . . . ascribe to them the qualities of Jews / J.-P. Sartre's statement (op. cit., p. 57) is similar, though less qualified.
What do we mean . . . uniquely close? / See above, p. 203.

205 'The love-affair . . . unrequited' / *Deutsche und Juden*, p. 41.

206 'Today there passed . . . one Jew' / Quoted from Heer, *Gottes erste Liebe*, p. 291.
'a second order of experience' / See Isaiah Berlin, 'Jewish Slavery and Emancipation', in *Herzl Institute Pamphlet* no. 18, New York 1961, p. 9.

207 It seems inconceivable . . . members of a totalitarian regime / See Hannah Arendt, op. cit., p. 21.
it is inconceivable that Hitler could have done without them / Hans Frank, however (see p. 306), believes that Hitler's popularity was such that he could have made peace with the Jews and thus given joy to the whole German people; but then, Hans Frank believed anything and nothing.

208 'But I am innocent' . . . 'the guilty usually say' / *Der Prozeß*, p. 222; see above, p. 127.
'However much malicious people . . . allowed to exist' / Quoted from Heer, *Gottes erste Liebe*, p. 560; however, Rathenau also wrote some of the most penetrating observations on the German–Jewish relationship, and Sir Isaiah Berlin's characterization of him (see 'Jewish Slavery and Emancipation', p. 10) is quite unjust.

209 'There must be a punitive expedition . . . root and branch!' /

Julius Streicher, quoted from the indictment against him in *Das Urteil von Nürnberg 1946*, p. 207.

210 'every other day . . . abandoned to their fate' / Helmuth Stieff to his wife, early in 1942. See 'Ausgewählte Briefe von General-major Helmuth Stieff', in *Vierteljahrshefte für Zeitgeschichte*, 2 (1954), p. 103. Stieff was executed after the July 1944 putsch. His personal conduct during his trial by Freisler (recorded on the film mentioned above – see note to p. 152) was exemplary.

The Commander of the Army . . . a minor war criminal / For this paragraph see H. C. Deutsch, *The Conspiracy against Hitler in the Twilight War*, Minneapolis 1968, pp. 185–8, and Wheeler-Bennett, *The Nemesis of Power*, pp. 462 and 604; for the text of Blaskowitz's memoir, see *Wir haben es gesehen*, pp. 86–8.

211 A company commander . . . 'ringing in our ears' / For this paragraph, including Erwin Bingel's deposition, see *Wir haben es gesehen*, pp. 124–6 (see below, note to p. 219).

I have already mentioned the clandestine leaflets . . . / See above, p. 137.

212 'We do not intend to say anything . . . dreadful and unworthy crimes?' / For the full text of the leaflets, see Petry, *Studenten aufs Schafott*, pp. 153–67. The first italics – 'Wozu wir dies Ihnen alles erzählen, da Sie es schon selber wissen, wenn nicht diese, so andere gleich schwere Verbrechen des fürchterlichen Untermenschentums?' – are mine. (See Petry, op. cit., p. 157.)

the reminiscences of Kunrat Hammerstein / See 'Höhere Führer ohne Befehlsnotstand', in *Neue Rundschau*, 1962, pp. 465–504; a brother of the general was dismissed from his post in the civil service for his political views, and died after being liberated from Mauthausen.

213 The picture that emerges . . . they knew, would not return / See Karl Jaspers's speech in *Deutsche und Juden* (essays by various hands), Frankfurt/M 1967, pp. 109–10.

the conversational habits of soldiers / For some observations on these habits, see J. P. Stern, 'Notes on the West German Army', in *German Life and Letters*, N. S. 19 (1966), pp. 89–115.

But this picture must . . . the euthanasia project of 1939–41 / The facts concerning this action are taken from B. Honolka, *Die Kreuzelschreiber: Euthanasie im Dritten Reich*, Hamburg 1961.

214 'premeditated killing' was the equivalent of murder / This – paragraph 211 of the old *Reichsstrafgesetzbuch* – is the law Bishop von Galen invoked in his sermon of 3 August 1941, mentioned below.

that astonishing belief to which I drew attention earlier / See above, p. 113.

215 in his comments about some of the Protestant clergy / See above, p. 92.
218 The notorious Army order . . . all captured Russian commissars / See, e.g., Domarus, p. 1683. For the original order of 31 March 1941, and its Army (OKW) supplementation of 12 May 1941 (i.e. still five weeks before the attack), see the Nuremberg indictment of General Wilhelm Keitel, in *Das Urteil von Nürnberg 1946*, dtv München 1961, pp. 188–93. When General Walter Warlimont was asked by a German court (11 December 1962) why there was no protest from any one of the 250 generals and admirals to whom the order was promulgated by Hitler, he replied that 'because of their inborn and inbred [*angeboren und anerzogen*] attitude they all assumed that the highest authority in the state and the Supreme Commander of the Wehrmacht, Adolf Hitler, being then regarded by all officers as worthy of veneration, could do no wrong'.
219 Soon after the order . . . attached to his university / See *Das Diktat der Menschenverachtung*, edited by A. Mitscherlich and F. Mielke, Heidelberg 1947, p. 99. It is not clear from this documentary collection how many heads the SS supplied at Wirth's request; a letter to Eichmann (see Mitscherlich, op. cit., pp. 101–2) indicates that some 115 persons were killed to provide skeletons for Wirth's collection.
a letter to Himmler (7 June 1943) / Professor Clauberg's letter is reprinted in Mitscherlich, op, cit., p. 159.
though of course private looting . . . common enough / The testimony comes from one of the SS guards, a Brazilian called Pery Broad, but I can see no reason for distrusting it; see *Wir haben es gesehen: Augenzeugenberichte über Terror und Judenverfolgung in Dritten Reich*, edited by G. Schoenberner, Hamburg 1962, p. 278.
220 its peak membership of eight millions / See David Childs, *Germany since 1918*, London 1971, p. 117.
Hitler was at first taken aback / At the news of the British ultimatum, 'Hitler sat immobile, gazing before him. He was not at a loss, as was afterwards stated, nor did he rage as others allege. He sat completely silent and unmoving. After an interval, which seemed an age, he turned to Ribbentrop, who had remained standing by the window. "What now?" asked Hitler . . .' – Paul Schmidt's report, quoted from Bullock, p. 550.
the mood of the people is said to have been sombre / See, e.g., Ulrich von Hassell's diary entry for 10 September 1939, in *Vom andern Deutschland*, Zürich 1946, p. 86.
221 It is clear . . . the war was lost / See Percy Ernst Schramm, *Hitler als militärischer Führer* (see note to p. 28 above), pp. 67–9.

he had discussed with his friend . . . twenty years before / See Nolte, pp. 406–7.

'the insatiable hatred . . . on 30 April 1945' / Quoted from Schramm, op. cit., p. 168.

222 There is no snobbery . . . the self-taught strategist / Most of the argument that follows is taken from sections of Erich von Manstein's memoirs, quoted from Schramm, op. cit., pp. 157–66.

223 'He was a man . . . strength of will behind it' / Quoted from Schramm, op. cit., p. 161.

'I walked round a mound . . . the napes of their necks' / Part of the account of a German engineer who was present at the killing of some 5000 Jews by the SS and the Ukrainian militia in Dubno on 5 October 1942; quoted from Fest, op. cit., p. 932.

Index